Communications in Computer and Information Science 537

More information about this series at http://www.springer.com/series/7899

Cerstin Mahlow · Michael Piotrowski (Eds.)

Systems and Frameworks for Computational Morphology

Fourth International Workshop, SFCM 2015
Stuttgart, Germany, September 17–18, 2015
Proceedings

 Springer

Editors
Cerstin Mahlow
Institut für Deutsche Sprache
Mannheim
Germany

Michael Piotrowski
Leibniz Institute of European History
Mainz
Germany

ISSN 1865-0929   ISSN 1865-0937   (electronic)
Communications in Computer and Information Science
ISBN 978-3-319-23978-1   ISBN 978-3-319-23980-4   (eBook)
DOI 10.1007/978-3-319-23980-4

Library of Congress Control Number: 2015947943

Springer Cham Heidelberg New York Dordrecht London

Printed on acid-free paper

Springer International Publishing AG Switzerland is part of Springer Science+Business Media
(www.springer.com)

Preface

This volume contains the papers presented at SFCM 2015: The Fourth International Workshop on Systems and Frameworks for Computational Morphology, held on September 17 and 18, 2015, at the University of Stuttgart, Germany.

From the point of view of computational linguistics, morphological resources form the basis for all higher-level applications. This is especially true for languages with a rich morphology like Czech, German, Finnish, Italian, Latin, Pali, Polish, Sanskrit, and Serbian, to name some of the languages targeted in this volume. A morphology component should thus be capable of analyzing single wordforms as well as whole corpora. For many practical applications not only morphological analysis but also generation is required, i.e., the production of surfaces corresponding to specific categories.

Apart from uses in computational linguistics, there are numerous practical applications that can benefit from morphological analysis and/or generation or even require it, for example in textual analysis, word processing, information retrieval, or dialog systems. These applications have specific requirements for morphological components, including requirements from software engineering, such as programming interfaces or robustness.

With the workshop on Systems and Frameworks for Computational Morphology (SFCM) we have established a place for presenting and discussing recent advances in the field of computational morphology. SFCM focuses on linguistically motivated morphological analysis and generation, computational frameworks for implementing such systems, and linguistic frameworks suitable for computational implementation. In 2015 the workshop took place for the fourth time. The main theme for SFCM 2009 was systems for a specific language, namely, German; SFCM 2011 looked at phenomena at the interface between morphology and syntax in various languages; SFCM 2013 discussed the role of morphological analysis and generation to improve the rather disappointing situation with respect to language technology for languages other than English. All workshop programs are accessible via the series website at http://www.sfcm.eu.

SFCM 2015 aimed at broadening the scope to include research on very under-resourced languages, interactions between computational morphology and formal, quantitative, and descriptive morphology, as well as applications of computational morphology in the Digital Humanities. For the first time, it was a two-day workshop and featured a special session dedicated to CLARIN ("Common Language Resources and Technology Infrastructure"). Dörte de Kok from CLARIN-D and Krister Lindén from FIN-CLARIN gave insights on CLARIN in general and how the German and Finnish CLARIN centers support computational morphology.

Based on the number of submissions and the number of participants at the workshop we can definitely state that the topic of the workshop has met with great interest from the community, both from academia and industry. The broader scope of this workshop as outlined in the call for papers is reflected in the broader variety of topics discussed and use cases described. We received 16 submissions describing complete works of research as well as novel challenges and visions, of which 10 were accepted after a thorough review by the members of the program committee. The peer review process was double-blind, and each paper received three independent reviews.

In addition to the regular papers, we had the pleasure of Magda Ševčíková from Charles University Prague giving an invited talk on the role of morphology in the Prague Dependency Treebank.

The discussions after the talks and during the demo session, as well as the final plenum, showed the interest in and the need and requirements for further efforts in the field of computational morphology. During the last years, we see more workshops and conferences following the lead idea of SFCM to bring together researchers with different perspectives interested in the common topic of morphological phenomena. We also see more events actively supporting the idea of a "workshop" by offering ample opportunity to demonstrate and discuss ongoing research in an informal atmosphere, where participants can get critical but supportive feedback, in addition to the traditional presentation of complete research by talks in front of a plenum. We are encouraged to continue the series of SFCM workshops by the advent of similar morphology-oriented events targeting specific languages (such as the "Greek Workshop on Frameworks and Systems for Computational Morphology" in 2013 on Rhodes) or addressing computational aspects in morphology from the linguistic point of view (such as the workshop on "Computational Methods for Descriptive and Theoretical Morphology" in 2015 in Vienna).

Topics of this Book

This book starts with the invited paper by Magda Ševčíková ("Morphology within the Multi-layered Annotation Scenario of the Prague Dependency Treebank"), presenting morphological annotation as an element in a large multi-layered treebank. Following the approach of relations between form and function, morphological information is represented as attributes at the tectogrammatical layer. This allows the use for practical applications like dependency-based machine translation and the creation of lexical databases.

The following paper, "Designing and Comparing G2P-Type Lemmatizers for a Morphology-Rich Language" by Steffen Egger, presents work on lemmatization of ancient Latin. He finds that general-purpose string-to-string transduction models as used for grapheme-to-phoneme conversion perform better than techniques based on suffix transformation. The lemmatizer is aimed to complement lexicon-based systems.

In the paper "Morphological Disambiguation of Classical Sanskrit," Oliver Hellwig targets another ancient language. He describes a system for tokenization and morphological analyzation of Sanskrit combining a morphological rule-base with statistical selection of the most probable analysis.

The third paper aiming at ancient languages is "Morphological Analysis and Generation for Pali" by David Alfter and Jürgen Knauth. They introduce a system for analyzing and generating Pali word forms. The system can be integrated into a general technical infrastructure and supports linguistic research on Pali.

The paper "A Universal Feature Scheme for Rich Morphological Annotation" by John Sylak-Glassman, Christo Kirov, David Yarowski, and Roger Que introduces a general set of features that represent fine distinctions in meaning expressed by inflectional morphology across languages. For evaluation, the texts of the Bible are used as a large parallel corpus. This work is in the field of typology and cross-linguistic morphology to improve NLP applications such as machine translation and information extraction.

In the paper "Dsolve—Morphological Segmentation for German using Conditional Random Fields," Kay-Michael Würzner and Bryan Jurish present a system for the segmentation of complex German word forms. Segmentation is handled as a classification task using conditional random fields. Unlike previous segmentation approaches, Dsolve also predicts types of morph boundaries, which boosts performance.

Maciej Janicki's paper "A Multi-purpose Bayesian Model for Word-Based Morphology" presents morphology as a systematic correspondence between full word forms without segmenting word forms into smaller units. The Bayesian models trained this way perform very well when evaluated for lexicon expansion and the generation of inflected forms in German and Polish.

In their paper "Using HFST—Helsinki Finite-State Technology for Recognizing Semantic frames," Krister Lindén, Sam Hardwick, Miikka Silfverberg, and Erik Axelson show the use of HFST as a comprehensive framework using the example of recognizing semantic frames. HFST is a toolkit for text analysis covering all steps from tokenization over morphological analysis up to semantic tagging. This paper emphasizes the usefulness of such toolkits for text analysis in the Digital Humanities.

The next paper, "Morpho-SLaWS: An API for Morphosyntactic Annotation of the Serbian Language" by Toma Tasovac, Saša Rudan, and Siniša Rudan, gives another insight into the use of NLP tools in Digital Humanities. The Serbian Lexical Web Service (SLaWS) offers a broad range of functions to be used as a resource-oriented web service. Morpho-SLaWS is the morphological component of this infrastructure and can be combined with other linguistic resources and tools.

Next, in their paper "Morphological Analysis and Generation of Monolingual and Bilingual Medical Lexicons," Serena Pelosi, Annibale Elia, and Alessandro Maisto describe the automatic creation of Italian–English medical lexical resources. They use finite-state transducers to analyze combinations of prefixes, confixes, and suffixes used in medical terms. This approach allows also for recognition of relevant neologisms and multi-word expressions.

Finally, the paper "Grammar Debugging" by Michael Maxwell argues for the representation of morphological and phonological features in a linguistic way that allows for automatic conversion into parsers. For debugging, he presents a tool that enables the linguist to follow each step during analysis and generation. Here again, linguists do not need programming skills but can adjust the parser on the linguistic level.

The contributions show that high-quality research is being conducted in the area of computational morphology: Mature systems are further developed and new systems and applications are emerging. Other languages than English are becoming more important. The papers in this book come from eight countries and two continents, discuss a wide variety of living and ancient languages, and illustrate that, in fact, morphological resources are indeed the basis for higher-level natural language processing applications.

The trend towards open-source developments still goes on and evaluation is considered an important issue. Making high-quality morphological resources freely available will help to advance the state of the art and allow for the development of high-quality real-world applications. Useful applications shown as use cases here with carefully conducted evaluation demonstrate to a broad audience that computational morphology might not be a solved problem but is mature enough to be used in research settings in the Digital Humanities. It also shows that computational morphology is an actual science with tangible benefits for society.

July 2015   Cerstin Mahlow
                                                           Michael Piotrowski

Acknowledgments

We would like to thank the authors for their contributions to the workshop and to this book. We also thank the reviewers for their effort and for their constructive feedback, encouraging and helping the authors to improve their papers. The submission and reviewing process and the compilation of the proceedings was supported by the EasyChair system. We thank Aliaksandr Birukou, the editor of the series *Communications in Computer and Information Science* (CCIS), and the Springer staff for publishing the proceedings of SFCM 2015. We are grateful for the financial support given by the German Society for Computational Linguistics and Language Technology (GSCL), the Institut für Deutsche Sprache, and CLARIN-D. We thank Jonas Kuhn and the staff from the Institute for Natural Language Processing (IMS) at the University of Stuttgart for hosting the workshop and for helping with local organization.

Organization

The Fourth International Workshop on Systems and Frameworks for Computational Morphology (SFCM 2015) was organized and chaired by Cerstin Mahlow and Michael Piotrowski. The workshop was held at the Institute for Natural Language Processing (IMS) at the University of Stuttgart, Germany.

Program Chairs

Cerstin Mahlow	Institut für Deutsche Sprache, Mannheim, Germany
Michael Piotrowski	Leibniz Institute of European History, Mainz, Germany

Program Committee

Delphine Bernhard	Université de Strasbourg, France
Bruno Cartoni	Google, Switzerland
Simon Clematide	University of Zurich, Switzerland
Thomas Hanneforth	University of Potsdam, Germany
Lauri Karttunen	Stanford University, USA
Kimmo Koskenniemi	University of Helsinki, Finland
Krister Lindén	University of Helsinki, Finland
Anke Lüdeling	Humboldt-Universität zu Berlin, Germany
Cerstin Mahlow	Institut für Deutsche Sprache, Germany
Günter Neumann	DFKI Saarbrücken, Germany
Michael Piotrowski	Leibniz Institute of European History, Germany
Yves Scherrer	University of Geneva, Switzerland
Helmut Schmid	Ludwig-Maximilians-Universität München, Germany
Angelika Storrer	University of Mannheim, Germany
Marcin Wolinski	Polish Academy of Science, Poland
Andrea Zielinski	Fraunhofer IOSB, Germany

Host

Jonas Kuhn	University of Stuttgart, Germany

Sponsoring Institutions

German Society for Computational Linguistics and Language Technology (GSCL)
University of Stuttgart, Germany
Institut für Deutsche Sprache, Mannheim, Germany
CLARIN-D

Contents

Morphology Within the Multi-layered Annotation Scenario of the Prague Dependency Treebank

Magda Ševčíková[✉]

Faculty of Mathematics and Physics, Institute of Formal and Applied Linguistics,
Charles University in Prague, Malostranské náměstí 25,
118 00 Prague, Czech Republic
sevcikova@ufal.mff.cuni.cz

Abstract. Morphological annotation constitutes a separate layer in the multi-layered annotation scenario of the Prague Dependency Treebank. At this layer, morphological categories expressed by a word form are captured in a positional part-of-speech tag. According to the Praguian approach based on the relation between form and function, functions (meanings) of morphological categories are represented as well, namely as grammateme attributes at the deep-syntactic (tectogrammatical) layer of the treebank.

In the present paper, we first describe the role of morphology in the Prague Dependency Treebank, and then outline several recent topics based on Praguian morphology: named entity recognition in Czech, formemes attributes encoding morpho-syntactic information in the dependency-based machine translation system, and development of a lexical database of derivational relations based partially on information provided by the morphological analyser.

Keywords: Annotation · Deep syntax · Lemma · Morphology · Multi-layered scenario · Part-of-speech tag · Surface syntax · Tagging

1 Introduction

The Prague Dependency Treebank (PDT) has a multi-layered scenario designed on the theoretical basis of Functional Generative Description (FGD). Though the theoretical framework itself focuses mainly on syntactic issues, the PDT annotation project started with annotation at the morphological layer. Information included at this layer was extensively used during annotation at both the layer of surface syntax and the deep-syntactic layer (tectogrammatics).

In the paper, the formal approach to Czech inflectional morphology is introduced first (see Sect. 2). An overview of tools for morphological analysis and disambiguation is followed by a description of the part-of-speech (POS) tags and morphological lemmas. The core of the paper presents annotation of morphological categories in PDT within the theoretical framework of FGD (Sects. 3.1

© Springer International Publishing Switzerland 2015
C. Mahlow and M. Piotrowski (Eds.): SFCM 2015, CCIS 537, pp. 1–26, 2015.
DOI: 10.1007/978-3-319-23980-4_1

and 3.2). A lemma and a positional POS tag capturing formally expressed inflectional categories were assigned manually to each token at the morphological layer (Sect. 3.3), and reinterpreted in a semi-automatic procedure during the annotation at the tectogrammatical layer; here, meanings of semantically relevant morphological categories were represented as values of special attributes (called grammatemes) assigned to nodes of the tectogrammatical tree (Sect. 3.4). PDT annotation scenario served as one of the resources for other treebanks mentioned in Sect. 3.5.

In Sect. 4, recent topics are outlined that are immediately connected with the presented approach to Czech morphology, namely named entity recognition in Czech, formemes encoding morpho-syntactic information in the dependency-based machine translation system, and development of a lexical database of derivational relations based partially on information provided by the morphological analyser.

2   Computational Morphology of Czech

2.1   Tools for Morphological Analysis and Disambiguation

Czech is a Slavic language with a complex system of both inflectional and derivational morphology. Though the traditional separation of inflections and derivations, which is documented in influential grammars of Czech, has been partially overcome in some NLP approaches to Czech, the main focus is still on inflectional morphology.

This section is limited to morphological analysis and morphological disambiguation (tagging) as two subtasks of morphological processing of Czech;[1] the former of them consists in assigning pairs of a tag and a lemma to an individual word form (usually regardless of the context) while the latter subtask is to select a single tag–lemma pair for the respective word form, mostly with respect to a (close) context.

Formulation of a computational approach to Czech morphology is dated back to the 1990s; cf. first experiments in automatic morphological analysis and disambiguation of Czech by Hladká and Hajič [13,18,23]. Morphological analysis was based on the Czech morphological dictionary (published now under the name MorfFlex CZ; [14]) which contains more than 350 thousand manually entered entries; the recogniser recognises about 12 million Czech word forms.

For first tagging experiments [23], it was possible to use manually annotated data, thanks to a pioneering corpus annotation project which was carried out at the Institute of the Czech Language of the Academy of Sciences of the Czech Republic from 1971 to 1985 (the corpus was called Korpus věcného stylu 'Practical Corpus' and, later on, converted into the Czech Academic Corpus with morphological and analytical annotation compatible with PDT; [24,66,67]).

---

[1] The issues of morphological synthesis, generation etc. go beyond the scope of the paper; see Hajič [11] for a complex description of computational approach to Czech morphology including formal definitions.

Table 1. Comparison of the taggers according to their accuracy on Czech (based on [51,56])

Tagger	Accuracy
Morče semi-supervised [51]	95.89 %
MorphoDiTa [56]	95.75 %
Combination of taggers [52]	95.70 %
Morče [68]	95.67 %
HMM [29]	94.82 %
Feature-based tagger [11]	94.04 %

The next, feature-based tagger was trained already on PDT data, which were manually annotated with positional POS tags and lemmas (Sects. 2.2 and 3.3). The tagger was based on a statistical algorithm with an exponential model [11], and distributed, along with a tool for morphological analysis, as a part of the PDT 2.0 release [16]. An implementation based on Hidden Markov Models is available as well [29].

In line with efforts to develop and to improve POS taggers for English and other languages inspired by Collins [6] and others, a tagger based on averaged perceptron, called Morče (an acronym of Morfologie češtiny 'Morphology of Czech'; [68]), was published in 2006. The Morče tagger was trained on manually annotated data of PDT, achieving a state-of-the-art performance on Czech, and later on, it was involved in experiments combining this tagger with the feature-based tagger, HMM tagger and a rule-based component [52], and in semi-supervised training experiments [51].[2] The semi-supervised version of the Morče tagger outperformed its original implementation as well as the combination with other taggers; see Table 1.

The most recent implementation, MorphoDiTa (Morphological Dictionary and Tagger; [53,56]), is an open-source tool for morphological analysis, tagging, and lemmatisation as well as for tokenisation and morphological generation; it is available along with trained linguistic models.

The feature-based tagger and the Morče tagger were used for morphological processing of large (100,000,000+ tokens) corpora of the SYN series, built at the Institute of Czech National Corpus.[3] Experiments with the rule-based disambiguation of large corpus data have been carried out [31,36,37,39]. Nevertheless, improvements in tagging have been reported recently by applying a combined disambiguation system including the Morče tagger and a rule-based component [40]; compare previous approaches to combining statistical and rule-based methods in [15,50], or [52].

---

[2] The semi-supervised version of Morče was published under the Compost project (http://ufal.mff.cuni.cz/legacy/compost/cz/). An implementation of the averaged perceptron algorithm was released in the Featurama project too (http://sourceforge.net/projects/featurama/).

[3] http://korpus.cz/.

Table 2. Positions of the positional POS tag

Position no.	Name	Description
1	POS	Part of speech
2	SUBPOS	Detailed part of speech
3	GENDER	Gender
4	NUMBER	Number
5	CASE	Morphological case
6	POSSGENDER	Possessor's gender
7	POSSNUMBER	Possessor's number
8	PERSON	Person
9	TENSE	Tense
10	GRADE	Degree of comparison
11	NEGATION	Negation
12	VOICE	Verbal voice
13	RESERVE1	Unused
14	RESERVE2	Unused
15	VAR	Variant, style, register, special usage

All the tools described above use compact tags or, predominantly, positional POS tags (both described in Sect. 2.2) as the output tag format.

An alternative system of encoding Czech morphology has been developed in the Natural Language Processing Centre at the Faculty of Informatics, Masaryk University in Brno, and implemented in the ajka analyser, which provides both inflectional and (to a limited extent) derivational analysis of Czech based on a large-coverage dictionary [44,45].

Last but not least a weakly-supervised (resource-light) approach to morphological analysis and tagging is to be mentioned, which substantially decreases requirements on cost-intensive manual input [8,20]. Though the weak supervision is often accompanied with a lower accuracy, the approaches are advantageous especially for underresourced languages.

2.2   Tag Sets for Czech, Positional POS Tag and Morphological Lemma Used in the Prague Dependency Treebank

There have been several tag sets used for Czech. From the chronological perspective, the tag set used in the original annotation of the Czech Academic Corpus (CAC; see Sect. 2.1) should be mentioned first [66,67].

In the original CAC tag set,[4] tags of maximum eight positions were used. At the first and second position, the part-of-speech class of the token was specified; the remaining positions were associated with morphological categories that are relevant for the particular part-of-speech class. Thus, for instance, in the fourth

---

[4] http://ufal.mff.cuni.cz/rest/CAC/tOrig.html.

tag position, mood is encoded with verb forms while gender with noun, adjectives, pronouns, and numerals. The values to be filled in at a particular position were defined with respect to the part-of-speech class as well and encoded with digits. Therefore, for instance, the same digit in the same position is to be interpreted differently with adjectives and with verbs. Compare the original CAC tags to be assigned to the tokens *Pokládáte* '(you) find', *za* 'for', and *standardní* 'standard' (the first three tokens from the sentence analysed in Table 3) and their interpretation:

Pokládáte	5251_19	verb – imperfective – 2nd person plural – indicative present active – [imperative:default] – one-word form – gender not expressed
za	774	preposition – primary – with accusative
standardní	22_414	adjective – primary – [subclass:default] – neuter – singular – accusative

A system of compact tags was defined by Hajič [11], and used in compilation of the morphological dictionary (MorfFlex CZ; [14]) and in tagging experiments, e.g. [13]. This tag system works with positions, specifying a combination (a "pattern") of relevant morphological categories (each associated with a tag position) for each part-of-speech (sub)class.[5] Compact tags for the same three tokens should be interpreted as follows:[6]

Pokládáte	VPp2A	verb – indicative present – plural – 2nd person – affirmative
za	R4	preposition – with accusative
standardní	ANS41A	adjective – neuter – singular – accusative – no gradation – affirmative

As an alternative to compact tags, a system of positional POS tags was developed and gradually preferred to the former one; cf. Hajič [11].[7] Positional POS tags, along with two-component lemmas (described below), were assigned to the PDT data at the morphological layer; see Sect. 3.3.

A positional POS tag consists of 15 positions: The part of speech and a (functionally or formally delimited) subpart of it are encoded in the first and second positions of the tag, respectively. Positions 3 to 12 are each associated with a particular morphological category, positions 13 and 14 are reserved for a potential extension of the tag information, and the 15th position captures information of variants, register features etc.; see Table 2.[8] Part-of-speech classes

---

[5] http://ufal.mff.cuni.cz/pdt1/Morphology_and_Tagging/Doc/compact_tags.pdf.
[6] The tag of the verb form is composed according to the pattern for present indicative forms: VPnpa (i.e., verb – indicative present – number – person – negation).
[7] http://ufal.mff.cuni.cz/pdt1/Morphology_and_Tagging/Doc/hmptagqr.pdf.
[8] An extended version of 16 positions was used in corpora of the Czech National Corpus. The 16th position is associated with the category of aspect which is, when using the tag with 15 positions, encoded in the technical lemma suffix described below.

Table 3. Morphological lemma and positional POS tag assigned to tokens of the sentence *Pokládáte za standardní, když se s Mečiarovou vládou nelze téměř na ničem rozumně dohodnout?* (lit.: Find for standard, when REFL with Mečiar's government is-not-possible almost on nothing reasonably agree?) 'Do you find it standard when almost nothing can be reasonably agreed on with Mečiar's government?' at the morphological layer of PDT, and conversion of the positional POS tags into the Interset interlingua attribute–value pairs (last column)

Token	Morphological lemma	Positional POS tag	Interset
Pokládáte	pokládat_:T	VB-P- - -2P-AA- - -	pos="verb", negativeness="pos", number="plur", person="2", verbform="fin", mood="ind", tense="pres", voice="act"
za	za-1	RR- -4- - - - - - - - -	pos="adp", adpostype="prep", case="acc"
standardní	standardní	AAIP4- - - -1A- - - -	pos="adj", negativeness="pos", gender="masc", animateness="inan", number="plur", case="acc", degree="pos"
,	,	Z:- - - - - - - - - - - -	pos="punc"
když	když	J,- - - - - - - - - - - - -	pos="conj", conjtype="sub"
se	se_^(zvr._zájmeno/částice)	P7-X4- - - - - - - - -	pos="noun", prontype="prs", reflex="reflex", case="acc", variant="short"
s	s-1	RR- -7- - - - - - - - -	pos="adp", adpostype="prep", case="ins"
Mečiarovou	Mečiarův_:;S_^(*2)	AUFS7M- - - - - - - -	pos="adj", poss="poss", gender="fem", number="sing", case="ins", possgender="masc"
vládou	vláda	NNFS7- - - - -A- - - -	pos="noun", negativeness="pos", gender="fem", number="sing", case="ins"
nelze	lze	VB-S- - -3P-NA- - -	pos="verb", negativeness="neg", number="sing", person="3", verbform="fin", mood="ind", tense="pres", voice="act"
téměř	téměř	Db- - - - - - - - - - - -	pos="adv"
na	na-1	RR- -6- - - - - - - - -	pos="adp", adpostype="prep", case="loc"
ničem	nic	PW- -6- - - - - - - - -	pos="adj—noun", prontype="neg", negativeness="neg", case="loc"
rozumně	rozumně_^(*1ý)	Dg- - - - - - -1A- - - -	pos="adv", negativeness="pos", degree="pos"
dohodnout	dohodnout_:W	Vf- - - - - - - -A- - - -	pos="verb", negativeness="pos", verbform="inf"
?	?	Z:- - - - - - - - - - - -	pos="punc"

as well as values of morphological categories were delimited in accordance with their description in the academic grammar of Czech [25].

In spite of combinatorial restrictions implied by the language itself,[9] there is a considerable number of combinations of the category values attested in the language data; cf. 1,574 different positional POS tags (and 71,503 different morphological lemmas) assigned to 1,957,247 tokens of the PDT 3.0 data annotated at the morphological layer. The positional POS tag, which allows for a combination of values of single categories, enables thus to describe the rich inflection in an economical way (compare, for instance, the POS tag set used in the Penn Treebank project [32]).

Besides a positional POS tag, each token was assigned a morphological lemma composed of two parts at the morphological layer of PDT. The first part of the lemma (so-called lemma proper) is a string of characters mostly corresponding to the base form of the word (namely, nominative singular form of nouns, nominative singular masculine of pronouns and numerals, nominative singular masculine positive form of adjectives, infinitive form of verbs, and positive form of adverbs).[10] Since the lemma was proposed as a unique identifier, ambiguous base forms were disambiguated with a digit attached by a hyphen to the string of characters (cf. Lemmas assigned to prepositions *za*, *s*, and *na* in Table 3).

The second part of the lemma is a technical suffix. It is attached to the lemma proper by an underscore. Technical suffixes do not occur with most lemmas; however, if needed, more technical suffixes are possible with a single lemma. The suffix contains either a comment on verbal aspect (cf. the suffix of the verb lemma *pokládat* in Table 3), or a comment explaining the respective meaning (suffix of the pronoun *se*), a label identifying the named entity type (_;S with the lemma *Mečiarův* identifying surnames), or derivational information (namely, formally encoded changes to be carried out to arrive at the base word; cf. _ ^(*2) with the same lemma: two characters should be removed in order to get the base word *Mečiar*).

Motivated by the needs of parsing, machine translation and other NLP subtasks, a method for conversion of different sets of POS tags has been developed: Interset is a set of universal morpho-syntactic features to which tag sets used in different corpora can be converted; it has been proposed as a sort of interlingua for POS tags [71]. The most recent Interset version covers 64 different tag sets of 37 languages [70]. See the positional POS tags used in PDT converted into the Interset attribute–value structures in Table 3.

---

[9] Generally speaking, there are typical nominal categories, such as case and gender, which do not combine with verbal categories, such as person, tense, mood, and voice. However, for instance, some Czech verb forms (past participle, transgressive) are marked for gender.

[10] With pluralia tantum nouns and other words with an incomplete or deficient paradigm, other forms are used instead of the canonical one; for instance, the plurale tantum *kalhoty* 'trousers' is assigned the nominative plural form as a lemma.

3 Annotation of Morphological Categories in the Prague Dependency Treebank

3.1 Theoretical Background of the Prague Dependency Treebank: Functional Generative Description

Functional Generative Description is a theoretical linguistic framework formulated in Prague in the 1960s [48,49]. It is rooted in the structuralist approach of the Prague Linguistic Circle; however, it has responded to similar stimuli as foreign approaches with fundamentally different backgrounds.

FGD decomposes the language system into several levels;[11] the "lowest" of them corresponds to linear text (either spoken or written) whereas the "highest" level represents the linguistic meaning of the sentence and is modelled as a dependency tree structure.[12] Between these two levels (phonetic and tectogrammatical level, respectively), another three levels were discerned in the original proposal, namely the morphonological level, morphological level, and level of surface syntax.

The theoretical fundamentals of FGD, to which – besides multiple levels – the dependency approach to syntax and the theory of valency belong, served as a starting point for the design of the annotation scenario of PDT [5]. Out of the set of levels differentiated in FGD, three layers have been included in the PDT scenario: the morphological layer, surface-syntactic layer, and tectogrammatical layer. Differences between the layout of the PDT layers and levels in FGD were motivated by the needs of NLP tasks, e.g. parsing, and were analysed by Štěpánek [65].

The formalised approach to morphology as a separate level of the language system model and the description of the meanings of morphological categories at the tectogrammatical level is a stable part of the FGD framework[13] and has been adopted into the annotation scenario of PDT as well.

---

[11] The present paper draws a terminological distinction between a *level* as a concept of the theoretical framework of FGD and a *layer* as a part of the annotation scenario of PDT.

[12] An opposite perspective, i.e. the text as a surface string which is assigned a deeper analysis, is justifiable as well; however, we stick to the perspective from the text as a basis on the top of which analyses are built.

[13] There are considerable similarities in dealing with morphology between FGD (and PDT) and the Meaning-Text Theory (MTT). As in MTT even more levels are distinguished than in FGD, the morphological level in FGD corresponds mainly to the deep-morphological representation in MTT but shares several features with the surface-syntactic representation of this framework [34]. The function of morphological categories is then a part of the deep-syntactic representation in MTT (the attributes are called grammemes in MTT and grammatemes in FGD); see Žabokrtský [74] for a more detailed comparison of these frameworks.

3.2 History of the Prague Dependency Treebank

The Prague Dependency Treebank is a collection of Czech newspaper texts from 1990s, processed at four layers. At the first (non-annotation) layer, called word layer, the source text is segmented into documents and paragraphs, tokens are associated with unique identifiers. At the morphological layer, as the lowest annotation layer, each token is assigned a positional POS tag and a lemma, see Table 3. At the surface-syntactic (analytical) layer, the syntactic structure of each sentence is represented as a dependency-tree structure. Nodes of the analytical tree are in a one-to-one correspondence to tokens at the morphological layer and are labelled with surface-syntactic functions (such as subject Sb, object Obj etc.; Fig. 1). At the tectogrammatical layer (the highest layer of annotation), the

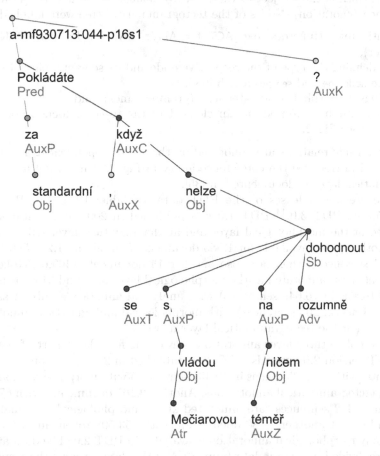

Fig. 1. Sentence *Pokládáte za standardní, kdyč se s Mečiarovou vládou nelze téměř na ničem rozumně dohodnout?* 'Do you find it standard when almost nothing can be reasonably agreed on with Mečiar's government?' annotated at the analytical layer of PDT 3.0. Nodes are labelled with word forms and surface-syntactic functions (e.g., Sb for subject, Adv for adverbials, the Aux labels are assigned to different types of function words)

underlying syntactic structure of the sentence is also represented as a dependency tree, which, however, differs from the analytical one in several aspects.

While every token annotated at the morphological layer has exactly one corresponding node in the analytical tree, the correspondence between the nodes of the tectogrammatical tree and the analytical tree, which is nevertheless explicitly recorded in the data in the form of cross-layer references, is not always one-to-one, since only content words are represented as tectogrammatical nodes, and new nodes are constructed for deletions (cf. the node with the lemma #PersPron representing the pro-dropped subject pronoun of the verb *pokládáte* in Fig. 2) or for grammatical elements which do play a role in the syntactic structure but cannot be expressed in the surface shape of the sentence (see the #Cor node in Fig. 2, which is the subject of the infinitive *dohodnout se* and is relevant for coreference annotation). Nodes of the tectogrammatical tree were labelled with

- semantic roles (functors; e.g. ACT for Actor, PAT for Patient, MANN for Manner),
- labels defining the type of the respective node and its semantic part of speech (cf. the nodetype and sempos attributes),
- meanings of morphological categories (grammatemes), and
- labels identifying the node as an element of the topic or focus part of the sentence; see Fig. 2.

Non-dependency relations are annotated on the top of dependencies in the tectogrammatical tree; see the coreference arrow in Fig. 2. Annotation at the tectogrammatical layer is documented in [35].

There are four releases of the PDT data available: PDT 1.0, PDT 2.0, PDT 2.5, and PDT 3.0.[14] PDT 1.0 was published in 2001 and contains data annotated at the morphological layer and at the analytical layer [19]. Annotation of both types is available for 1,583 documents (containing 1,255,590 tokens in 81,614 sentences); there are also another 14 documents (469,652 tokens in 29,561 sentences) annotated at the morphological layer only and 314 documents (251,743 tokens in 16,649 sentences) with analytical annotation only. A sample of 3,490 tokens (in 203 sentences) with morphological and analytical annotation is annotated at the tectogrammatical layer as well.

The complete three-layer annotation is available for a large part of the data from PDT version 2.0 onwards. PDT 2.0, published in 2006 [16], contains 3,165 documents (with 833,195 tokens in 49,431 sentences) with morphological, analytical, and tectogrammatical annotations. Another 2,165 documents (with 670,544 tokens in 38,482 sentences) are annotated at the morphological and analytical layer, and for yet another 1,780 documents (with 453,508 tokens in 27,931 sentences) only morphological annotation is available in PDT 2.0. The data at each layer were divided into train data (app. 80 % of the data set with the respective annotation combination), development-test data (app. 10 %), and evaluation-test data (app. 10 %).

---

[14] A preliminary, test version of the treebank (PDT 0.5), containing 450 thousand tokens in 26 thousand sentences, was compiled for the Summer Workshop on Language Engineering at the Johns Hopkins University in Baltimore in 1998.

In PDT 2.5 and PDT 3.0 (released in 2011 and 2013, respectively),[15] the texts of PDT 2.0 are enriched with new annotations at the tectogrammatical and analytical layer, but neither the size of the data nor the portions of the data annotated at individual layers have changed; particular mistakes were corrected in the recent releases as well [3,4]. The following annotations were new in the PDT 2.5 as compared to PDT 2.0:

- annotation of multiword expressions at the tectogrammatical layer,
- a new grammateme identifying a special usage of plural forms of nouns (pair/group meaning) at the tectogrammatical layer,
- clause segmentation at the analytical layer.

For the PDT 3.0 release, the tectogrammatical layer was further modified:

- changes in the modality grammatemes,
- an extended annotation of coreference and bridging anaphora,
- annotation of discourse relations,
- genre specification.

Table 4. Values of the nodetype attribute assigned to each tectogrammatical node

nodetype values	Description
complex	Complex nodes represent nouns, adjectives, verbs, adverbs, and pronouns and numerals; they are the only nodes assigned with grammatemes
root	The root of the tectogrammatical tree is a technical node labelled with a unique identifier of the sentence
atom	Atomic nodes represent rhematisers, modal modifications (with functors RHEM, MOD, respectively) etc.
coap	Roots of coordination and apposition constructions are, according to the FGD convention, assigned a lemma of the coordinating conjunction or an artificial lemma of a punctuation symbol (e.g. #Comma)
fphr	Nodes with the FPHR functor are parts of foreign phrases, i.e. they are components of phrases that do not follow rules of Czech grammar
dphr	Dependent parts of phrasemes represent words that constitute a single lexical unit with their parent node (with the DPHR functor); the meaning of this unit is not a sum of the meanings of its component parts
list	Roots of foreign and identification phrases (with lemmas #Forn and #Idph) were added into the tree as parent nodes of foreign phrases (i.e., nodes with nodetype=fphr) or as parents of a multi-word named entity
qcomplex	Quasi-complex nodes represent obligatory verbal complementations that are not present in the surface sentence (they are mostly labelled with the same functors as complex nodes but have a special lemma, e.g. #Gen)

---

[15] Syntactically annotated PDT data of the particular versions are publicly accesible via the PML Tree Query environment (https://lindat.mff.cuni.cz/services/pmltq/; [38]) for searching.

3.3 Morphology as a Layer of Annotation in the Prague Dependency Treebank

As one can see from the history of the PDT releases, data of PDT were annotated at the morphological layer first. Each token was assigned a positional POS tag and a morphological lemma within a manual procedure which was preceded by an automatic morphological analysis.

The manual annotation was carried out by eight annotators [21]. Each file was annotated by two annotators in parallel, their task was a manual disambiguation of results of the morphological analysis using the DA and LAW (Lexical Annotation Workbench) editors of morphological annotations.[16] When the lemma was not offered by the tagger, it was created manually by the annotator and, subsequently, included into the morphological dictionary. After the parallel annotation was finished, instances of disagreement were decided by a third annotator. See the morphological annotation of a sentence in Table 3.

Annotation at the morphological layer was used during annotation at the analytical and, more importantly, at the tectogrammatical layer, being the main source of information for automatic assignment of grammatemes.

Morphological annotation, after a separate checking at this layer, was involved in the cross-layer checking of analytical and tectogrammatical annotations before the public release of the data. Štěpánek [64] gives examples of rather simple comparisons of POS tag values with surface-syntactic functions at the analytical layer and with functors at the tectogrammatical layer (e.g. with conjunctions), and describes checking of named entity information involved in the technical suffix of the morphological lemma against the tectogrammatical annotation, or a complex verification whether all valency slots defined by the valency lexicon are filled in with tectogrammatical nodes representing the requested word forms.

Table 5. Frequency of the nodetype values in the PDT 3.0 data annotated at all three layers

nodetype value	Frequency
complex	550,909
root	49,431
qcomplex	45,995
coap	35,742
atom	34,032
fphr	4,553
list	2,515
dphr	1,283

---

[16] https://bitbucket.org/jhana/feat-morph/wiki/Home.

3.4   Morphological Meanings at the Tectogrammatical Layer

Following the Praguian tradition of distinguishing form and function, functions (meanings) of morphological categories are captured by grammateme attributes in the tectogrammatical tree. The inclusion of grammatemes into the tectogrammatical layer responds to the claim of self-containedness and unambiguity of the sentence representation at each layer. If, for instance, meanings conveyed by the grammatical number with nouns, degree of comparison with adjectives, or tense with verbs were not specified at the tectogrammatical layer, several semantically different sentences could be generated from a single tectogrammatical tree.

Since morphological meanings are conveyed only by some nodes of the tectogrammatical tree and, moreover, not all grammatemes are relevant for all nodes, tectogrammatical nodes were classified in two subsequent steps. First, eight general types of nodes were distinguished according to their functor and/or tectogrammatical lemma in a fully automatic procedure. Grammatemes are relevant for nodes of just one type (for complex nodes); cf. the nodetype values and their frequency in PDT 3.0 in Tables 4 and 5.

Second, complex nodes were subdivided into four groups, called semantic parts of speech (semantic nouns, semantic adjectives, semantic verbs, and semantic adverbs) within which 19 more specific subgroups were discerned automatically. Accordingly, the sempos attribute with 19 values was defined (Table 6). Each subgroup was associated with a set of relevant grammatemes.

Table 6. Frequency of the sempos values in the PDT 3.0 data annotated at all three layers

sempos value	Frequency	sempos value	Frequency
n.denot	236,890	n.pron.def.demon	4,760
adj.denot	101,057	adj.pron.indef	3,383
v	88,026	adv.pron.indef	3,107
n.pron.def.pers	32,938	adv.pron.def	2,928
adj.quant.def	19,428	adj.quant.grad	1,865
n.denot.neg	18,832	adv.denot.grad.nneg	1,139
n.pron.indef	11,342	adv.denot.grad.neg	1,073
adv.denot.ngrad.nneg	8,996	adv.denot.ngrad.neg	751
n.quant.def	7,993	adj.quant.indef	655
adj.pron.def.demon	5,745		

As annotation of grammatemes was the last task in the PDT 2.0 annotation procedure, it could profit from the annotation at lower layers as well as from annotations already done at the tectogrammatical layer (mainly from the tree structure, functors, and coreference).

Nearly 1,600,000 grammateme values in total (with more than 550 thousand complex nodes) were assigned at the tectogrammatical layer of PDT 2.0, most of them automatically. Manual annotation, carried out by two annotators in parallel, with a follow-up decision by a third annotator in cases of disagreement, is responsible for approximately 17,500 out of the grammateme values [42].

The set of grammatemes and values assigned at the tectogrammatical layer was based on the FGD framework [49]. However, the repertoire has been revisited and changed according to the recent linguistic research during the annotation of individual PDT releases. In this paper, we present the grammateme annotation which is available in PDT 3.0.

There are 15 grammatemes annotated at the tectogrammatical layer of PDT 3.0. Grammatemes number, gender, person, politeness, and typgroup were assigned to nodes classified as semantic nouns. The grammatemes degcmp, negation, numertype, and indeftype were annotated with semantic nouns and with semantic adjectives. Semantic adverbs were assigned grammatemes degcmp, negation, and indeftype. Semantic verbs were assigned a special subset of verbal grammatemes: tense, aspect, factmod, deontmod, diatgram, and iterativeness.

Seven out of the 15 grammatemes correlate with morphological categories which are traditionally addressed in the grammatical description of Czech. Nevertheless, the grammateme values cannot be mostly interpreted from a single word form (its POS tag), but a more complex structure including auxiliaries had to be involved in the value assignment procedure (cf. grammatemes tense, factmod, deontmod, or diatgram described below), or manual annotation was needed, for instance, to assign number with pluralia tantum, absolute usage of comparative forms of adjectives and adverbs, or polite usage of 2nd person plural verbs.

- The number grammateme captures the number of entities to which the particular noun refers. In most cases, the value (sg or pl) correlates with the morphological category but is different, for instance, with pluralia tantum nouns (e.g., *otevřel dveře*.sg *na terasu* 'he opened the door to the terrace' vs. *několikery dveře*.pl 'several doors').
- Values of the gender grammateme (anim for animate masculines, inan for inanimates, fem and neut) correspond to the morphological gender of nouns, but if the grammatical gender does not coincide with the natural gender, the grammateme value was chosen according to the former one (cf. the neuter noun *děvče* 'girl').
- The person grammateme (values 1 for the speaker, 2 for the hearer, and 3 for a person/object it is talked about) was assigned with nodes representing pronouns. The grammateme values were non-trivially interpreted from agreement markers expressed by relevant verb forms.
- Values pos (positive), comp (comparative), and sup (superlative) of the degcmp grammateme correspond mostly to the category of degree of comparison, but comparative forms with an absolute (non-comparative) meaning were identified manually and assigned the third value acomp (e.g., *starší žena* 'an elder(ly) woman').

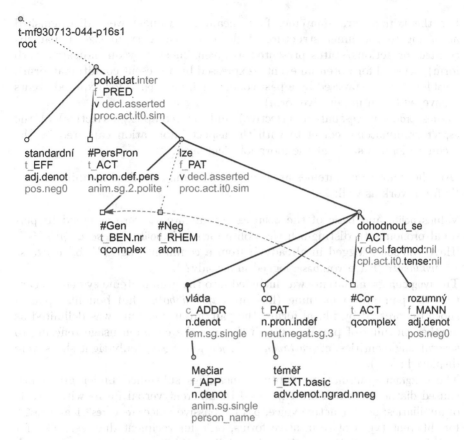

Fig. 2. Sentence *Pokládáte za standardní, když se s Mečiarovou vládou nelze téměř na ničem rozumně dohodnout?* 'Do you find it standard when almost nothing can be reasonably agreed on with Mečiar's government?' annotated at the tectogrammatical layer of PDT 3.0. Nodes are labelled with a tectogrammatical lemma, with a functor (e.g. ACT, MANN), topic-focus annotation (in front of the functor), a nodetype value (e.g., root or qcomplex), or a semantic part of speech and grammatemes (only with complex nodes, displayed under the functor). The predicate node of the tree (functor PRED) was assigned a sentence modality value (here, inter for interrogative sentences)

– Values of the tense grammateme distinguish the presented actions/states according to whether they preceded the moment of utterance or another action (ant), followed it (post), or happened simultaneously with it (sim). If the particular node represented a more complex verb form, the grammateme value had to be interpreted carefully. For example, future verbal tense in Czech is expressed by a simple inflected form (with perfectives; *dohodne se* '(he) will-agree'), or by an auxiliary verb (imperfectives; *bude pokládat* '(he) will find'), or by prefixing (lexically limited; cf. the future form *pojede* '(he) will-go' of the verb *jet* 'to go').

- For the factmod grammateme, four meanings (values) were distinguished according to the inner structure of the mood category in Czech, namely, asserted for actions/states presented as given (mostly by an indicative verb form), potential for potential events (expressed by a present conditional form), irreal for events expressed by a past conditional, and appeal for required events (conveyed by an imperative form).
- Values proc (processual/imperfective) and cpl (complex/perfective) of the aspect grammateme correlate with the aspect information captured by the technical lemma suffix at the morphological layer.

Another four grammatemes are considered grammaticalised meanings in the FGD framework as well:

- Values polite and basic of the politeness grammateme were assigned to personal pronouns to distinguish the polite form (*Vy*.polite *jste se už přihlásil?* 'Have you.polite logged in already?') from a common usage (*Vy*.basic *jste se už přihlásili?* 'Have you.basic logged in already?').
- The typgroup grammateme was included into the grammateme system to capture the pair/group meaning (like in *koupil si boty* '(he) bought a-pair-of shoes') expressed by plural forms; the pair/group meaning was delimited as another meaning of plural in Czech (besides the common usage reffering to several single entities, cf. *vystaveny byly jen pravé boty* 'only right shoes were displayed'; [58]).
- The diatgram grammateme captures meanings subsumed under grammaticalised diatheses, which are expressed by different verbal forms with a scale of auxiliaries: act for active voice, pas for passive voice, res1, res2.1 and res2.2 for different types of resultative forms, recip for recipient diathesis, disp for verb forms expressing dispositional modality, and deagent for deagentive verb forms.
- The deontmod grammateme was used to represent modal verbs as auxiliaries at the tectogrammatical layer; seven values were delimited according to modal meanings of necessity, possibility etc.

Even subsumed under the term of grammatemes, the following attributes capture derivational morphology,[17] rather than inflections:

- The iterativeness grammateme enables to represent an iterative verb by the tectogrammatical lemma of its non-iterative counterpart.
- The negation grammateme represents the negative meaning (expressed mostly by the *ne-* prefix) of nouns, adjectives and adverbs.[18]
- The indeftype grammateme made it possible to reduce pronouns and pronominal adverbs to a small set of lemmas at the tectogrammatical layer, exploiting the semantically relevant regularities within this closed class [62]. Cf. the node

---

[17] These derivations are subtypes of lexical derivation according to Kuryłowicz [30].

[18] Negated verb forms are analysed differently at the tectogrammatical layer, namely, they are decomposed into two nodes; cf. the verbal node with the lemma *lze* and node with the artificial lemma #Neg representing the negation in Fig. 2.

with the lemma *co* 'what' in Fig. 2, which represents the pronoun *(na) ničem* '(on) nothing' (the negative semantic feature was captured by the negat value).
– Similarly, the numertype is used to capture the specific meanings of different types of numerals (e.g. ordinal numerals, multipliers) that are represented by the tectogrammatical lemma of the corresponding cardinal numeral.

In addition to the approach described above for selected derivational relations captured by grammatemes, two types of highly regular derivatives, namely possessive adjectives and deadjectival adverbs, were converted into their base words, i.e., into nouns and adjectives, respectively. Since both these types of derivatives differ from their base words just in the function they play within the tectogrammatical structure,[19] it is sufficient to use the functor to encode the difference between the derived word and the base; see the nodes with the lemma *Mečiar* and *rozumný* 'reasonable' in Fig. 2.

Possible extension of the annotation of derivational morphology at the tectogrammatical layer is discussed in Sect. 4.3.

3.5 PDT-Style Annotations in Other Treebanks

Czech Academic Corpus, mentioned above in Sect. 2, has been converted from the original annotation (carried out in the 1970s and 1980s) into the PDT annotation scheme after the PDT 2.0 release; cf. CAC 1.0 [67] and CAC 2.0 [66]. CAC 2.0 contains morphological and analytical annotation for nearly 500 thousand tokens (and another data portion with morphological annotation only) which is now fully compatible with PDT.

Besides CAC, PDT annotation scenario has been used also for Arabic [17] and English [12], and has served as one of the resources for annotation schemes for Slovak (Slovak Treebank, which is a part of the Slovak National Corpus), Slovenian (Slovene Dependency Treebank),[20] Ancient Greek and Latin (Ancient Greek and Latin Dependency Treebanks),[21] and as an inspiration for other treebanking projects.

In 2011, an important project of bringing treebanks of different languages (some of them just mentioned) under a common annotation scheme has been proposed under the acronym HamleDT (HArmonized Multi-LanguagE Dependency Treebank). Treebanks were harmonised into the Prague Dependencies annotation style (based on analytical PDT annotation; [73]) and, recently, converted into Stanford Universal Dependencies [33]. Thirty treebanks are available in HamleDT 2.0 [43, 72].[22]

---

[19] They belong to syntactic derivation as defined by Kuryłowicz [30].
[20] http://nl.ijs.si/sdt/.
[21] http://nlp.perseus.tufts.edu/syntax/treebank/.
[22] Stanford Universal Dependencies, the Interset interligua (mentioned in Sect. 2.2), and Google universal POS tags [41] served as a basis for the annotation scheme of the Universal Dependencies treebank project, the current version of which (Universal Dependencies 1.1; [1]) contains dependency annotated data for 18 languages including Czech.

4   Morphology in Named Entity Recognition, Dependency-Based Machine Translation, and in a Database of Derivational Relations in Czech

4.1   Named Entity Recognition in Czech

In a pilot approach to named entity (NE) classification and recognition, started only in 2007 [60], technical suffixes of morphological lemmas were used as an important resource for this task. Based on a survey of previous NE research using a low number of coarse-grained categories (such as [9]) on the one hand, or detailed categories (preferred in semantically oriented tasks, cf. [47]) on the other, a two-level classification has been proposed for Czech, which is convenient for both a robust processing and research interested in more subtle categorisation.

At the first level of the classification, ten rough categories were distinguished and, at the second level, further subclassified into 62 detailed categories. For instance, within the category of geographical names, subcategories of names of continents, states, towns, hydronyms etc. were discerned. This classification was used in the Czech Named Entity Corpus (CNEC), which consists of 6 thousand sentences with more than 150 thousand tokens manually assigned with NE categories [57,61]. The data were used for development of several recognisers of NE in Czech texts; cf. [26–28,55,60], and the most recent of them, NameTag [54,56], which is an open-source tool for NE recognition, distributed along with trained linguistic models.

4.2   Formemes in Dependency-Based Machine Translation

The complex dependency deep-syntactic analysis has been used as a transfer layer in a machine translation system developed at the Institute of Formal and Applied Linguistics, Faculty of Mathematics and Physics, Charles University in Prague. The MT system, originally called TectoMT [75], has been extended with a number of modules into a modular NLP framework Treex, which is either available for installation from CPAN,[23] or can be run on-line under the LIN-DAT/CLARIN repository [46]. Recently, the Treex framework has been used, for instance, in the QTLeap European machine translation project.[24]

The deep-syntactic analysis provided by the Treex framework has introduced a special type of attributes, called formemes, into the deep-syntactic tree. Formemes are node attributes in which the form of the word represented by respective node is encoded by a combination of morphological and syntactic features. Taking the example of the prepositional phrase *s (Mečiarovou) vládou* in Fig. 2 and its English equivalent *with (Mečiar's) government*, the formeme n:with+X is to be assigned to the tectogrammatical node representing the (source) phrase *with government* within the English-to-Czech machine translation, while the node representing the (target) phrase *s vládou* is assigned the formeme n:s+7

---

[23] See http://ufal.mff.cuni.cz/treex.

[24] http://qtleap.eu/.

in which the morphological case (7 for instrumental) is specified in addition to the particular preposition. A complete list of formemes implemented in Treex can be found in [7].

From the perspective of the PDT annotation scheme, information encoded in formemes is a combination of information involved in POS tags at the morphological layer and in surface-syntactic functions at the analytical layer of PDT with selected auxiliary words (e.g., prepositions).

4.3 Derivational Morphology in Czech

Besides a basic NE annotation, the technical suffix of the morphological lemma provides information on regular derivational relations as well.[25] In PDT, derivational information involved in the lemma suffix at the morphological layer was extended by derivational information captured in selected grammatemes or in functors at the tectogrammatical layer (see Sect. 3.4).

This rather preliminary approach to interconnection of Czech derivational morphology with inflections on the one hand, and with syntax on the other has indicated the way how to overbridge the separation of derivations from inflectional morphology which is documented in all representative grammars of Czech.[26]

In order to put the annotation of derivations in PDT on a solid basis but, primarily, to build a reliable resource of derivational data for Czech, a lexical network of derivationally related words (DeriNet; [59]) is being developed. The current version DeriNet 0.9 contains more than 305 thousand lexemes which were connected with more than 117 thousand links that correspond to derivational relations between pairs of lexemes (i.e., between a base lexeme and a lexeme derived from it).[27] The pairs of derivationally related lexemes can be arranged into a tree graph; see the derivational tree with the root *standard* 'standard' (displayed by DeriNet Viewer)[28] in Fig. 3.

The network was initialised with a set of lexemes whose existence was supported by corpus evidence. As the data were morphologically processed by the Morče tagger, technical suffixes including derivational information were available, and were extensively used in creating derivational links in the network. This starting annotation phase has been followed by several rounds of semi-automatic annotation within which special attention had to be devoted to vowel and consonant alternations that occur very frequently during derivation in Czech. Since some of the alternations are involved in the inflectional paradigm as well, recent efforts in exploiting the inflectional morphological dictionary seem to make it

---

[25] A limited derivational analysis is carried out also by the ajka analyser (see Sect. 2.1).

[26] In Czech linguistics, derivation is separated from inflectional morphology, being described as the core part of word-formation, which is kept apart from the grammatical module; only inflectional morphology and syntax are supposed to constitute the grammatical structure of Czech.

[27] http://ufal.mff.cuni.cz/derinet.

[28] http://ufal.mff.cuni.cz/derinet/viewer.

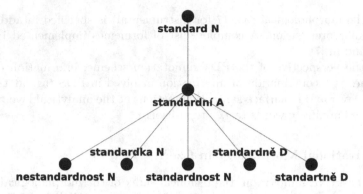

Fig. 3. The derivational tree of the noun *standard* 'standard' in the lexical network DeriNet

possible to build a model of alternations which will enable to couple derivationally related lexemes automatically with a high precision even if they differ substantially due to the alternations.[29]

Though DeriNet is still being developed (besides exploitation of the inflectional data, the main focus is on addition of new edges and correction of mistakes),[30] it is, to the best of our knowledge, the most complex and the only freely available resource of derivational data for Czech, and it belongs to a relative small number of derivational resources in general (cf. CELEX [2] for English, German and Dutch, DerivBase for German [69], DerivBase.Hr for Croatian [63], or most recently, the Démonette network for French [22]).

After arriving at a final version of the DeriNet data, semantic labelling of the derivational relations is proposed as the next step. Here, dealing with ambiguity and homonymy is expected to be the biggest challenge.[31]

The DeriNet network enriched with semantic labels is then envisaged to be used as the main resource for an extension of the derivational annotation of tectogrammatical data in PDT. Nevertheless, it is expected that only the most frequent semantic classes of derivatives with a transparent derivational meaning will be processed in order not to "overload" the data and to keep them usable for both NLP tasks and linguistic research.

---

[29] For instance, one of the changes occurring during derivation of the adjective *sněžný* 'snowy' from the noun *sníh* 'snow' is present in the inflectional paradigm of the noun (*sníh*.nom.sg – *sněhu*.gen.sg).

[30] One of the current mistakes is documented in the tree in Fig. 3: the noun *nestandardnost* 'non-standardness' is to be captured as derived either from the noun *standardnost* 'standardness', or from the adjective *nestandardní* 'non-standard' (which is not included in the network, though).

[31] For instance, the suffix *-ka* is used both in diminutives and female nouns (e.g. *skříň* 'cupboard' > *skříňka* 'small cupboard', *učitel* 'teacher' > *učitelka* 'female teacher'), and, on the other hand, several meanings are expressed by formally different affixes in Czech (e.g. female nouns are derived by the suffixes *-ka*, *-yně*, *-ice*, *-ovna* and several others).

5 Conclusions

The aim of the present paper was to put together a complex picture of the role of morphology in the richly annotated data of the Prague Dependency Treebank. Morphological annotation constitutes a separate layer in the treebank, nevertheless, it has been used as a source of information encoded at the higher, structural layers of annotation. Correlations between morphological categories captured at the morphological layer and grammateme attributes included in the tectogrammatical tree were analysed in detail.

Though tagging has been discussed to be a sort of solved task for at least "sufficiently resourced" languages [10], probably including Czech, it is still an interesting and appealing task since, particularly in a morphologically rich language like Czech, a high-quality lemmatisation and POS tagging are considered a common prerequisite of most NLP tasks.

In the paper we briefly outlined several topics that are based on morphological tools, and on morphologically annotated data as well. An outlook, concerning the proposed extension of the tectogrammatical annotation with derivations, documents the importance of morphology in efforts to deepen the syntactic analysis of language data.

Acknowledgements. The research reported on in the paper has been supported by the LINDAT-Clarin project of the Ministry of Education of the Czech Republic (LM2010013).

References

1. Agić, Ž., Aranzabe, M.J., Atutxa, A., Bosco, C., Choi, J., de Marneffe, M.-C., Dozat, T., Farkas, R., Foster, J., Ginter, F., Goenaga, I., Gojenola, K., Goldberg, Y., Hajič, J., Johannsen, A.T., Kanerva, J., Kuokkala, J., Laippala, V., Lenci, A., Lindén, K., Ljubešić, N., Lynn, T., Manning, C., Martínez, H.A., McDonald, R., Missilä, A., Montemagni, S., Nivre, J., Nurmi, H., Osenova, P., Petrov, S., Piitulainen, J., Plank, B., Prokopidis, P., Pyysalo, S., Seeker, W., Seraji, M., Silveira, N., Simi, M., Simov, K., Smith, A., Tsarfaty, R., Vincze, V., Zeman, D.: Universal Dependencies 1.1. LINDAT/CLARIN digital library at Institute of Formal and Applied Linguistics, Charles University in Prague (2015). http://hdl.handle.net/11234/LRT-1478
2. Baayen, R.H., Piepenbrock, R., Gulikers, L.: The CELEX lexical database (release 2), Data/software. Linguistic Data Consortium, Philadelphia (1995)
3. Bejček, E., Hajič, J., Panevová, J., Mírovský, J., Spoustová, J., Štěpánek, J., Straňák, P., Šidák, P., Vimmrová, P., Šťastná, E., Ševčíková, M., Smejkalová, L., Homola, P., Popelka, J., Lopatková, M., Hrabalová, L., Kluyeva, N., Žabokrtský, Z.: Prague Dependency Treebank 2.5. LINDAT/CLARIN digital library at Institute of Formal and Applied Linguistics, Charles University in Prague (2011). http://hdl.handle.net/11858/00-097C-0000-0006-DB11-8

4. Bejček, E., Hajičová, E., Hajič, J., Jínová, P., Kettnerová, V., Kolářová, V., Mikulová, M., Mírovský, J., Nedoluzhko, A., Panevová, J., Poláková, L., Ševčíková, M., Štěpánek, J., Zikánová, Š.: Prague Dependency Treebank 3.0. LINDAT/CLARIN digital library at Institute of Formal and Applied Linguistics, Charles University in Prague (2013). http://hdl.handle.net/11858/00-097C-0000-0023-1AAF-3

5. Böhmová, A., Hajič, J., Hajičová, E., Hladká, B.: The Prague dependency treebank: a three-level annotation scenario. In: Abeillé, A. (ed.) Treebanks: Building and Using Syntactically Annotated Corpora, pp. 103–128. Kluwer Academic Publishers, Dordrecht (2003)

6. Collins, M.: Discriminative training methods for hidden markov models: theory and experiments with perceptron algorithms. In: Proceedings of the ACL 2002 Conference on Empirical Methods in Natural Language Processing (EMNLP 2002), vol. 10, pp. 1–8. Association for Computational Linguistics, Philadelphia (2002)

7. Dušek, O., Žabokrtský, Z., Popel, M., Majliš, M., Novák, M., Mareček, D.: Formemes in english-czech deep syntactic MT. In: Proceedings of the Seventh ACL Workshop on Statistical Machine Translation, pp. 267–274. Association for Computational Linguistics, Montréal (2012)

8. Feldman, A., Hana, J.: A Resource-Light Approach to Morpho-Syntactic Tagging. Rodopi, Amsterdam (2010)

9. Fleischman, M., Hovy, E.: Fine-grained classification of named entities. In: Proceedings of the 19th International Conference on Computational Linguistics (COLING), vol. I, pp. 267–273. Association for Computational Linguistics, Taipei (2002)

10. Giesbrecht, E., Evert, S.: Part-of-speech tagging - a solved task? an evaluation of POS taggers for the Web as corpus. In: Proceedings of the 5th Web as Corpus Workshop (WAC5), San Sebastian, pp. 27–35 (2009)

11. Hajič, J.: Disambiguation of Rich Inflection: Computational Morphology of Czech. Karolinum, Prague (2004)

12. Hajič, J., Hajičová, E., Panevová, J., Sgall, P., Cinková, S., Fučíková, E., Mikulová, M., Pajas, P., Popelka, J., Semecký, J., Šindlerová, J., Štěpánek, J., Toman, J., Urešová, Z., Žabokrtský, Z.: Prague Czech-English Dependency Treebank 2.0. LINDAT/CLARIN digital library at Institute of Formal and Applied Linguistics, Charles University in Prague (2012). http://hdl.handle.net/11858/00-097C-0000-0015-8DAF-4

13. Hajič, J., Hladká, B.: Probabilistic and rule-based tagger of an inflective language - a comparison. In: Proceedings of the 5th Conference on Applied Natural Language Processing, pp. 111–118. Association for Computational Linguistics, Washington, DC (1997)

14. Hajič, J., Hlaváčvá, J.: MorfFlex CZ. LINDAT/CLARIN digital library at Institute of Formal and Applied Linguistics, Charles University in Prague (1990). http://hdl.handle.net/11858/00-097C-0000-0015-A780-9

15. Hajič, J., Krbec, P., Oliva, K., Květoň, P., Petkevič, V.: Serial combination of rules and statistics: a case study in Czech tagging. In: Proceedings of the 39th Annual Meeting of the Association of Computational Linguistics (ACL 2001), pp. 260–267. Association for Computational Linguistics, Tolouse (2001)

16. Hajič, J., Panevová, J., Hajičová, E., Sgall, P., Pajas, P., Štěpánek, J., Havelka, J., Mikulová, M., Žabokrtský, Z., Ševčíková-Razímová, M., Urešová, Z.: Prague Dependency Treebank 2.0. Data/software. Linguistic Data Consortium, Philadelphia (2006)

17. Hajič, J., Smrž, O., Zemánek, P., Pajas, P., Šnaidauf, J., Beška, E., Kracmar, J., Hassanová, K.: Prague Arabic Dependency Treebank 1.0. LINDAT/CLARIN digital library at Institute of Formal and Applied Linguistics, Charles University in Prague (2009). http://hdl.handle.net/11858/00-097C-0000-0001-4872-3

18. Hajič, J., Vidová Hladká, B.: Czech language processing - PoS tagging. In: Proceedings of the 1st International Conference on Language Resources and Evaluation (LREC 1998), pp. 931–936. ELRA, Granada (1998)

19. Hajič, J., Vidová Hladká, B., Panevová, J., Hajičcová, E., Sgall, P., Pajas, P.: Prague Dependency Treebank 1.0. Data/software. Linguistic Data Consortium, Philadelphia (2001)

20. Hana, J., Feldman, A.: Resource-light approaches to computational morphology. Part 1: monolingual approaches. Lang. Linguist. Compass **6**, 622–634 (2012)

21. Hana, J., Zeman, D., Hajič, J., Hanová, H., Hladká, B., Jeřábek, E.: Manual for Morphological Annotation, Revision for the Prague Dependency Treebank 2.0. Technical report no. 2005/TR-2005-27, FAL MFF UK, Prague (2005)

22. Hathout, N., Namer, F.: Démonette, a French derivational morpho-semantic network. Linguist. Issues Lang. Technol. **11**, 125–168 (2014)

23. Hladká, B.: Software Tools for Large Czech Corpora Annotation. Master thesis. MFF UK, Prague (1994)

24. Hladká, B., Králík, J.: Proměny Českého akademického korpusu. Slovo a Slovesnost **67**, 179–194 (2006)

25. Komárek, M., Kořenský, J., Petr, J., Veselková, J., et al.: Mluvnice češtiny 2. Tvarosloví. Academia, Prague (1986)

26. Konkol, M., Konopík, M.: Maximum entropy named entity recognition for czech language. In: Habernal, I., Matoušek, V. (eds.) TSD 2011. LNCS, vol. 6836, pp. 203–210. Springer, Heidelberg (2011)

27. Konkol, M., Konopík, M.: CRF-based Czech named entity recognizer and consolidation of Czech NER research. In: Habernal, I., Matoušek, V. (eds.) TSD 2013. LNCS, vol. 8082, pp. 153–160. Springer, Heidelberg (2013)

28. Kravalová, J., Žabokrtský Z.: Czech named entity corpus and SVM-based recognizer. In: Proceedings of the 2009 Named Entities Workshop: Shared Task on Transliteration (NEWS 2009), pp. 194–201. Association for Computational Linguistics, Suntec (2009)

29. Krbec, P.: Language Modelling for Speech Recognition of Czech. Ph.D. thesis. MFF UK, Prague (2005)

30. Kuryłowicz, J.: Dérivation lexicale et dérivation syntaxique. Bull. de la Société de Linguistique de Paris **37**, 79–92 (1936)

31. Květoň, P.: Rule-based Morphological Disambiguation. Ph.D. thesis. MFF UK, Prague (2006)

32. Marcus, M., Santorini, B., Marcinkiewicz, M.A.: Building A Large Annotated Corpus of English: The Penn Treebank. Technical reports (CIS), Paper 237 (1993). http://repository.upenn.edu/cis_reports/237/

33. de Marneffe, M.-C., Dozat, T., Silveira, N., Haverinen, K., Ginter, F., Nivre, J., Manning, C.: Universal stanford dependencies: a cross-linguistic typology. In: Proceedings of the 9th International Conference on Language Resources and Evaluation (LREC 2014), pp. 4585–4592. ELRA, Reykjavík (2014)

34. Mel'čuk, I.A.: Dependency Syntax: Theory and Practice. State University of New York Press, New York (1988)

35. Mikulová, M., Bémová, A., Hajič, J., Hajičová, E., Havelka, J., Kolářová, V., Kučová, L., Lopatková, M., Pajas, P., Panevová, J., Razímová, M., Sgall, P., Štěpánek, J., Urešová, Z., Veselá, K., Žabokrtský, Z.: Annotation on the tectogrammatical level in the Prague Dependency Treebank. Annotation manual. Technical report no. 2006/30, ÚFAL MFF UK, Prague (2006)
36. Oliva, K., Květoň, P., Ondruška, R.: The computational complexity of rule-based part-of-speech tagging. In: Matoušek, V., Mautner, P. (eds.) TSD 2003. LNCS (LNAI), vol. 2807, pp. 82–89. Springer, Heidelberg (2003)
37. Oliva, K., Hnátková, M., Petkevič, V., Květoň, P.: The linguistic basis of a rule-based tagger of Czech. In: Sojka, P., Kopeček, I., Pala, K. (eds.) TSD 2000. LNCS (LNAI), vol. 1902, pp. 3–8. Springer, Heidelberg (2000)
38. Pajas, P., Štěpánek, J., Sedlák, M.: PML Tree Query. LINDAT/CLARIN digital library at Institute of Formal and Applied Linguistics, Charles University in Prague (2009). http://hdl.handle.net/11858/00-097C-0000-0022-C7F6-3
39. Petkevič, V.: Reliable morphological disambiguation of Czech: rule-based approach is necessary. In: Šimková, M. (ed.) Insight into the Slovak and Czech Corpus Linguistics, pp. 26–44. Veda, Bratislava (2006)
40. Petkevič, V.: Problémy automatické morfologické disambiguace češtiny. Naše řeč **97**, 194–207 (2014)
41. Petrov, S., Das, D., McDonald, R.: A universal part-of-speech tagset. In: Proceedings of the 8th International Conference on Language Resources and Evaluation (LREC 2012), pp. 2089–2096. ELRA, Istanbul (2012)
42. Razímová, M., Žabokrtský, Z.: Annotation of grammatemes in the prague dependency treebank 2.0. In: Proceedings of the LREC Workshop on Annotation Science, pp. 12–19. ELRA, Genova (2006)
43. Rosa, R., Mašek, J., Mareček, D., Popel, M., Zeman, D., Žabokrtský, Z.: HamleDT 2.0: thirty dependency treebanks stanfordized. In: Proceedings of the 9th International Conference on Language Resources and Evaluation (LREC 2014), pp. 2334–2341. ELRA, Reykjavík (2014)
44. Sedláček, R.: Morfologický analyzátor češtiny. Master thesis. FI MU, Brno (1999)
45. Sedláček, R., Smrž, P.: A new Czech morphological analyser ajka. In: Matoušek, V., Mautner, P., Mouček, R., Tauser, K. (eds.) TSD 2001. LNCS (LNAI), vol. 2166, pp. 100–107. Springer, Heidelberg (2001)
46. Sedlák, M.: Treex::Web. LINDAT/CLARIN digital library at Institute of Formal and Applied Linguistics, Charles University in Prague (2014). http://hdl.handle.net/11858/00-097C-0000-0023-44AF-C
47. Sekine, S.: Sekine's Extended Named Entity Hierarchy (2003). http://nlp.cs.nyu.edu/ene/
48. Sgall, P.: Generativní Popis Jayzka a Česká Deklinace. Academia, Prague (1967)
49. Sgall, P., Hajičová, E., Panevová, J.: The Meaning of the Sentence in its Semantic and Pragmatic Aspects. Reidel Publishing Company, Dordrecht (1986)
50. Spoustová, D.: Kombinované statisticko-pravidlové metody značkování češtiny. Ph.D. thesis. MFF UK, Prague (2007)
51. Spoustová, D., Hajič, J., Raab, J., Spousta, M.: Semi-supervised training for the averaged perceptron POS tagger. In: Proceedings of the 12th Conference of the European Chapter of the ACL (EACL 2009), pp. 763–771. Association for Computational Linguistics, Athens (2009)
52. Spoustová, D., Hajič, J., Votrubec, J., Krbec, P., Květoň, P.: The best of two worlds: cooperation of statistical and rule-based taggers for Czech. In: Proceedings of the Workshop on Balto-Slavonic Natural Language Processing 2007, pp. 67–74. Association for Computational Linguistics, Prague (2007)

53. Straka, M., Straková, J.: MorphoDiTa: Morphological Dictionary and Tagger. LINDAT/CLARIN digital library at Institute of Formal and Applied Linguistics, Charles University in Prague (2014). http://hdl.handle.net/11858/00-097C-0000-0023-43CD-0

54. Straka, M., Straková, J.: NameTag. LINDAT/CLARIN digital library at Institute of Formal and Applied Linguistics, Charles University in Prague (2014). http://hdl.handle.net/11858/00-097C-0000-0023-43CE-E

55. Straková, J., Straka, M., Hajič, J.: A new state-of-the-art Czech named entity recognizer. In: Habernal, I. (ed.) TSD 2013. LNCS, vol. 8082, pp. 68–75. Springer, Heidelberg (2013)

56. Straková, J., Straka, M., Hajič, J.: Open-source tools for morphology, lemmatization, POS tagging and named entity recognition. In: Proceedings of 52nd Annual Meeting of the Association for Computational Linguistics (ACL 2014): System Demonstrations, pp. 13–18. Association for Computational Linguistics, Baltimore (2014)

57. Straková, J., Straka, M., Ševčíková, M., Žabokrtský, Z.: Czech Named Entity Corpus. In: Ide, N., Pustejovsky, J. (eds.) Handbook of Linguistic Annotation. Springer, Heidelberg (in press)

58. Ševčíková, M., Panevová, J., Smejkalová, L.: Specificity of the number of nouns in Czech and its annotation in prague dependency treebank. Prague Bull. Math. Linguist. **96**, 27–47 (2011)

59. Ševčíková, M., Žabokrtský, Z.: Word-formation network for czech. In: Proceedings of the 9th International Conference on Language Resources and Evaluation (LREC 2014), pp. 1087 1093. ELRA, Reykjavík (2014)

60. Ševčíková, M., Žabokrtský, Z., Krůza, O.: Named entities in Czech: annotating data and developing NE tagger. In: Matoušek, V., Mautner, P. (eds.) TSD 2007. LNCS (LNAI), vol. 4629, pp. 188–195. Springer, Heidelberg (2007)

61. Ševčíková, M., Žabokrtský, Z., Straková, J., Straka, M.: Czech Named Entity Corpus 1.1. LINDAT/CLARIN digital library at Institute of Formal and Applied Linguistics, Charles University in Prague (2014). http://hdl.handle.net/11858/00-097C-0000-0023-1B04-C

62. Ševčíková Razímová, M., Žabokrtský, Z.: Systematic parameterized description of pro-forms in the prague dependency treebank 2.0. In: Proceedings of the Fifth International Workshop on Treebanks and Linguistic Theories (TLT 2006), pp. 175–186. Institute of Formal and Applied Linguistics, Prague (2006)

63. Šnajder, J.: DerivBase.Hr: a high-coverage derivational morphology resource for croatian. In: Proceedings of the 9th International Conference on Language Resources and Evaluation (LREC 2014), pp. 3371–3377. ELRA, Reykjavík (2014)

64. Štěpánek, J.: Post-annotation checking of prague dependency treebank 2.0 data. In: Sojka, P., Kopeček, I., Pala, K. (eds.) TSD 2006. LNCS (LNAI), vol. 4188, pp. 277–284. Springer, Heidelberg (2006)

65. Štěpánek, J.: Závislostní zachycení větné struktury v anotovaném syntaktickém korpusu (nástroje pro zajištění konzistence dat). Ph.D. thesis. MFF UK, Prague (2006)

66. Vidová Hladká, B., Hajič, J., Hana, J., Hlaváčová, J., Mírovský, J., Raab, J.: Czech Academic Corpus 2.0. Data/software. Linguistic Data Consortium, Philadelphia (2008)

67. Viová Hladká, B., Hana, J., Hajič, J., Hlaváčová, J., Mírovský, J., Votrubec, J.: Czech Academic Corpus 1.0. Data/software. Karolinum, Prague (2007)

68. Votrubec, J.: Volba vhodné sady rysů pro morfologické značkování češtiny. Master thesis. MFF UK, Prague (2005)

69. Zeller, B., Šnajder, J., Padó, S.: DerivBase: inducing and evaluating a derivational morphology resource for German. In: Proceedings of the 51st Annual Meeting of the Association for Computational Linguistics (ACL 2013), pp. 1201–1211. Association for Computational Linguistics, Sofia (2013)

70. Zeman, D.: Lingua: Interset 2.026. LINDAT/CLARIN digital library at Institute of Formal and Applied Linguistics, Charles University in Prague (2014). http://hdl.handle.net/11234/1-1465

71. Zeman, D.: Reusable tagset conversion using tagset drivers. In: Proceedings of the 6th International Conference on Language Resources and Evaluation (LREC 2008), pp. 213–218. ELRA, Marrakech (2008)

72. Zeman, D., Mareček, D., Mašek, J., Popel, M., Ramasamy, L., Rosa, R., Štěpánek, J., Žabokrtský, Z.: HamleDT 2.0. LINDAT/CLARIN digital library at Institute of Formal and Applied Linguistics, Charles University in Prague (2014). http://hdl.handle.net/11858/00-097C-0000-0023-9551-4

73. Zeman, D., Mareček, D., Popel, M., Ramasamy, L., Štěpánek, J., Žabokrtský, Z., Hajič, J.: HamleDT: to parse or not to parse? In: Proceedings of the 8th International Conference on Language Resources and Evaluation (LREC 2012), pp. 2735–2741. ELRA, Istanbul (2012)

74. Žabokrtský, Z.: Resemblances between meaning-text theory and functional generative description. In: Proceedings of the 2nd International Conference of Meaning-Text Theory, pp. 549–557. Slavic Culture Languages Publishers House, Moskva (2005)

75. Žabokrtský, Z., Ptáček, J., Pajas. P.: TectoMT: highly modular MT system with tectogrammatics used as transfer layer. In: Proceedings of the Third ACL Workshop on Statistical Machine Translation, pp. 167–170. Association for Computational Linguistics, Columbus (2008)

Designing and Comparing G2P-Type Lemmatizers for a Morphology-Rich Language

Steffen Eger[(⊠)]

Text Technology Lab, Goethe University, Frankfurt am Main, Germany
steeger@em.uni-frankfurt.de

Abstract. We consider the statistical lemmatization problem in which lemmatizers are trained on (word form, lemma) pairs. In particular, we consider this problem for ancient Latin, a language with high degree of morphological variability. We investigate whether general purpose string-to-string transduction models are suitable for this task, and find that they typically perform (much) better than more restricted lemmatization techniques/heuristics based on suffix transformations. We also experimentally test whether string transduction systems that perform well on one string-to-string translation task (here, G2P) perform well on another (here, lemmatization) and vice versa, and find that a joint n-gram modeling performs better on G2P than a discriminative model of our own making but that this relationship is reversed for lemmatization. Finally, we investigate how the learned lemmatizers can complement lexicon-based systems, e.g., by tackling the OOV and/or the disambiguation problem.

1 Introduction

Lemmatization can be defined as the normalization task of mapping the inflected forms of lexical words to their canonical form, i.e., their *lemma* (cf. [5,6,12]). A related problem is *stemming*, in which the variability of word forms is reduced by mapping different variants to a common root or *stem*, which may be a crude abstraction that does not need to correspond to any valid linguistic unit.[1] Lemmatization and stemming are important preprocessing steps in information retrieval, text mining, and knowledge discovery.

In this work, we view the lemmatization problem within the general string-to-string translation setup of mapping arbitrary strings $\mathbf{x} \in \Sigma^*$ to arbitrary other strings $\mathbf{y} \in \Gamma^*$, where Σ and Γ are arbitrary alphabets (finite sets). While this setup would also include other natural language processing (NLP) tasks such as

- *grapheme-to-phoneme conversion (G2P)* [2,11], in which $\mathbf{x}$ is a letter-string and $\mathbf{y}$ is a string of phonemes,
- *transliteration* [21], in which $\mathbf{x}$ is a word form in one script (e.g., Cyrillic, Hebraic, Latin, etc.) and $\mathbf{y}$ is a corresponding form in another script, or
- *spelling error correction* [4], in which $\mathbf{x}$ is a wrongly spelled word form and $\mathbf{y}$ its desired correction,

---

[1] In stemming, all that typically matters is that related words map to the same (linguistic or even non-linguistic) object.

© Springer International Publishing Switzerland 2015
C. Mahlow and M. Piotrowski (Eds.): SFCM 2015, CCIS 537, pp. 27–40, 2015.
DOI: 10.1007/978-3-319-23980-4_2

our focus is, as indicated, on the lemmatization task in which $\mathbf{x}$ is a word form and $\mathbf{y}$ its lemma. Our statistical problem is to *learn* mappings $\mathbf{x} \mapsto \mathbf{y}$ from pairs of strings $\{(\mathbf{x}_i, \mathbf{y}_i) \mid i = 1, 2, 3, \ldots\}$.

As [12] point out, the difficulty of the lemmatization problem heavily depends on the types of natural languages involved. While lemmatization is considered relatively easy in highly analytical languages such as English, the problem becomes considerably more difficult in languages that exhibit sufficient morphological variability, such as the Slavic languages or ancient Greek and Latin. In these, "stems can combine with many different suffixes, and the selection of appropriate ending and its combination with the stem depends on morphological, phonological and semantic factors" [12]. In the present work, our focus is on lemmatization in ancient Latin, because, on the one hand, ancient Latin is a prime exemplar of a language with rich morphology in which more than hundred distinct forms may be associated with a single (e.g., verb) lemma. On the other hand, we are currently actively developing several NLP tools for ancient Latin,[2] of which a lemmatizer (as well as, in subsequent steps, a POS tagger and a parser) is an integral part.

Arguably, the most well-researched domain within the field of string-to-string translation is G2P and it is tempting to simply apply one of the existing G2P toolkits to the problem. Our approach in this work is indeed to evaluate how standard G2P models perform on the lemmatization task and how their performance relates to standard statistical lemmatizers. As one of our results, we will show that two of the general G2P models that we review, a standard joint n-gram model and a discriminative model of our own making, not only perform orders of magnitude better than two off-the-shelf lemmatizers on the G2P problem, but also considerably better on the lemmatization task. We also show that ordering of performance relationships is not necessarily preserved across string transduction problems. More precisely, we show that the joint n-gram modeling that we test is considerably better on G2P conversion than our own discriminative model, but that this relationship is reversed on the lemmatization task. After reviewing the models in Sect. 2, we briefly outline our data base in Sect. 3, and conduct performance comparisons in Sect. 4. In this section, we also investigate how our learned lemmatizers may complement lexicon-based lemmatizers, e.g., by tackling the out-of-vocabulary (OOV) problem and/or by disambiguation. We conclude in Sect. 5.

Concerning related work, Porter stemmer [19] is a rule-based heuristic for solving the stemming problem in English. The approaches that we survey in the current work are much more closely related to modern machine learning approaches for string transduction. For instance, Dreyer and Eisner [6] present a discriminative log-linear model learning latent classes and apply it to lemmatization. Gesmundo and Samardzic [9] reformulate lemmatization as a tagging problem in a setting where they assume that lemmas are derived from word forms by prefix and suffix transformations and the tag label encodes the substitution patterns. Toutanova and Cherry [23] show that considering lemmatization

---

[2] See, e.g., https://prepro.hucompute.org/.

and part-of-speech tagging *jointly* may be mutually beneficial. Their character-based lemmatization module is similar to the G2P-type lemmatizers we consider below but only considers one-to-one character transformations plus a heuristic for dealing with suffixes.

2   Models

In this study, we rely on the following software/models for learning the lemmatization problem.

- *Phonetisaurus* [18] implements a joint n-gram model [2] in a weighted finite state transducer setup, and has originally been designed for G2P conversion. Like our own modeling, Phonetisaurus can be used in a more general setting, however, to learn to transduce arbitrary input sequences into arbitrary output sequences. Phonetisaurus seems to perform on par or better than competitors on the G2P problem and trains and decodes orders of magnitudes faster [18].[3]
- *LemmaGen* [12,13] is a lemmatizer that learns 'if-then' rules from $(\mathbf{x}, \mathbf{y})$ pairs as shown in Table 4. To transduce/lemmatize a new input form, rules (and their exceptions) are ordered, and the first condition that is satisfied fires the corresponding rule [12]. Importantly, LemmaGen learns to transduce word form *suffixes* into lemma *suffixes*, so it might be prone to committing errors, e.g., when initial or middle parts of word forms need to be adjusted to generate the correct lemma.
- *Mate* [3] provides a full pipeline of lemmatization, tagging, morphological tagging, and dependency parsing. It is trainable on appropriate input format. In our context, we only train the lemmatizer module of the pipeline.

Our own modeling implements a two-stage tagging procedure to translate input strings into output strings. In the first stage, an input word is *segmented* into parts using a sequence labeler (tagger) that maps input character sequences to ones or zeros, depending on whether a split occurs at the given character position. In the second stage, each part of the segmented input string is tagged with an output string subsequence. Table 1 illustrates. The training data for both sequence labelers is taken from *monotone many-to-many aligned* input strings as in Table 2.[4] The second stage tagger directly trains on the aligned data, while the first stage tagger learns sequence segmentations from the segmented $\mathbf{x}$ sequences in the alignments using a binary coding scheme (cf. [1,7]). Table 3 illustrates this—note that we encode a split as a '1' and a non-split (continuation) as a '0'.

As a **tagging model**, we use linear chain conditional random fields (CRF) [14].[5] This allows us to include arbitrary features in the tagging process. We use the following:

---

[3] In our experiments below, we choose an n-gram order of size 6 for Phonetisaurus. Increasing n-gram order size did not lead to better performance in preliminary tests.

[4] We use the alignments produced by the Phonetisaurus toolkit.

[5] Although CRFs are rather old and typically not always the best-performing sequence labeling models [17], we use them here mainly for practical reasons. In particular, the CRF package we are using, available from https://code.google.com/p/crfpp/, provides a very convenient interface to modeling sequence labeling.

Table 1. Sample decoding phase.

præformet ⤳ p-r-æ-f-o-r-m-et	passvrarum ⤳ p-a-ss-vra-rum
↓ ↓ ↓ ↓ ↓ ↓ ↓ ↓	↓ ↓ ↓ ↓ ↓
p-r-ae-f-o-r-m-o	p-a-ti- o - r

Table 2. Sample aligned input string pairs $(\mathbf{x}, \mathbf{y})$.

d-i-s-s-o-n-verat	d-i-s-s-o-n-o
c-o-n-r-e-ct-v-s	c-o-n-r-i-g-e-o
j-m-p-e-d-i-o	i-m-p-e-d-i-o
c-o-m-p-u-t-aris	c-o-m-p-u-t-o
t-e-r-r-e-batvr	t-e-r-r-e-o
a-d-i-u-t-o-rivm	a-d-i-u-t-o-r
p-r-a-e-p-e-d-i-m-e-n-t-a	p-r-a-e-p-e-d-i-m-e-n-t-um
u-n-d-e-c-i-m-am	u-n-d-e-c-i-m-a
d-u-l-c-i-l-o-c-u-t-i-ssimarum	d-u-l-c-i-l-o-c-u-t-u-s

Table 3. Word forms $\mathbf{x}$ from Table 2, corresponding segmentations and binary encodings of the segmentations.

Word form	Segmentation	Binary encoding
dissonverat	d-i-s-s-o-n-verat	01111110000
conrectvs	c-o-n-r-e-ct-v-s	011111011
jmpedio	j-m-p-e-d-i-o	0111111
computaris	c-o-m-p-u-t-aris	0111111000
terrebatvr	t-e-r-r-e-batvr	0111110000
adiutorivm	a-d-i-u-t-o-rivm	0111111000
praepedimenta	p-r-a-e-p-e-d-i-m-e-n-t-a	0111111111111
undecimam	u-n-d-e-c-i-m-am	011111110
dulcilocutissimarum	d-u-l-c-i-l-o-c-u-t-i-ssimarum	0111111111110000000

(1) *Contextual features*: for each input symbol (a character or a subsequence of characters), we include all character subsequence m-grams (unigrams, bigrams, trigrams, etc.) that fit inside a window of size 6 around the current input symbol position.[6] To illustrate, when the second stage tagger views the current input position e in the input word form c-o-n-r-e-ct-v-s, it sees that the next position contains ct, the previous position contains r, etc.; the next two positions contain (ct,v), etc.

---

[6] Increasing window size typically does not lead to better performance, as we verified in preliminary experiments.

(2) *Linear-chain and transition features*: These include features between subsequent output symbol characters (character subsequences) as is the defining property of linear chain conditional random fields.

(3) *Intra-subsequence-character features*: We also include features that allow the second stage tagger to not only see the character subsequence at the current input position but also the characters that constitute it. For example, rather than merely knowing that the last input position of *d-i-s-s-o-n-verat* is *verat*, the tagger would also know that *verat* is made up of the characters *v*, *e*, *r*, *a*, *t*. This may help the classifier in case longer character subsequences are sparse. Since additional features increase computational costs, we only include unigram intra-subsequence-character features.

We call the system that includes features (1) and (2) *AliSeTra* (for align-segment-translate), while we refer to the system that in addition includes features (3) as *AliSeTra++*. We also note that our design of phrasing string transduction as a (two-stage) sequence labeling approach is, per se, nothing novel — it is one of the standard paradigms in G2P (cf., e.g., [10,11]).

3 Data

Our data base is a huge Latin lexicon containing almost 10 million distinct word forms subsumed under more than 100,000 lemmas [8,15]. This lexicon has been semi-automatically created from several freely available Web resources and via lexical expanders and subsequent manual correction (where necessary). Of these forms, almost 80 % belong to the open word classes nouns, verbs, and adjectives, on which we will focus in the remainder of this work.[7] Our task will be to learn to lemmatize Latin word forms falling under the named word classes from pairs of examples as shown in Table 4.

Table 4. Example string pairs in the data base. (Potential) substitution patterns highlighted for clarity of exposition.

Verbs		Nouns		Adjectives	
ingem**uistis**	ingemisco	princ**ipibvs**	princps	denuntia**tissimam**	denuntiatus
exmact**auissetis**	exmacto	fragi	fragum	perrectas	perrectus
con**rectvs**	con**rigeo**	chyrogrillio	chyrogrillius	dedola**tiores**	dedolatus
emund**atarum**	emundo	adversa**tvm**	adversatus	praestan**tioribvs**	praestans
superinte**xere**	superinte**go**	erupturus	erupturus	infortuna**tissimvs**	infortunatus
dispute**bant**	disputeo	sciotheri**corvm**	sciothericum	reso**niores**	resonus

---

[7] Typically, word forms in other word classes are also not inflectional, so that the learning problem would be trivial.

4   Evaluation

We now evaluate the four described systems. We start with an evaluation on a G2P conversion task, in order to see how the systems perform in a string-to-string translation setting different from lemmatization. We train and evaluate all systems on the General American (GA) variant of the Combilex [20] G2P data set. Throughout our evaluation settings, we use *word accuracy* as our evaluation measure, defined as the fraction of correctly transduced forms in the test set, i.e., it is defined as the number of strings $\mathbf{x}_i$ in the test set that satisfy $\hat{\mathbf{y}}_i = \mathbf{y}_i$, divided by the size of the test set. Here $\mathbf{x}_i$ is an input form, $\mathbf{y}_i$ is the gold standard reference and $\hat{\mathbf{y}}_i$ is the prediction of a specific system. Word accuracy is a strict measure that penalizes even tiny deviations from the gold standard, but is nowadays the most common in G2P and related fields.

4.1   Testing G2P Performance

Table 5 gives results when we train the systems on training sets of size 2,000, 5,000, and 10,000, respectively, and test them on a disjoint set of string pairs of size 28,609. Phonetisaurus is clearly best in all settings, with a margin of about 7–20 % over AliSeTra, depending on training set size. AliSeTra++ performs slightly worse than AliSeTra in two out of three training set size cases, indicating that the additional features tend to harm in this case, which could be due to the fact that the system now must estimate additional (possibly irrelevant) parameters and due to stronger overfitting given the additional degrees of freedom (see also the discussion below). In any case, difference between AliSeTra++ and AliSeTra is marginal. Both AliSeTra/++ and Phonetisaurus perform strikingly better than each of LemmaGen and Mate on the G2P conversion task. For example, at a training set of size 10,000, Phonetisaurus has about 66 % of the test inputs correct, while LemmaGen has only 6.82 % correct (i.e., accuracy is about 10 times higher for Phonetisaurus) and Mate 1 %.

Table 5. Word accuracy in % as a function of training set size. G2P data.

	2,000	5,000	10,000
AliSeTra++	38.33	51.98	61.26
AliSeTra	36.64	52.43	62.13
Phonetisaurus	**44.60**	**57.62**	**66.67**
LemmaGen	2.29	4.42	6.82
-last-4-chars	15.30	22.33	36.82
Mate	0.39	0.76	1.00
-on-training	89.17	97.49	95.26

Looking at the reasons for this discrepancy, we find that, as we have already outlined when introducing the systems, LemmaGen can essentially only transform the endings of strings, which results in errors for virtually all long words. In fact, when we test accuracy comparing only the last four characters of $\hat{y}_i$ with the last four of y_i, we find that the accuracy of LemmaGen increases substantially, but is still at a much lower level than either Phonetisaurus or AliSeTra. For instance, at a training set size of 10,000, word accuracy of Phonetisaurus (AliSeTra) is still 81 % (68 %) higher than that of LemmaGen, even in this favorable setting for LemmaGen. The performance of Mate is even (considerably) worse than that of LemmaGen. This is not due to the fact that input and output alphabets are different in G2P conversion, as the performance on the training data shows. Here, Mate achieves accuracy of up to 97 %, indicating that the system may be entirely overfitting the training data (e.g., storing training data instances as lexical entries and learning minimal transformation regularities).[8]

4.2   Testing Lemmatization Performance

Next, we investigate performance on the lemmatization task. Figure 1 shows learning curves—accuracy as a function of training set size—for all systems when the systems are exclusively trained and tested on verbs. We distinguish two modes of testing:

- *In-domain-testing*: In in-domain testing, training and test data contain forms that belong to the same lemma. For example, the training data might contain the form *amavisse*, while the test data might contain the form *amas*, both of which have *amo* as a lemma (however, no *form* in the test data also occurs in the training data).
- *Out-domain-testing*: In out-domain testing, the test data contains only forms whose lemmas do not underlie any form in the training data.

In-domain and out-domain testing intend to address different application scenarios. If a statistical lemmatizer is primarily used for lemmatizing out-of-vocabulary (OOV) forms,[9] out-domain-testing would be the more relevant criterion for suitability of the lemmatizer. In a less restricted application scenario for the lemmatizer, results of in-domain-testing would likely be the more relevant statistic, particularly if training sets are large enough, since in this case, most forms to be lemmatized in a text will either have been seen in the training data or, at least, may be expected to be morphologically related to forms in the training data.

The figure shows that AliSeTra++ performs best now, with a slight but consistent margin over AliSeTra. Particularly in out-domain testing, AliSeTra/++ perform substantially better than Phonetisaurus where difference in performance

---

[8] In fact, it seems that Mate simply stores input strings that occur fewer than 5 times, rather than learning substitution patterns from these (personal communication with Bernd Bohnet). Thus, the evaluation scenario adopted in this work puts Mate at a general disadvantage, since we generally train systems on arbitrary lists of word pairs selected from a lexicon rather than on the distributions found in 'real' text.

[9] E.g., when the lemmatizer is developed to assist a lexicon-based lemmatizer.

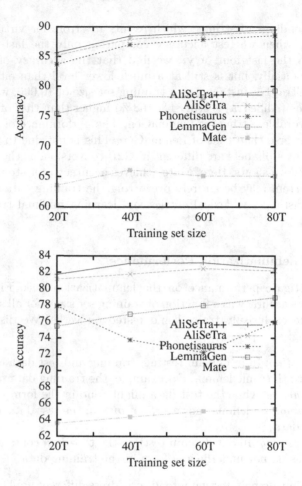

Fig. 1. Word accuracy as a function of training set size. Left: In-domain testing. Right: Out-domain testing. Verbs.

is between 5 and 12 %. Again, all three of the general string transduction systems have considerably higher word accuracies than either LemmaGen or Mate, but differences are much less pronounced than on the G2P conversion task. In fact, in out-domain-testing, LemmaGen performs even better than Phonetisaurus, for particular training set sizes. It is also worthy to note that LemmaGen and Mate perform relatively stable over in-domain vs. out-domain testing, while AliSe-Tra/++ and Phonetisaurus seem to suffer more from overfitting (put positively: can better adapt to the distribution of the training data).

As to why AliSeTra++ performs better than AliSeTra on the verb lemmatization task, an intuitive explanation would be that average segment length in the string transduction task is correlated with effectiveness of the intra-subsequence-character features, since longer segments are sparser and therefore harder to estimate as whole chunks. In fact, average length of a segment in verb lemma-

Table 6. Test set sizes.

	Verbs	Nouns	Adjectives
In-domain	20,000	20,000	20,000
Out-domain	206,347	39,454	83,295

tization is 1.53, with a maximum segment length of 10—cf. the aligned pair *(m-i-r-arenturque,m-i-r-o)*—while average length of a segment in the G2P data set is 1.14, with a maximum length of 2—cf. the aligned pair *(gu-a-r-a-n-t-ee-d, g-a-r-@-n-t-i-d)*.

In Tables 7, 8, and 9, we report word accuracies for the different systems on the three word classes verbs, nouns, and adjectives. Each system is trained ten times, on randomly extracted and not necessarily disjoint training sets of size 40,000. These training sets contain only (word form, lemma) pairs that belong to the respective word classes. The tables report average and simple majority vote results when each system is tested on in-domain and out-domain data, as before. Test set sizes are indicated in Table 6. Generally, the same conclusions as for the values shown in Fig. 1 apply—namely, that AliSeTra/++ and Phonetisaurus perform considerably better than LemmaGen and Mate, and that AliSeTra/++ typically perform best among all systems (particularly in the out-domain setting).

Table 7. Word accuracy in % for different systems, *verbs*. Each system is trained on 10 random subsets of the training data of size 40,000 each. Average and simple majority vote results indicated. In bold: Statistically indistinguishable best performances.

	Avg-InDomain	Maj-InDomain	Avg-OutDomain	Maj-OutDomain
AliSeTra	87.89	89.07	81.78	82.94
AliSeTra++	**88.42**	**89.72**	**83.09**	**84.51**
Phonetisaurus	86.98	89.64	73.78	78.40
LemmaGen	78.23	81.45	76.91	80.19
Mate	66.10	67.98	64.36	66.63

Error Analysis. For verbs, typical errors are mismatches of *-or/-o* endings. Such distinctions are very hard to learn for the statistical lemmatizers because it requires to know whether a verb is a *deponent verb*, that is, lacks active forms. This can actually not be regularly predicted from the characters that constitute a form, but would require lexical knowledge. Also, mismatches between conjugation classes is a common source of error. For example, the verb *transpicio* ('look through') is third conjugation class, for which the *-i-* ending of the stem is characteristic. A wrong lemmatization might assign a form in the morphological paradigm of *transpicio* the lemma *transpico*, which contains the characteristic ending for the (most common) first conjugation class. For nouns, the decoding

Table 8. Word accuracy in % for different systems, *nouns*. Each system is trained on 10 random subsets of the training data of size 40,000 each. Average and simple majority vote results indicated. In bold: Statistically indistinguishable best performances.

	Avg-InDomain	Maj-InDomain	Avg-OutDomain	Maj-OutDomain
AliSeTra	**78.25**	79.98	74.11	75.84
AliSeTra++	77.76	**80.96**	**74.31**	**75.92**
Phonetisaurus	76.74	79.28	72.98	75.64
LemmaGen	75.37	78.09	72.74	75.85
Mate	72.90	73.53	70.26	71.98

Table 9. Word accuracy in % for different systems, *adjectives*. Each system is trained on 10 random subsets of the training data of size 40,000 each. Average and simple majority vote results indicated. In bold: Statistically indistinguishable best performances.

	Avg-InDomain	Maj-InDomain	Avg-OutDomain	Maj-OutDomain
AliSeTra	**92.13**	**93.18**	**87.21**	**87.94**
AliSeTra++	91.50	92.14	**87.28**	**87.90**
Phonetisaurus	91.80	**93.57**	84.57	86.09
LemmaGen	85.37	86.20	84.49	85.77
Mate	71.16	71.70	70.32	71.67

problem is even more difficult for the statistical lemmatizers because gender (e.g., *-us* (masculine) vs. *-um* (neuter) lemma ending) is, to a significant degree, arbitrary and therefore unpredictable. Moreover, many declination classes have identical endings for forms in certain slots of the morphological paradigms (e.g., *-is* ending in dative plural for nouns that belong to both first as well as second declension), which is another source of difficult-to-predict error. In many of these instances, a lexicon could act as a filtering device (see below).

As to why the joint m-gram modeling Phonetisaurus performs worse than the discriminative model in the lemmatization task but not the G2P setting, we find that there are significantly more distinct 'graphones' (pairs of corresponding input-output subsequences such as (a,a) or $(arenturque,o)$) in a comparable quantity of aligned $(\mathbf{x}, \mathbf{y})$ pairs (e.g., 1,217 vs. 725 distinct graphones in a lemma vs. G2P data set, respectively, in a list of 10,000 aligned pairs), so that the basic entity of the joint m-gram model, the graphone, is harder to estimate.

4.3   Text Evaluation

We also present an evaluation of 'real-world' lemmatization, i.e., when the presented lemmatizers are used for the lemmatization of word forms in the context of sentences. To this end, we extract all words in all sentences from Perseus [22]. We discard all upper-case forms (since upper case forms generally do not occur

Table 10. Word accuracy for different systems. Each is trained 10 times on 120,000 (word form, lemma) pairs as described in the text. Type accuracy is the fraction of unique word forms lemmatized correctly, while token accuracy also takes frequency of word forms into account (irregular forms, which are harder to learn, are typically much more frequent). In bold: Statistically indistinguishable best performances.

		AliSeTra++	Phonetisaurus	LemmaGen	Mate
Type	Average	**61.09**	57.67	53.07	46.71
	Majority	63.83	60.96	57.40	49.12
Token	Average	**54.38**	50.04	47.01	41.43
	Majority	57.07	52.09	52.11	44.12

in the above outlined training data), and all word forms that the Perseus gold standard does not classify as either verbs, adjectives, or nouns.

Instead of training lemmatizers separately on each word class and then trying to resolve the resulting ambiguity upon lemmatizing a new test form **x**, we directly train lemmatizers on word forms from all word classes.[10] Hence, we train each lemmatizer on a total of 120,000 word forms, consisting of 40,000 verb pairs, 40,000 noun pairs, and 40,000 adjective pairs each. Results are shown in Table 10. As can be seen, AliSeTra++ performs again best and the ordering of systems is (about) the same as in the previous experiments, i.e., AliSeTra++ > Phonetisaurus > LemmaGen > Mate. We omit indicating the results of AliSeTra because the CRF typically takes hours to days to train on the given training set size.

To say a word on why results appear relatively weak compared to the previously outlined, we note the following:

- Perseus sometimes indicates lemma variants as gold standard for input forms (e.g., in Latin i/j and u/v alternation are typically considered free variants). We count such phenomena as errors although, from a linguistic point of view, these would not constitute real errors. Still, from an evaluation perspective, this does not matter since conditions for all systems are the same.
- Most importantly, note that our training distributions do not represent the actual distributions of word forms in text. For example, we include equal numbers of verbs, nouns, and adjectives in training, but such a distribution is not likely to hold for real text.
- We note, however, that when we increase training set size from 120,000 word pairs to more than 3 million word pairs, type accuracy for LemmaGen increases from about 53 % to more than 76 % and token accuracy increases from about 47 % to more than 74 %. Training the other lemmatizers on much more data would be the logical next step, but is omitted in this evaluation because training times are considerable.

---

[10] We also performed the alternative decoding strategy where lemmatizers are separately trained, but found it to perform worse.

Table 11. Combining a lexicon and statistical lemmatizer.

	Type	Token
Lexicon	72.21	69.11
Lexicon + AliSeTra++	76.22	71.38

Table 12. TreeTagger lemma token accuracy on a subpart of the PL and accuracy values when the lemmatizer is complemented by our trained lemmatizers.

	Token Accuracy
TreeTagger	86.23 %
TreeTagger + AliSeTra++	88.56 %
TreeTagger + LemmaGen	89.37 %

Finally, we address **two more questions** in the context of real-world lemmatization. The first is how a *lexicon* can be combined with the trained lemmatizers that we have outlined. To this end, we (a) lemmatize each word in Perseus with simple lexicon look-up: if the word form is in our lexicon (see Sect. 3), retrieve the corresponding lemma. If several lemmas are associated with the form, pick one of them randomly. This strategy leads to a word type accuracy of 72.21 % (average over ten runs). Most problems in this case are due to lemma ambiguity: while the lexicon has an OOV rate of only 1.03 %, each form is on average associated with 1.49 lemmas. For example, for the form *canis* the lexicon outputs the lemma suggestions *canes, cania, cano, canum, canus, canis*. Alternatively, (b) for each form to lemmatize, we let AliSeTra++ output its k-best lemma suggestions (we choose $k = 10$) and choose the first-best that occurs in the lexicon. If none of the k best is in the lexicon, we simply choose the first-best suggestion of AliSeTra++. Table 11 shows that this leads to a type accuracy of 76.22 %, which is not only considerably better than AliSeTra++'s performance without a lexicon (61.09 %) but also better than the lexicon itself.

Secondly, we ask how our trained lemmatizer can complement an existing tagger or lemmatizer. To this end, we download the Latin TreeTagger from Gabriele Brandolini[11] and have it lemmatize (and tag) a subpart of the Patrologia Latinae (PL) [16].[12] This tagger and lemmatizer has a token lemma accuracy of 86.23 % on the indicated text. About 50 % of all errors are unknown word forms. If, for each unknown word form, we substitute the prediction of AliSeTra++ (trained on 120,000 pairs), or LemmaGen (trained on more than 3 million pairs), lemma token accuracy increases to 88.56 % and 89.37 %, respectively, which constitute improvements of about 2.7 % and 3.6 %, respectively. See Table 12 for a summary.

---

[11] Available at http://www.cis.uni-muenchen.de/~schmid/tools/TreeTagger/.

[12] We could not use Perseus because the TreeTagger was trained on Perseus.

5 Conclusion

We have considered the statistical lemmatization problem in which lemmatizers are trained on (word form, lemma) pairs, which enables them to learn the morphological processes involved in lemmatization. We have investigated whether general purpose string-to-string transduction models are suitable for this task, and have seen that they typically perform (much) better than more restricted lemmatization techniques/heuristics based on suffix transformations. We have also investigated how the learned lemmatizers can complement lexicon-based systems, e.g., by tackling the OOV and/or the disambiguation problem.

Our next step is to train the described lemmatizers on the full size of our database, from which we expect huge accuracy gains, since they have been concurrently been trained only on a tiny fraction of it (much less than 10 %). For the CRF based models, training them on the full size of our database is actually a scaling challenge since they must then learn hundreds of millions of features, but this can be accommodated by training many subsystems on disjoint portions of the data and a subsequent aggregation step. For real world lemmatization, this also requires to train the systems on distributions that reflect those found in 'real' text rather than on random word pair lists retrieved from a lexicon, as done here. Finally, by combining the so-enhanced lemmatizers with our lexicon, very high accuracy lemmatizers can be expected.

References

1. Bartlett, S., Kondrak, G., Cherry, C.: Automatic syllabification with structured SVMs for letter-to-phoneme conversion. In: McKeown, K., Moore, J.D., Teufel, S., Allan, J., Furui, S. (eds.) ACL, pp. 568–576. Association for Computational Linguistics, Morristown (2008)
2. Bisani, M., Ney, H.: Joint-sequence models for grapheme-to-phoneme conversion. Speech Commun. **50**(5), 434–451 (2008)
3. Bohnet, B.: Top accuracy and fast dependency parsing is not a contradiction. In: Proceedings of the 23rd International Conference on Computational Linguistics (Coling 2010), Coling 2010 Organizing Committee, Beijing, China, pp. 89–97, August 2010. http://www.aclweb.org/anthology/C10-1011
4. Brill, E., Moore, R.C.: An improved error model for noisy channel spelling correction. In: Proceedings of the 38th Annual Meeting on Association for Computational Linguistics, ACL 2000, pp. 286–293. Association for Computational Linguistics, Stroudsburg (2000)
5. Daelemans, W., Groenewald, H.J., Huyssteen, G.B.V.: Prototype-based active learning for lemmatization. In: Angelova, G., Bontcheva, K., Mitkov, R., Nicolov, N., Nikolov, N. (eds.) RANLP, pp. 65–70. RANLP 2009 Organising Committee/ACL, Morristown (2009)
6. Dreyer, M., Smith, J., Eisner, J.: Latent-variable modeling of string transductions with finite-state methods. In: EMNLP, pp. 1080–1089. ACL (2008)
7. Eger, S.: Sequence segmentation by enumeration: an exploration. Prague Bull. Math. Linguist. **100**, 113–132 (2013)

40   S. Eger

8. Eger, S., vor der Brück, T., Mehler, A.: Lexicon-assisted tagging and lemmatization in Latin: a comparison of six taggers and two lemmatization methods. In: Latech 2015. Association for Computational Linguistics (2015, accepted)
9. Gesmundo, A., Samardzic, T.: Lemmatisation as a tagging task. In: Proceedings of the 50th Annual Meeting of the Association for Computational Linguistics (vol. 2: Short Papers), pp. 368–372. Association for Computational Linguistics (2012). http://aclweb.org/anthology/P12-2072
10. Jiampojamarn, S., Cherry, C., Kondrak, G.: Joint processing and discriminative training for letter-to-phoneme conversion. In: Proceedings of ACL-08: HLT, pp. 905–913. Association for Computational Linguistics, Columbus, June 2008. http://www.aclweb.org/anthology/P/P08/P08-1103
11. Jiampojamarn, S., Cherry, C., Kondrak, G.: Integrating joint n-gram features into a discriminative training framework. In: NAACL-HLT, pp. 697–700. Association for Computational Linguistics (2010)
12. Juršič, M., Mozetič, I., Lavrač, N.: Learning ripple down rules for efficient lemmatization. In: Mladenić, D., Grobelnik, M. (eds.) Proceedings of the 10th International Multiconference Information Society, pp. 206–209. IJS, Ljubljana (2007)
13. Juršič, M., Mozetič, I., Lavrač, N.: LemmaGen: multilingual lemmatisation with induced ripple-down rules. J. Univ. Comput. Sci. **16**, 1190–1214 (2010)
14. Lafferty, J., McCallum, A., Pereira, F.: Conditional random fields: probabilistic models for segmenting and labeling sequence data. In: Proceedings of 18th International Conference on Machine Learning, pp. 282–289. Morgan Kaufmann, San Francisco (2001)
15. Mehler, A., vor der Brück, T., Gleim, R., Geelhaar, T.: Towards a network model of the coreness of texts: an experiment in classifying Latin texts using the ttlab Latin tagger. In: Biemann, C., Mehler, A. (eds.) Text Mining: From Ontology Learning to Automated text Processing Applications. Theory and Applications of Natural Language Processing, pp. 87–112. Springer, Berlin (2015)
16. Migne, J.P. (ed.): Patrologiae Cursus Completus: Series Latina, vol. 1–221. Chadwyck-Healey, Cambridge (1844–1855)
17. Nguyen, N., Guo, Y.: Comparisons of sequence labeling algorithms and extensions. In: Ghahramani, Z. (ed.) ICML. ACM International Conference Proceeding Series, vol. 227, pp. 681–688. ACM, New York (2007)
18. Novak, J.R., Minematsu, N., Hirose, K.: WFST-based grapheme-to-phoneme conversion: open source tools for alignment, model-building and decoding. In: Proceedings of the 10th International Workshop on Finite State Methods and Natural Language Processing, pp. 45–49. Association for Computational Linguistics, Donostia-San Sebasti, July 2012. http://www.aclweb.org/anthology/W12-6208
19. Porter, M.: An algorithm for suffix stripping. Program Electron. Libr. Inf. Syst. **14**(3), 130–137 (1980)
20. Richmond, K., Clark, R.A.J., Fitt, S.: Robust LTS rules with the Combilex speech technology lexicon. In: INTERSPEECH, pp. 1295–1298. ISCA (2009)
21. Sherif, T., Kondrak, G.: Substring-based transliteration. In: Carroll, J.A., van den Bosch, A., Zaenen, A. (eds.) ACL. Association for Computational Linguistics, Morristown (2007)
22. Smith, D.A., Rydberg-Cox, J.A., Crane, G.R.: The Perseus project: a digital library for the humanities. Literary and Linguistic Computing **15**(1), 15–25 (2000). http://llc.oxfordjournals.org/content/15/1/15
23. Toutanova, K., Cherry, C.: A global model for joint lemmatization and part-of-speech prediction. In: Su, K.Y., Su, J., Wiebe, J. (eds.) ACL/IJCNLP, pp. 486–494. Association for Computational Linguistics, Morristown (2009)

Morphological Disambiguation
of Classical Sanskrit

Oliver Hellwig[✉]

University of Düsseldorf, Düsseldorf, Germany
hellwig7@gmx.de

Abstract. Sanskrit, the "sacred language" of Ancient India, is a morphologically rich Indo-Iranian language that has received some attention in NLP during the last decade. This paper describes a system for the tokenization and morphosyntactic analysis of Sanskrit. The system combines a fixed morphological rule base with a statistical selection of the most probable analysis of an input text. After an introduction into the research history and the linguistic peculiarities of Sanskrit that are relevant to the task, the paper describes the present architecture of the system and new extensions that increase its accuracy when analyzing morphologically ambiguous forms. The algorithms are tested on a gold-annotated data set of 3,587,000 words.

1 Introduction

Sanskrit, an Old Indo-Aryan (OIA) language, whose first texts date back to around 1.500 BCE, has produced one of the largest premodern text corpora in the world. Taking an oversimplifying approach, there are two relevant linguistic layers of Sanskrit. The earlier layer contains the Vedic corpus that may have been created between 1.500 and the middle of the first millenium BCE and that has probably preserved a spoken form of Sanskrit.[1] The later layer of Classical Sanskrit is written in a language that is largely regulated by the famous grammar of Pāṇini (details in Sect. 2). The term "Sanskrit" only refers to this classical stage of the language throughout this paper.

While the oldest Vedic layer has been the subject of numerous detailed linguistic studies, the later layer of Classical Sanskrit, which contributes the vast majority of transmitted texts, has been studied only scarcely from a linguistic point of view. There are several reasons for this inequally distributed research interest, some of them originating in the fascination of traditional philology for the old, "authentic" layers of the language. In addition, the early codification of Sanskrit in the grammar of Pāṇini has led to the assumption that Classical Sanskrit is mainly interesting for the content it produced, but not for its linguistic features. This view will not hold stand when the numerous interactions with other South-Asian languages are taken into account (Sect. 3). Another obstacle that prevented

---

[1] Bloch [2] gives an introduction into the linguistic history of Sanskrit. More details about the Vedic layer are found in Witzel [34].

© Springer International Publishing Switzerland 2015
C. Mahlow and M. Piotrowski (Eds.): SFCM 2015, CCIS 537, pp. 41–59, 2015.
DOI: 10.1007/978-3-319-23980-4_3

the large-scale linguistic study of Classical Sanskrit is the mere size of the litera-ture it produced. A computer based approach will facilitate access to this corpus and its underlying linguistic structures, and may be helpful in moving scholarly attention to the numerous linguistic peculiarities of Classical Sanskrit. This paper describes a lexical and morphological parser for Classical Sanskrit whose output allows a strictly corpus-based, data driven approach to this language.

The paper is organized as follows. Section 2 gives an overview of formal sys-tems of Sanskrit grammar and modern NLP related research in processing Clas-sical Sanskrit. Section 3 summarizes some of the central issues that complicate the automatic analysis of Sanskrit. Section 4 describes the basic architecture of the tokenizer and morphological analyzer. Extensions of the basic system and improvements in the accuracy and coverage of the morphological analysis are reported in Sect. 5. Section 6 summarizes the paper.

2   Previous Research and Resources

Sanskrit has a long tradition of formal language description and analysis that predates any modern Western attempts in this field by millenia. This tradition was started by the grammarian Pāṇini, who probably lived around 350 BCE in Northwestern India (a general overview in [29]). His grammar Aṣṭādhyāyī ("eight [aṣṭan] chapters [adhyāya]") provides an extremely concise description of a late Vedic level of Sanskrit and may reflect a dialect of Sanskrit spoken at his time (details of the discussion in [4]). This conciseness was made possible by introduc-ing methods such as thematic roles, rewrite rules, abstract derivation levels, and pre-concepts of phonemes and morphemes, all of which are crucial for contem-porary linguistics [13].[2] Pāṇini's methods of language description were expanded and refined by his followers in works such as the Mahābhāṣya (Patañjali, 150 BCE) or the Siddhāntakaumudī (16. c. CE; refer to Scharfe for a history of grammatical research in India [29]).

Given the sophisticated formal methods that are provided by the Indian grammatical tradition and that were "rediscovered" in Western linguistics only in the 20th century, it is not surprising that some researchers try to transpose the Pāṇinian system of morphosyntactic analysis, more or less directly, into an NLP tool. These approaches frequently face problems with overgeneration (refer to Kulkarni's study from the area of phonetics [17]) and with the order in which the rules of the Aṣṭādhyāyī need to be applied.[3] Mishra handles these problems

---

[2] In a recent research project, the Aṣṭādhyāyī has been fully annotated on the mor-phological, lexical and word-semantic level to make it easier accessible for Western researchers without knowledge of Sanskrit [25]. A web platform that gives access to this database is available at http://panini.phil-fak.uni-duesseldorf.de/panini/.

[3] The rules of the Aṣṭādhyāyī are not given in the order in which they need to be applied for generating a valid Sanskrit word. Instead, it is generally assumed that their order minimizes the resulting rule base. The Indian grammar uses the concept of anuvṛtti ("following") rules for regulating the order in which rules and their elements are applied. These rules are not part of the text of the Aṣṭādhyāyī, but are recorded – and heavily discussed – in the commentary literature; refer to [4, 187ff.] for details about rule order in the Aṣṭādhyāyī, and to [26] for the proof of minimality in a subset of Pāṇinian rules.

by reformulating the rules of the Aṣṭādhyāyī in terms of set theory [21]. Huet [12] and Kulkarni [16] combine formal methods from the Aṣṭādhyāyī with a statistical scorer. Mittal estimates the probability of Sandhi splits from a parallel corpus of sandhied and unsandhied texts [22].[4] He combines a finite state automaton built from the parallel corpus, estimations of word frequencies, and a morphological analyzer with a scoring function that calculates a joint lexical and phonological weight for a given analysis of a Sanskrit sentence. The author reports that his system selects the best split of a given Sanskrit string in 92.8 % percent of all cases. Hellwig presents a statistical lexical and morphological analyzer [8], but misses the opportunity to give reliable performance data of this system [10].

In recent years, NLP has become increasingly interested in the processing of morphologically rich languages, and Sanskrit fits well into this extended scope of research. From among the more popular languages, Hebrew has similar challenges for NLP as Sanskrit. According to Adler, Hebrew has a rich and highly ambiguous morphology, and its morphological tag set is by far more comprehensive than that of English [1]. Shacham and Wintner combine results of classifiers that are each specialized on a subset of all morphological tags for Hebrew, and report an improvement over the baselines found in former papers on the topic [30]. Yuret describes an algorithm for the morphological disambiguation of Turkish, which has a similar proportion of morphologically ambiguous forms as Sanskrit [35]. By training decision lists with local, non-lexical features, the author achieves a disambiguation accuracy of nearly 96 % on a small test set. Lee proposes a graphical model for the joint morphological analysis and parsing of morphologically rich languages such as Latin and Czech [19], and obtains slight improvements over a baseline generated by separate training on the two tasks.

Basic computational resources were missing almost completely when the first versions of the system presented in this paper were created. The relational lexicographic database (Sect. 4.1) had to be extracted from a digitized version of the dictionary of Monier-Williams [23]. Although the majority of entries could be converted automatically by using regular expressions, preparing a usable database version of this dictionary still required considerable manual correction due to inconsistencies in the formatting of the original dictionary and of its digitized text version. Moreover, the Monier-Williams was designed as a typical reference-oriented printed dictionary. This means that it recorded numerous compounds with purely compositional meaning (e.g., *mahāgiri*, "high mountain", consisting of the adjective *mahā* "high" and the noun *giri* "mountain"). Such lexicon entries may be useful in printed editions, but complicate the lemmatization that focuses on decomposed primitives.

Similar problems are also encountered when building computational processors for other premodern Indian languages as, for example, for Pāli [14] or for Old Marathi, for which a morphological analyzer is currently developed. Lack of

---

[4] Refer to page Subsect. 3.3 for the phonological phenomenon of Sandhi.

resources further pertains to large, consistently formatted digital text corpora[5] and to gold annotated training and test data from any level of linguistic analysis, although the research community has begun to compile such resources on a small scale during the last years [31].

3 Linguistic Background and Challenges

Sanskrit poses a number of challenges for the automatic linguistic analysis, some of which are not found in the languages typically examined in current NLP. This section gives an overview of the most important of these phenomena.

3.1 Morphology

Sanskrit has a rich and partly ambiguous morphology. Nouns and adjectives inflect for three numbers (SG., DU., and PL.), eight cases (NOM., ACC., VOC., GEN., DAT., INS., ABL., LOC.), and a frequent and productive stem form (CO.) that is used to create compounds.[6] The finite forms of the verbal system differentiate between present (indicative present, imperative, imperfect), future (future, conditional, periphrastic future), perfect, and seven classes of aorists. Each of the tenses builds forms for three persons, three numbers, and the active and medium voices. These forms are supplemented by infinite forms such as fully declinable participles of the present, future, perfect, and of the past, and indeclinable forms (infinitive, absolutive). With a few exceptions, the derivation of nominal and verbal forms from their respective stems is regular. The complex, interacting rules that guide these derivational processes are formulated in the Aṣṭādhyāyī.

While the rich inflexion of Sanskrit, in principle, promotes a reliable morphological analysis of Sanskrit texts, there are a few high-frequency morphemes

---

[5] The GRETIL web repository (http://gretil.sub.uni-goettingen.de/) contains less than 20 million strings. Several of the texts are not usable for automatic processing due to excessive formatting of their editors, as described in Sect. 3.6.

[6] The following abbreviations are used in this paper: NOM.: nominative; ACC.: accusative; INS.: instrumental; DAT.: dative; GEN.: genitive; LOC.: locative; VOC.: vocative; CO.: compound; SG.: singular; DU.: dual; PL.: plural; MSC.: masculine; FEM.: feminine; NEU.: neuter; IND.: indeclinable; PRES.: present; IMPF.: imperfect; PERF.: perfect tense; PROH.: prohibitive (a kind of imperative that is only used in negated phrases); PASTPART.: past participle, frequently with a passive sense; PRESPART.: present participle

Ambiguities in a morphological analysis are expressed by a regex-style notation, with | denoting the operator OR and round brackets a set of options. So, (NOM.|ACC.|VOC.)PL.NEU.means that a form is a neuter plural either in nominative or accusative or vocative.

The plus operator + is used to separate elements of compounds, the ampersand sign & to indicate Sandhi at word boundaries (Sect. 3.3).

Further abbreviations: `tri`: trigram based model for morphological disambiguation; `crf`: Conditional Random Fields; `me`: Maximum Entropy.

whose phonetic ambiguity complicates the morphological tagging. Most important among them is the word final sequence -*am*, which marks NOM., ACC., and VOC.SG. of the noun class -*a* neuter, ACC.SG. of the noun class -*a* masc. and ACC.SG. of nominal stems that end with consonants. Such morphological ambiguities gain in importance through the phenomenon of *bahuvrīhi* compounding, which can change the gender of a nominal compound (refer to Sect. 3.2). In addition, the phonetic process of Sandhi can "obfuscate" the output forms of the inflectional endings (Sect. 3.3).

3.2 Compounding

Although compound formation does not seem to interfere with morphological analysis at first view, the long ranges covered by many compounds, e.g., in philosophical and scientific texts, complicate the estimation of transition weights for sequence based algorithms. In addition, Sanskrit knows a class of compounds called *bahuvrīhi* ("(a person who has) much rice") that produce adjectives with a possessive meaning.[7] During this compounding process, the original nominal compound is transformed into an adjective, and the gender of the final member of the compound is adopted to the gender of the noun the *bahuvrīhi* refers to. In example 1, the phrase *pāpakarmabhiḥ* can be interpreted as a "default" compound ("by bad actions", INS.PL.NEU., *tatpuruṣa* interpretation) or, more correctly, as a *bahuvrīhi* adjective refering to the anaphoric masculine pronoun *taiḥ*. During adjectivization, the gender of the compound is changed from the original neuter to the masculine of the pronoun:

(1) *nihśeṣo*   *hi*   *kṛto*
   without remainder-NOM.SG.MSC. because-IND. make-PASTPART.NOM.SG.MSC.
   vaṃśo   *mama*   *taiḥ*
   family-NOM.SG.MSC. my-GEN.SG.   they-INS.PL.(MSC.|NEU.)
   pāpakarmabhiḥ
   bad-CO.+actions-INS.PL.(MSC.|NEU.)

"Because my family was completely destroyed by these bad persons (lit.: by them, who have bad actions), . . ." (Mahābhārata, 13.31.25).[8]

3.3 Phonetic Rules (Sandhi)

Sanskrit uses a large set of euphonic rules called Sandhi ("connection"), whose formulation is another major contribution of the Aṣṭādhyāyī. Most of these rules

---

[7] Note that the word *bahuvrīhi* is itself an example of a *bahuvrīhi* compound. In its "default interpretation" as a so-called *tatpuruṣa* ("his man", an instance of relational compounding) compound, it means just "much rice.".

[8] From a purely grammatical point of view, the sentence can also be translated as "... destroyed by these bad actions." Numerous references of the *bahuvrīhi* solution with unambiguous case endings (e.g., in NOM.PL.MSC.) make the proposed interpretation much more plausible.

combine two phonemes into one or two other phonemes to produce a "smoother pronounciation".[9] Sandhi occurs inside of words during the derivational process and at the boundary between words during the construction of the sentence from the inflected lemmata. For an example of how word boundary Sandhi works, consider the three inflected Sanskrit words *tān* (ACC.PL.MSC. of pronoun *tad*, "they"), *cet* (IND., "if"), and *jayati* (3rdSG.PRES. of verb *ji*, "to win"). The word-final *n* of *tān* and the initial *c* of *cet* produce the Sandhi *ṃśc*, while the word-final *t* of *cet* and the initial *j* of *jayati* produce *jj*. Using these two Sandhis, the three separate forms are merged into a single string *tāṃścejjayati* ("if (s)he overcomes them").

Sandhi tends to "obfuscate" morphological terminations. This phenomenon is, for instance, observed in the phrase *pāṇḍavā api* (NOM.PL.MSC. of the noun *pāṇḍava*, "name of a famous family", and *api*, IND., "also"), where the original word final letter *ḥ* of *pāṇḍavāḥ* has been elided through boundary Sandhi. A morphological analyzer must be able to reconstruct the pre-sandhied form *pāṇḍavāḥ* based on the right context *api*, before it starts the actual morphological analysis.

While, theoretically, Sandhi must be used whenever applicable, real texts show a lot of divergence from this rule. Sanskrit epics, for example, do not adhere strictly and consistently to these rules ("Epic Sandhi").[10] Much more frequently, however, deviations from these rules may have been caused by errors of the author or the scribe of a text due to an insufficient knowledge of these euphonic rules. It should be needless to emphasize that Sandhi rules complicate the automatic analysis of Sanskrit massively, because they introduce ambiguity into tokenization (refer to Sect. 4) and tend to overgenerate possible analyses of a string. A working system used for real texts must be able to cope with the full set of standard Sandhi rules, but also with irregular situations as found in the epics, and it should not interrupt analysis when a Sandhi rule has not been applied.

3.4 Word Order

Word order is another problematic area, because it is explored intensively in NLP models for English, while its role in South-Asian languages is far less prominent. Staal claims that there are virtually no rules for word order in Sanskrit [32], without supporting his theory with quantitative data. Gillon, who claims that unmarked Sanskrit sentences show a tendency for verb-finality [7], has certainly arrived at a more realistic picture of word order in Sanskrit prose texts. Although prose texts seem to prefer a certain word order, it is by far not as strictly regulated as, for instance, in English. Features exploring the order of words may,

---

[9] Though slightly outdated, the grammar of Stenzler still provides a good introduction into Sanskrit Sandhi rules [33, 3ff.].

[10] Refer to [24, 1ff.] for a detailed linguistic description with several examples. Brockington locates the epics, especially the Mahābhārata, in a continuum "of dialects and language registers from classical or Pāṇinian Sanskrit at one end to colloquial MIA [Middle Indo-Aryan] at the other" [3, 83] and makes this linguistic situation responsible for the irregular application of Sandhi in epic texts.

therefore, not contribute as significantly to the accuracy of the morphological analysis as they do for English [6].

3.5 The Lexicon

Classical Sanskrit has built up an extremely rich vocabulary that covers topics as diverse as religion, philosophy, science (grammar, medicine, mathematics), poetry, and popular tales. Apart from OIA terms and their derivatives, Sanskrit included words from several "substrate languages" such as Dravidian, Middle (Prākṛts, Apabhraṃśa) and even New Indo-Aryan languages.[11] Because Sanskrit was used as a literary language by most authors, and because most authors were well aware of its long-standing literary tradition, one can observe a tendency to revive older strata of the vocabulary and to incorporate them into new texts.[12] From the perspective of NLP, the richness of the vocabulary contributes to the sparsity of lexicographic data, and complicates the estimation of lexical parameters of ML models.

3.6 Orthography

A closely connected area is the general lack of a strict orthography and the missing reliability of punctuation. Many algorithms for language analysis require full sentences as the basic input units. Sanskrit uses a vertical line called *daṇḍa* ("staff", "stick") for marking breaks in the metrical structure and in the general discourse structure of texts. However, the *daṇḍa*, which is rendered by a backslash (/) in this paper, frequently does not coincide with the termination of complete sentences. Example 2 contains two *daṇḍa*s that mark the end of the metrical units. Here, only the second *daṇḍa* after *adhitiṣṭhati* coincides with the termination of a full sentence, while the first one separates the verbal form *uvāca* from its subject (Mahābhārata, 13.28.10):

(2) ... *gardabhī*   *putragṛddhinī*   /   *uvāca*
    ... she-ass-NOM.SG.FEM. son-CO.+caring-NOM.SG.FEM. *daṇḍa* say-3rdSG.PERF.
    mā   *śucaḥ*   *putra*
    not-IND. worry-PROH.SG. son-VOC.SG.MSC.
    caṇḍālastvādhitiṣṭhati   /
    Caṇḍāla-NOM.SG.MSC.&you-ACC.SG.&ride-3rdSG.PRES. *daṇḍa*

"The she-ass, who was sorried about her son, said: 'Don't worry, son! A Caṇḍāla[13] is riding on you.'"

Algorithms for detecting the true sentence breaks in Sanskrit have not yet been developed. NLP systems must either rely on sentences with manually

---

[11] Emeneau describes the basic parameters of the interaction between Indo-Iranian and Dravidian languages [5]. A quantitative overview of the major influences that is based on Mayrhofer's etymological dictionary [20] is given in [9].

[12] A quantitative evaluation of the reuse of Pāṇinian vocabulary is presented in [11].

[13] A member of a low caste.

marked borders, which involves time consuming manual annotation, or must be able to handle the lack of orthographic information appropriately. To increase the readability, the term "sentence" will, nevertheless, denote a sequence of strings that is terminated by a *daṇḍa* in this paper. Such a "sentence" may thus contain parts of a sentence or of sentences, a full sentence, or several concatenated sentences.

At an even more basic level, traditional editions of Sanskrit texts insert blank spaces between non-mergable strings sparingly, if at all. On the contrary, Western editors frequently even resolve boundary Sandhis to increase the readability of the text, thereby producing syllable sequences that are invalid from an Indian point of view. Therefore, the text of the second sentence in Example 2 could also be written as *uvācamāśucaḥputracaṇḍālastvādhitiṣṭhati* (traditional Indian style) or *uvāca mā śucaḥ putra caṇḍālas tvā adhitiṣṭhati* (Western style).

4 Architecture of the System

This section gives an overview of how a Sanskrit sentence is analyzed in the proposed system. Because the core functionality of the tagger has been described in [8], this section only summarizes the central components (Sect. 4.1) and processing steps (Sect. 4.2). Section 4.3 gives a short evaluation of the algorithm for joint tokenization and lemmatization.

4.1 Basic Components

The system consists of five core components.

1. The lexical database stores lemmata, their grammatical categories, meanings, word semantic information, and inflected verbal forms. The database currently contains 174,190 distinct lemmata with 313,725 meanings and 104,811 connections to a word semantic repository that is derived from OpenCyc[14].
2. The corpus stores the Sanskrit texts along with their lexicographic, morphological and word semantic gold annotations.[15] There are 273 texts in the corpus database, 69 of which are completely annotated. The texts contain 2,674,000 strings that are split into 3,587,000 lexical tokens with morphological gold annotations. The corpus data are used to train statistical models for lexico-morphological analysis and disambiguation. As can be seen in Table 1, the corpus mainly contains texts from the epic-Purāṇic traditions[16] and from science, including medicine, alchemy, and gemmology. The type-token-ratios

---

[14] http://opencyc.org/.

[15] As these data are only checked by one annotator and have not been adjudicated, they should rather be called semi-gold annotations.

[16] The Mahābhārata and the Rāmāyaṇa are the two central epic texts written in Sanskrit. The term Purāṇa ("old (story)") denotes a group of works dealing with virtually everything; refer to Rocher for an introduction [28].

(TTR)[17] vary strongly between the topic levels, with the highest value not surprisingly found in lexicography.

3. The linguistic models comprise (1) a hard-coded rule base for Sandhi resolution and for determining morphological categories of nouns, and (2) learned parameters of the statistical algorithms that are created using the training data extracted from the corpus. Sanskrit nouns are inflected by adding terminations to the roots of words in a similar way as in Latin or Ancient Greek. Morphological analysis of nominal forms is performed by removing possible inflectional suffixes from a string at runtime, and looking up the remaining word root in the noun section of the lexical database. Inflected verbal forms have a special role in the system. They are synthesized automatically for each (prefixed) verbal root, checked manually, and then stored in the verb section of the lexical database along with their morphological information (tense, mode, person, number). At runtime, morphological analysis of verbal forms is performed by looking up an input string in the verb section of the database, and returning the associated morphological information, if it is found. Although Sanskrit verbal forms can be analyzed using a rule based system (refer, for instance, to [21]), the current solution was chosen to speed up the creation of the initial system, because a thorough handling of the verbal forms would have required a formalization of large ranges of the Aṣṭādhyāyī.

Table 1. Composition of the corpus, grouped by topics. %: percentage of lemma tokens in texts with a given topic in relation to the number of all lemma tokens in the corpus; TTR: averaged type-token-ratio for each topic.

Topic	%	TTR
Buddhist	1.51	0.34
darśana ("philosophy")	1.62	0.3322
dharma ("law")	4.07	0.4095
Grammar	0.52	0.314
Epic-Purāṇic	55.33	0.2145
Lexicography	2.13	0.5966
Poetry	4.88	0.4308
Religious	4.37	0.414
Science	23.8	0.347
śruti (late Vedic texts)	1.78	0.3576

4. The tag set consists of tags for indeclensibles, nouns and verbal forms. The indeclensible tag covers particles, interjections, and conjunctions. The noun

---

[17] The TTRs found in the third column of Table 1 are obtained by calculating the TTRs for each text, and then averaging these values over the topic levels. Because text lengths have not been used as normalizing factors, the TTRs of underrepresented topic levels such as *śruti* or Buddhist literature are most probably too high.

tags represent substantives and adjectives in one of the three genders, three numbers and eight cases, plus the 3 respective stem forms. The tags for the verbal system differentiate between present, future, and past tenses in the three persons and numbers. The verbal tags are thus less fine-grained than the nominal ones: While each morphological category of nouns is mapped to its own tag, tags for verbal forms focus on person and number distinction, but differentiate only roughly between the tenses (refer to Sect. 3.1 for the tense system of Sanskrit). Because the morphological ambiguity in the verbal system is much lower than in the nominal one, this design decision reduces the number of tags and simplifies the task of automatic morphological analysis.
5. The linguistic processor uses the models and the lexical database to analyze a sentence. The resulting analysis can be checked manually (creation of gold-annotated data) and stored in the corpus to increase the size of the training database.

4.2   Tokenization and Morphological Analysis

The algorithm that performs tokenization, lemmatization, and morphological analysis works in two main steps. The first step tries to generate the correct lemmatization of the input text, which includes Sandhi resolution and compound splitting. The second step performs a fine-tuning of the morphological analysis of the highest scoring lemmatization obtained in the first step. The disambiguation methods dealt with in this paper are part of the second step.

In the first step, each input string s is scanned from left to right (refer to [8] for details). If a (combination of) phoneme(s) at position i in s is found in the list of possible Sandhi results, s is tentatively split at i, and its left part is analyzed lexically and morphologically after its final Sandhi has been undone. If the left part is a valid Sanskrit form, the right part of s is analyzed in the same way. If this recursive algorithm reaches the end of the string, all proposed analyses are inserted in a hypothesis lattice. After the full input sentence has been processed, Viterbi decoding is used to find the most probable sequence of lexical tokens in the resulting lattice.

For Viterbi decoding, all morpho-lexical analyses LM_j are extracted for each possible split string j. The split string *vanam*, for example, produces the three analyses $LM_{j1} = (\text{Nom.Sg.Neu.}, vana, \text{"forest"})$, $LM_{j2} = (\text{Acc.Sg.Neu.}, vana, \text{"forest"})$, and $LM_{j3} = (\text{Voc.Sg.Neu.}, vana, \text{"forest"})$. Although the first step is concerned with lemmatization, morphological information is included at this point because it helps to distinguish between different lexical derivations of ambiguous surface strings such as *te*, which can be derived from *tvat* ("you", Dat. or Gen.Sg.) or *tat* ("this", Nom.Pl.Msc.). The decoding process uses the probabilities of bigrams (LM_{j-1}, LM_j) whose frequencies are estimated from the annotated corpus and smoothed using the method proposed by Kneser and Ney [15]. To make analysis paths of different lengths comparable to each other, the sums of logarithmized transition probabilities resulting from Viterbi decoding are divided by the lengths l of their paths, which is equivalent to taking the lth root from the unlogarithmized path probabilities. When T denotes the set of all possible tokenizations t of a given sentence, the winning tokenization of a sentence fulfills the condition $\underset{t \in T}{\mathrm{argmax}} \frac{1}{|t|} \left(\sum_{i=1}^{|t|} \log p(LM_i | LM_{i-1}) \right)$.

4.3 Evaluation of the Tokenization

The quality of the joint tokenization and lexical disambiguation was assessed by calculating the Levenshtein edit distance between gold sequences of lexemes from the corpus and the corresponding silver sequences of lexemes generated by the system. For testing, a set of 10.000 sentences was drawn randomly from the corpus. The parameters of the tokenizer were re-estimated from the remaining part of the corpus, and the retrained model was applied to the 10.000 holdout sentences.

As can be seen in Table 2, the model produces the correct lexical tokenization for 94.4 % of the holdout sentences, and one error for 3.3 % of them. To get an idea of how the topics of the texts influence tokenization accuracy, the numbers of edit operations were grouped by the texts from which the sentences were drawn, and some of the most voluminous texts were labeled with the same coarse-grained domain tag set that was used for creating Table 1. Table 3 shows that tokenization works well for texts from the epic-Purāṇic literature. These texts are mostly written in an easy, unpretentious style, they share a large core vocabulary, and they constitute one of the thematic focus areas of the corpus (refer to Table 1). A similar picture emerges for the Āyurvedic (medical) texts, which are, however, linguistically and especially lexicographically much more demanding than the epic-Purāṇic literature, as indicated by the higher type-token-ratio shown in Table 1. The alchemical texts, in contrast, show higher error rates, although the alchemical tradition has actually developed from Āyurveda. This fact can possibly be explained by rare lexemes used in these texts (e.g., in the Rasādhyāya, a late text showing strong influences from NIA languages) and by the low literary quality of many alchemical texts. The Aṣṭādhyāyī produces the worst tokenization score in the evaluation, because the text uses Sanskrit as a metalanguage for encoding its grammar, and some of these metalinguistic phenomena are not handled by the regular processing pipeline of the program to avoid overgeneration. In addition, Table 1 shows that the grammatical texts constitute the smallest thematic section of the corpus. Adding more texts from the grammatical tradition may improve the unsupervised tokenization of the Aṣṭādhyāyī.

The evaluation has shown that the lemmatization produces acceptable results for texts from domains for which enough training data is available. The morphological analysis resulting from the first step of the decoding process, however, is frequently wrong. Therefore, another level of morphological Viterbi decoding is added for the highest-scoring lexical path, using only smoothed trigrams of morphological tags, but no lexical information. Column 3 (`tri`) of Table 5 reports the global accuracy of this approach, grouped by the number of different proposals per lexical item. As could be expected, the accuracy of this approach decreases with the number of morphological options per word. The next section

Table 2. Length of sentences (rows) and numbers of edit operations needed to transform silver in gold tokenization (Levenshtein), tested on a holdout set of 10.000 sentences. Values in percent of all 10.000 sentences.

	Number of edits			
	0	1	2	≥ 3
≤ 5	14.47	0.19	0.26	0.04
6–10	75.63	2.91	1.43	0.28
11–15	3.58	0.16	0.17	0.01
≥ 16	0.75	0.04	0.04	0.03
$\sum$	94.43	3.3	1.9	0.36

describes experiments for improving the performance of the system for ambiguous morphological analyses.

5 Improvements and Evaluation

As noted in Sect. 4.2, words in the best lexical path can be annotated with more than one morphological solution. Column 2 of Table 5 shows that such ambiguous solutions occur for approximately $100\% - 58\% = 42\%$ of all words in the test set. Resolving these ambiguities is, therefore, crucial for the accurate morphological tagging of Classical Sanskrit. This section describes a set of experiments that aim at improving the morphological analysis of ambiguous cases. Subsection 5.1 sketches the feature extraction. Subsection 5.2 describes which ML models are used for learning. Section 5.3 describes how the test and training sets are created. Results and error analysis are presented in Sect. 5.4.

5.1 Features

The features are built from the two pieces of information that are available after the first stage of linguistic analysis has been completed: (1) the lexical information about each word in the highest scoring path, and (2) the morphological solutions that the analyzer has proposed for each lexeme in this path. The proposals for the morphological analysis are merged into an ordered set of distinct morphological classes. This merged set is used as a single feature M of the word under consideration. If, for example, the analyzer has detected that a word can be (NOM.|ACC.)PL.(MSC.|FEM.), these four proposals are unfolded into the single feature ACC.PL.FEM.|ACC.PL.MSC.|NOM.PL.FEM.|NOM.PL.MSC., using alphabetical ordering of the names of the morphological tags.

Before extracting the features from the training set, frequency thresholds are applied to remove lexical items L with a total frequency of less than 10 and combined morphological solutions M that occur with a total frequency of less than 50 in the training corpus. If only one morphological solution is proposed

Table 3. Number of edit operations for individual texts; refer to Table 1 for the topic labels. Abbreviations: med.: medical (Āyurveda); alchem.: alchemical (*rasaśāstra*); narr.: narrative

Text	Number of tested sent	Number of edits				Domain
		0	1	2	≥ 3	
Mahābhārata	3071	94.86	3.35	1.69	0.1	Epic-Purāṇic
Rāmāyaṇa	774	95.61	2.71	1.68	0	Epic-Purāṇic
Liṅgapurāṇa	395	93.92	4.05	1.52	0.51	Epic-Purāṇic
Suśrutasaṃhitā	347	98.27	0.86	0.86	0	Science (med.)
Aṣṭāṅgahṛdayasaṃhitā	289	94.12	2.77	2.42	0.69	Science (med.)
Ānandakanda	243	92.18	4.94	2.88	0	Science (alchem.)
Bṛhatkathāślokasaṃgraha	189	95.77	4.23	0	0	Poetry (narr.)
Carakasaṃhitā	172	95.93	2.33	1.16	0.58	Science (med.)
Rasaratnākara	163	93.87	3.07	1.84	1.23	Science (alch.)
Rājanighaṇṭu	141	91.49	4.96	2.84	0.71	Lexicography
Manusmṛti	122	95.08	3.28	0.82	0.82	*dharma*
Viṣṇusmṛti	75	90.67	2.67	5.33	1.33	*dharma*
Hitopadeśa	58	93.1	3.45	3.45	0	Poetry (narr.)
Rasendracintāmaṇi	36	91.67	5.56	2.78	0	Science (alch.)
Aṣṭādhyāyī	35	57.14	14.29	22.86	5.71	Grammatical
Rasādhyāya	24	87.5	8.33	4.17	0	Science (alch.)

for a word (58 % of all cases), this solution is assumed to be the correct one, and the true morphological class of this word is replaced by a dummy variable to reduce the complexity of the training process.[18] The full feature vector v_i for the word at position i is the union of all lexical and morphological features of words with a maximal distance of 3 from i (context window).[19] Consider, as an example, the trivial sentence *sa vanaṃ gacchati* ("he goes into the forest") with a context window of size 1. The first step of the analysis has proposed the following highest scoring sequence: (*sa* = (NOM.SG.MSC., lemma *tad*, "he")), (*vanam*[20] = ((NOM.|ACC.|VOC.)SG.NEU., *vana*, "forest")), (*gacchati* = ((3rdSG.PRES.|(LOC.SG.(MSC.|NEU.), PRESPART.)), *gam*, "to go")). The first word has the local features L=*tad* and M=(NOM.SG.MSC.), the second word has L=*vana* and M=(NOM.SG.NEU.|ACC.SG.NEU.|VOC.SG.NEU.), and the third

---

[18] The one-solution case predicts the correct morphological category in about 99.8 % of all cases. The errors are caused by irregular word forms.

[19] The parameter 3 for the window size was chosen after comparing disambiguation results for window sizes between 1 and 7. Window sizes above 3 did not consistently increase the accuracy, but required higher training times.

[20] The final Sandhi *ṃ* has been transformed into the pausa form *m*.

Table 4. Features and target classes for the sentence *sa vanaṃ gacchati*. X denotes the dummy variable used for words with only one morphological analysis. (NOM.) ...: local features of *vanam*, i.e. (NOM.|ACC.|VOC.)SG.NEU.; 3rdSG.PRES. ...: local features of *gacchati*, i.e. 3rdSG.PRES.|(LOC.SG.(MSC.|NEU.))

Word		1 *sa*	2 *vanam*	3 *gacchati*
Local	L	*tad*	*vana*	*gam*
features	M	NOM.SG.MSC.	(NOM.|ACC.|VOC.)SG.NEU.	3rdSG.PRES. ...
Full feature vector		{X}	{L_{-1} = tad, L_0 = vana, L_{+1} = gam, M_{-1} = NOM.SG.MSC., M_0 = (NOM. ..., M_{+1} = 3rdSG.PRES. ... }	{L_{-1} = vana, L_0 = gam, L_{+1} = ∅, M_{-1} = (NOM. ..., M_0 = 3rdSG.PRES. ..., M_{+1} = ∅}
Target class		X	ACC.SG.NEU.	3rdSG.PRES.

one L=*gam* and M=(3rdSG., past tense|LOC.SG.MSC.|LOC.SG.NEU.). The target classes, on which the classifiers are trained, are the correct morphological tags according to the gold standard for the ambiguous solutions, or the dummy variable X in case of unambiguous solutions. The full feature vectors and the target classes for each word are given in Table 4, where the numeric subscripts denote the distance from the respective focus word at position i. These full vectors are the input for the ML methods that are described in Sect. 5.2.

5.2   Models

The ML models that are used to resolve the morphological ambiguities must be able to handle high-dimensional feature vectors of varying size from a nominal scale. The size of the feature vectors is variable because (1) all lexical and morphological context information of words with an unambiguous morphological analysis is replaced by the dummy variable X, and (2) lexical and morphological context information can be pruned away when their frequencies are below the thresholds given in Sect. 5.1. Two models that fulfill these requirements are Maximum Entropy Classifiers (ME, [27])[21] and Conditional Random Fields (CRF, [18]).[22] While ME is trained and evaluated on single words, CRF is a sequential model that takes information about the preceding word into account. Because the local morphological and lexical context presumably influences the analysis of a word, it may be expected that the sequential CRF performs better than the non-sequential ME, even if they are trained with the same data.

---

[21] Used in the Java implementation of the OpenNLP package; settings: smoothing factor: 0.001, 100 iterations.

[22] Used in the C++ implementation from http://www.chokkan.org/software/crfsuite/; settings: L2 regularization: 2.0, one-dimensional architecture.

5.3   Test Design

Training and test sets are constructed by first extracting those sentences from the corpus whose gold analysis contains between 2 and 20 lexical items. Longer sentences are excluded to limit the time needed for data creation. The resulting set S consists of approximately 475,000 sentences. Each sentence in S is tokenized by using the first step of the analysis algorithm described in Sect. 4.2. If the lexical silver annotation proposed after the first step is identical with the lexical gold annotation from the corpus, the features described in Sect. 5.1 are extracted from the sentence, and the sentence is added, along with its features, to a set F. This set F is split randomly into a training set containing 95 % and a test set containing 5 % of all sentences in F.

It should be kept in mind that the final test and training sets contain only sentences that have been analyzed correctly on the lexical level. This restriction was introduced to simplify the creation of the test data, but it could have a negative effect when the final system is confronted with real-world sentences whose first-step lemmatization contains errors. Another caveat concerns the testing method. Because considerable time is needed for training the models, no cross-validation of the results is performed for this paper.

5.4   Evaluation and Error Analysis

Table 5 shows the accuracy rates of all three tested classifiers, i.e. the number of correctly classified items divided by the number of all items in the respective category, depending from the number of morphological categories proposed by the system. As could be expected, the two sequence based algorithms (tri, crf) consistently outperform the me model, although this model is also trained with context features. Among the sequence based classifiers, crf is superior to tri.

The column called fallback shows that it is possible to improve over the accuracy of crf for some frequent classes when the decisions of tri and crf are merged. As crf outputs a probability p along with its decision, a threshold for p that maximizes the accuracy of the crf result is searched on a holdout set. If the probability for a solution from the test set is below this treshold, the output of crf is replaced with that of tri. A simple majority voting with all three classifiers tri, crf and me does not increase the accuracy (last column in Table 5).

Table 6 gives a more detailed evaluation of precision, recall, and F-score for the most frequent target tags in the test set. Two observations are relevant. First, crf generates the best solutions for most tags, as indicated by the numbers printed in bold. For some cases, such as the notoriously difficult NOM.SG.MSC. (second row), one can observe a strong increase in P, R, and F when compared to the values of tri and me. Second, there are large differences between the target tags that can be explained by the underlying morphological ambiguities and their statistical distributions. The most frequent tag CO.MSC., for example, is identical with VOC.SG.MSC. in many cases. Nevertheless, the chance of confounding the two forms is low, because vocatives are comparatively rare in

Table 5. Number of proposed morphological categories and accuracy of the tested classifiers. Refer to Footnote 6 for the abbreviations.

No. of solutions	Proportion	tri	crf	me	fallback	majority
1	58.04	–	–	–	–	–
2	15.74	92.04	93.12	87.56	93.79	93.22
3	9.09	82.48	88.52	82.1	88.56	87.43
4	9.38	77.89	82.94	79.15	82.78	82.56
5	2.98	89.56	91.42	87.18	91.85	91.65
6	1.76	85.82	89.8	82.76	90.76	88.84
7	0.69	85.7	89	86.55	88.88	88.63
8	0.25	76.49	83.44	78.15	84.77	79.14
9	1.51	83.03	84.21	75.03	85.39	83.54
≥ 10	0.54	84.45	86.47	80.72	88.18	85.54

the corpus. Similarly good results are achieved for ambiguous verbal forms, most of which have one "dominant" interpretation. So, the form *uvāca* ("I/he said") is almost exclusively used as 3rd SG.PERF. (and not 1st SG.PERF.), and *gacchati* is mostly used as 3rd SG.PRES. of the root *gam* ("to go") and not as LOC.SG.MSC. of the present participle of *gam*. On the contrary, the rates for (NOM.|ACC.)SG.NEU. and ACC.SG.MSC. are low, because the frequent noun classes on -*a* have the same endings for these three forms. This situation is further complicated by *bahuvrīhi* formation (Sect. 3.2) and sentences extending over *daṇḍa* boundaries (Sect. 3.6). *bahuvrīhi* formation is also responsible for errors in classifying forms such as INS.SG.MSC. and NEU. (not in the table), because it can change their genders during the compounding process.

6 Summary and Perspectives

The paper has described a system for joint tokenization, lemmatization and morphological analysis of Sanskrit, and it has reported performance rates for the tokenization task (Sect. 4.3, Tables 2 and 3). By using crf as an additional sequential classification layer, it is possible to improve the analysis of morphologically ambiguous forms. It should be emphasized that the numbers reported in this paper are only valid for the test set. They will probably be lower in unsupervised analysis, because the input for building the features (Sect. 5.1) may contain errors. Future research should concentrate on improving the quality of the features with which the model is trained, and on integrating more linguistic tasks such as syntactic parsing into the model, as proposed for Latin by Lee [19]. On the engineering side, deep neural learning models co-trained on several tasks should be tested for a morphologically complex language such as Sanskrit.

From a more general point of view, the linguistic analysis of Sanskrit opens perspectives in two areas. First, Sanskrit is a typical representative of resource-poor

Table 6. Precision (P), recall (R) and F score (F) for the three classifiers and the most frequent morphological tags (frequency $\geq 2\%$ of all ambiguous cases in the test set). The highest values for P, R and F per line are printed in bold. Prop.: Proportion of this gold tag in all gold tags of ambiguous cases. v. n.: verbal noun

Tag	Prop.	crf			tri			me		
		P	R	F	P	R	F	P	R	F
Co.Msc.	14.34	98.52	**99.62**	**99.07**	98.8	97.38	98.08	93.54	98.88	96.14
Nom.Sg.Neu.	11.22	**80.92**	**88.07**	**84.34**	73.2	79.09	76.03	75.83	84.29	79.84
Acc.Sg.Neu.	9.11	**81.94**	**76.24**	**78.99**	72.44	69.13	70.75	71.54	74.7	73.09
Nom.Pl.Msc.	7.00	93.91	**98.36**	**96.08**	94.4	95.54	94.97	89.79	95.34	92.48
Acc.Sg.Msc.	4.47	**84.4**	79.87	**82.07**	83.08	**80.01**	81.52	75.14	75.96	75.55
3.Sg.Past	3.09	98.9	**99.8**	**99.35**	99.28	99.41	99.34	93.51	97.65	95.54
Gen.Sg.Msc.	2.90	90.02	**97.02**	**93.39**	92.36	93.96	93.15	89.02	91.67	90.33
Loc.Sg.Neu.	2.86	92.21	89.09	90.62	**93.51**	**90.29**	**91.87**	86.74	85.64	86.19
Nom.Sg.Msc.	2.76	**92.66**	**96.65**	**94.61**	92.31	92.71	92.51	89.41	91.69	90.54
Loc.Sg.Msc.	2.44	85.25	91.09	88.07	**87.57**	**91.25**	**89.37**	82.87	83.83	83.35
3.Sg.Pres.	2.44	**98.28**	**99.09**	**98.68**	96.22	98.68	97.43	92.78	97.53	95.1
Nom.Sg.Msc. (v.n.)	2.38	**82.39**	**93.16**	**87.44**	80.81	85.65	83.16	76.81	87.51	81.81
Co.Fem.	2.37	94.31	**95.75**	**95.02**	94.82	88.62	91.62	92.12	91.33	91.72
Nom.Sg.Fem.	2.19	**92.47**	91.2	**91.83**	84.36	89.46	86.84	87.21	85.61	86.4
Ins.Sg.Msc.	2.08	89.39	**93.02**	**91.17**	90.27	90.79	90.53	86.33	85.66	85.99
Ins.Pl.Msc.	2.08	87.89	**95.55**	91.56	**92.64**	92.64	**92.64**	86.57	86.74	86.65

languages – both in its linguistic embedding in South Asia and in its status as a classical language that is not spoken anymore. Solutions found for the linguistic analysis of Sanskrit may, therefore, be applicable both for other South Asian languages and for similar studies in classical European languages. Second, NLP has been focussing stronger on morphologically rich languages with a weakly regulated word order during the past few years, and it may profit from insights gained from the study of "off-track" languages such as Sanskrit.

References

1. Adler, M., Elhalad, M.: An unsupervised morpheme-based HMM for Hebrew morphological disambiguation. In: Proceedings of the 21st International Conference on Computational Linguistics, pp. 665–672 (2006)
2. Bloch, J.: Indo-Aryan from the Vedas to Modern Times. Librarie d'Amérique et d'Orient, Paris (1965)
3. Brockington, J.: The Sanskrit Epics. Brill, Leiden (1998)
4. Cardona, G.: Pāṇini. A Survey of Research. Mouton, The Hague - Paris (1976)
5. Emeneau, M.: Dravidian and indo-aryan: the indian linguistic area. In: Emeneau, M.B. (ed.) Language and Linguistic Area, pp. 167–196. Stanford University Press, Stanford (1980)
6. Gillon, B.S.: Review of "Natural Language Processing: A Paninian Perspective" by A. Bharati, V. Chaitanya, and R. Sangal. Prentice-Hall of India 1995. Computational Linguistics **21**(3), 419–421 (1995)

7. Gillon, B.S.: Word order in classical Sanskrit. Indian Linguist. **57**(1–4), 1–35 (1996)
8. Hellwig, O.: SadnskritTagger: a stochastic lexical and POS tagger for Sanskrit. In: Huet, G., Kulkarni, A., Scharf, P. (eds.) Sanskrit CL 2007/2008. LNCS, vol. 5402, pp. 266–277. Springer, Heidelberg (2009)
9. Hellwig, O.: Etymological trends in the Sanskrit vocabulary. Literary Linguist. Comput. **25**(1), 105–118 (2010)
10. Hellwig, O.: Performance of a lexical and POS tagger for Sanskrit. In: Jha, G.N. (ed.) SCL. LNCS, vol. 6465, pp. 162–172. Springer, Heidelberg (2010)
11. Hellwig, O., Petersen, W.: What's Pāṇini got to do with it? The use of gaṇa-headers from the Aṣṭādhyāyī in Sanskrit literature from the perspective of corpus linguistics. In: Proceedings of the WCS 2015 (forthcoming)
12. Huet, G.: A functional toolkit for morphological and phonological processing, application to a Sanskrit tagger. J. Funct. Program. **15**(04), 573–614 (2005)
13. Kiparsky, P.: On the architecture of Pāṇini's grammar. In: Huet, G., Kulkarni, A., Scharf, P. (eds.) SCL. Lecture Notes in Computer Science, vol. 5402, pp. 33–94. Springer, Heidelberg (2009)
14. Knauth, J., Alfter, D.: A dictionary data processing environment and its application in algorithmic processing of Pali dictionary data for future NLP tasks. In: Proceedings of the 5th Workshop on South and Southeast Asian NLP, pp. 65–73 (2014)
15. Kneser, R., Ney, H.: Improved backing-off for m-gram language modeling. In: Proceedings of the International Conference on Acoustics, Speech, and Signal Processing, pp. 181–184 (1995)
16. Kulkarni, A., Shukla, D.: Sanskrit morphological analyser: some issues. Indian Linguist. **70**(1–4), 169–177 (2009)
17. Kulkarni, M.: Phonological overgeneration in paninian system. In: Huet, G., Kulkarni, A., Scharf, P. (eds.) SCL. LNCS, vol. 5402, pp. 306–319. Springer, Heidelberg (2009)
18. Lafferty, J.D., McCallum, A., Pereira, F.C.N.: Conditional random fields: probabilistic models for segmenting and labeling sequence data. In: Proceedings of the Eighteenth International Conference on Machine Learning, pp. 282–289 (2001)
19. Lee, J., Naradowsky, J., Smith, D.A.: A discriminative model for joint morphological disambiguation and dependency parsing. In: Proceedings of the 49th Annual Meeting of the Association for Computational Linguistics: Human Language Technologies, vol. 1, pp. 885–894 (2011)
20. Mayrhofer, M.: Kurzgefaßtes etymologisches Wörterbuch des Altindischen. Carl Winter Universitätsverlag, Heidelberg (1982)
21. Mishra, A.: Simulating the Pāṇinian system of Sanskrit grammar. In: Huet, G., Kulkarni, A., Scharf, P. (eds.) SCL. LNCS, vol. 5402. Springer, Heidelberg (2009)
22. Mittal, V.: Automatic Sanskrit segmentizer using finite state transducers. In: Proceedings of the ACL 2010 Student Research Workshop, pp. 85–90. Association for Computational Linguistics, Stroudsburg (2010)
23. Monier-Williams, M.: Sanskṛit -English Dictionary, 3rd edn. Munshiram Manoharlal Publishers Pvt. Ltd., New Delhi (1988)
24. Oberlies, T.: A Grammar of Epic Sanskrit. De Gruyter (2003)
25. Petersen, W., Soubusta, S.: Structure and implementation of a digital edition of the Aṣṭādhyāyī. In: Kulkarni, M. (ed.) Recent Researches in Sanskrit Computational Linguistics, pp. 84–103. D.K. Printworld, New Delhi (2013)
26. Petersen, W.: Zur Minimalität von Pāṇinis Śivasūtras: eine Untersuchung mit Methoden der formalen Begriffsanalyse. Ph.D. thesis, Universität Düsseldorf (2008)

27. Ratnaparkhi, A.: Maximum Entropy Models for Natural Language Ambiguity Resolution. Ph.D. thesis, University of Pennsylvania (1998)
28. Rocher, L.: The Purāṇas, A History of Indian Literature, vol. II, Fasc. 3. Otto Harrassowitz, Wiesbaden (1986)
29. Scharfe, H.: Grammatical Literature. A History of Indian Literature, Volume 5, Fasc. 2, Otto Harrassowitz, Wiesbaden (1977)
30. Shacham, D., Wintner, S.: Morphological disambiguation of Hebrew: a case study in classifier combination. In: Proceedings of the 2007 Joint Conference on Empirical Methods in Natural Language Processing and Computational Natural Language Learning, pp. 439–447. Association for Computational Linguistics, Prague (2007)
31. Shukla, P., Kulkarni, A., Shukl, D.: Geeta: Gold standard annotated data, analysis and its application. In: Proceedings of ICON (2013)
32. Staal, J.: Word Order in Sanskrit and Universal Grammar. Foundations of Language, Supplementary Series, vol. 5. D. Reidel Publishing Company, Dordrecht (1967)
33. Stenzler, A.F.: Elementarbuch der Sanskrit-Sprache. Max Mälzer, Breslau (1872)
34. Witzel, M.: Early indian history: linguistic and textual parametres. In: Erdosy, G. (ed.) The Indo-Aryans of Ancient South Asia. Language, Material Culture and Ethnicity, vol. 1, pp. 85–125. Walter de Gruyter, Berlin (1995)
35. Yuret, D., Türe, F.: Learning morphological disambiguation rules for Turkish. In: Proceedings of HLT-NAACL (2006)

Morphological Analysis and Generation for Pali

David Alfter[✉] and Jürgen Knauth

Universität Trier, Trier, Germany
alfter.david@gmx.net

Abstract. In this paper we describe a system that performs morphological generation and analysis for Pali. We discuss the morphological aspects of the tasks our system performs with emphasis on Pali specific characteristics and difficulties and present insights into how this system is integrated into a technical infrastracture used in research about Pali.

1   Introduction

Pali is a historical language from the group of Middle Indo-Aryan languages that is still widely studied because of the many buddhist scriptures that are written in Pali [3,4]. However, Pali has not been intensely studied with regard to its computational processing. This is certainly also due to technical reasons, like the lack of a dictionary suitable for computational linguistic tasks and the lack of a Pali corpus in a good machine readable format. Part of our work as researchers therefore involves the preparation of data for computational tasks in general.

Pali is a fusional language; besides a base meaning expressed by a stem or a root, further morphological information is expressed by adding affixes [1]. Thus, in the word DEVO, the stem DEV- expresses the meaning 'god/deity' while the ending -O expresses 'noun, singular, a-declension, masculine, nominative.'

We propose in this work a system for the morphological generation and analysis of Pali. This system has been developed in the context of the SeNeReKo project where the authors of this paper are involved in. After that we describe how we can treat the morphophonological phenomenon of *sandhi*. We further address the problem of irregular morphological forms and how we can efficiently cope with such problems.

The resources available in Pali are few and insufficient for regular computational processing tasks: Pali is a low-resource language. Especially the lack of a dictionary has caused us problems. A central aspect of our work therefore has been how to progress with our goals of data processing under those conditions.

2   Related Work

A team of the University of Copenhagen has previously tried to process and use the dictionary data. They wanted to create a new digitized version of the

© Springer International Publishing Switzerland 2015
C. Mahlow and M. Piotrowski (Eds.): SFCM 2015, CCIS 537, pp. 60–71, 2015.
DOI: 10.1007/978-3-319-23980-4_4

dictionary, but did not succeed and stopped after having edited three letters of the Pali alphabet [10].

Some problems that occur in Pali have been addressed in the related language Sanskrit [7–9,11–13]. However, the resources available for Sanskrit are of a different quality and quantity than the resources available for Pali.

Kulkarni et al. [11] for example use sandhi rules to split sandhi compounds and a morphological analyzer to validate the results. For Pali, the morphological analyzer is only in the phase of being built. However, they also aknowledge that generating all possible splits results in the generation of thousands of splits, 90 % of which are not morphologically valid [11].

In many Sanskrit systems, dictionaries play one of the key roles and solutions for Sanskrit cannot simply be adapted to Pali for lack of a suitable dictionary. Huet [9] proposes a sandhi splitter that has recourse to databases which do not exist for Pali, such as a database with all finite root forms, including primary conjugations and secondary conjugations [9].

3   Preliminaries

3.1   The Data

Our work presented in this paper uses the Pali Canon provided by the Vipassana Research Institute in 2012 as a basis [14]. This corpus comprises the fundamental texts of the Therevada Buddhism and constitutes much of the historic Pali that is left.

As a basis for a dictionary we use the digitized copy of the dictionary of Stede and Davids (1997) which has been provided by the University of Chicago [5].

We processed the data in various ways (especially pattern matching) in order to arrive at dictionary entries structured in such a way that we can identify all lemmas and get some information about word classes.

3.2   Overall Technical System Architecture

Any kind of data is not very useful if it is not maintained by a technical infrastructure, especially dictionary data. While we could maintain the corpus data in the form of files, the dictionary data had to be inserted into a database for ease of use.

Because of the unstructured form of each dictionary entry, we chose to stor this data in the NoSQL database management system MongoDB under the control of a small application server running on NodeJS. Therefore the data is managed in a document-based fashion so that we have more flexibility with respect to data models. The server provides a REST interface for easy access by computer programs, enabling us to build a small variety of technical tools using this data. Besides the dictionary server, we created a server addressing the Pali morphology (which is the focus of this paper), a data processor to infer PoS from plaintext dictionary entries, an editor for manual lookup and editing of dictionary entries, and other minor tools.

4 Morphological Generation in Pali

In this chapter we discuss the theoretical and technical aspects of our morphological generator (which is implemented as a server as mentioned above).

4.1 Overall Generation Process

The morphological generation component generates inflected forms of a lemma.

When generating, we first have to distinguish between regular generation and irregular word forms. For regular generation, we combine the paradigm endings with the stem of the word to obtain morphological forms. At this stage, we can also perform small sound changes and stem modifications according to grammatical conventions in Pali. The next section describes regular generation in more detail.

For irregular forms, we perform a table lookup as described below in Sect. 4.4.

4.2 Generation of Regular Forms

When generating regular forms according to the paradigm, we take a lemma and, if possible, its word class. Our first task is to derive a stem from the lemma (to the be able to inflect it in a following step). For this process of deriving the stem, the word class is important because the word classes have different lemma endings, and this ending has to be removed from the lemma to form the word stem.

Nouns and adjectives have a special "lemma ending" which often does not occur in the word's paradigm. By "ending" we mean the termination character sequence of a word which does not always need to match a pure linguistic concept of "ending" in Pali. This "ending" thus explicitly marks a word as lemma. In contrast, pronouns use the first person masculine singular form as lemma, and verbs use the third person active singular indicative present tense form. Entries in our Pali dictionary represent these lemmas and follow these conventions.

If we cannot supply the word class of a lemma at generation time, a dedicated word class guesser tries to guess the most probable word class by comparing the ending of the lemma with word class specific lemma endings. In the optimal case, only one word class can be singled out and returned as hypothesis. However, often two or more word classes are possible.

Then, the paradigm which matches the current word's word class is selected. The stem is combined with every ending of the paradigm and the morphological information is saved together with the generated form. Before combining, we check whether the ending performs changes on the stem, and, if this is the case, we apply these changes before adding the ending.

For example, the word MANAS 'mind' is a noun lemma. From the surface form, we can infer that it belongs to the "as" declension group. The stem is formed by removing the lemma ending of the "as" group, which is "as." We arrive at the stem "man-." We combine the stem with every ending as specified by the paradigm for nouns of the "as" declension group.

For verbs, some forms are constructed with the base, which is similar to the stem of nouns, while others are constructed with the *root*. A verb has a root, which is not a full free morpheme. For example PACATI 'to cook,' has the stem 'paca-' and the root $\sqrt{pac}$. The root $\sqrt{pac}$ belongs to the first division of the first conjugation which form the base by adding 'a' to the root. There are seven different declension classes that derive the base differently. Sometimes, more than one base can be derived from a root, e.g., the root $\sqrt{rudh}$ 'to obstruct' has five bases: rundhati, rundhiti, rundhīti, rundheti, rundhoti.

As an example of a regular verb formation, let us consider the following. From $\sqrt{kar}$, base karo 'to make,' we can form the singular forms of the present indicative as follows: karomi 'I make,' karosi 'you make,' karoti 's/he/it makes.'

According to this concept in technical implementation we have chosen paradigms as data model in XML format, for example:

```
<paradigm type="noun">
  <number type="singular">
    <declension type="as">
      <gender type="neuter">
        <case type="nominative">
          <ending>o</ending>
        </case>
        <case type="vocative">
          <ending>a</ending>
          <ending>o</ending>
          ...
        </case>
      </gender>
    </declension>
  </number>
</paradigm>
```

The innermost nodes contain the ending morpheme while the nodes traversed in order to reach an innermost node express the morphological information of that node. In this example we have the ending 'o' which expresses *noun, singular, declension 'as,' neuter, nominative* and the endings 'a' and 'o' which in this specific case express *noun, singular, declension 'as,' neuter, vocative.* If we have the lemma MANAS 'mind,' we can, given this excerpt of a paradigm, generate the forms MANO and MANA with the respective morphological information.

The example given above addresses nouns. Morphological information about other word classes are specified similarly.

4.3 Regular Deviations from the Paradigm

Let us now consider the lemma PACATI 'to cook.' This is a verb lemma, thus the stem is paca-. We can form the singular forms of the present indicative as follows: pacami, pacasi, pacati. The problem is that in this case, the first form is wrong and should be pacāmi with a lengthening of the a. The other forms (pacasi, pacati) are correct. Indeed, the ending -mi of the singular first person indicative present active lengthens the preceding letter if that letter is 'a.' In the above example with karo, no lengthening takes place. This is a regular deviation from the regular paradigm in a technical sense.

Regular deviations from the paradigm can be encoded in the paradigm in the form of conditional rules. The basic concept of these rules are that we specify pairs consisting of:

– a pattern that specifies where the modifications in a generated form should be applied
– the concrete modifications that shall be applied.

The following are examples of endings with rules.

```
(1) <ending type="Drare">asi</ending>
(2) <ending type="Cm2">anto</ending>
(3) <ending type="Cl1a">mi</ending>
```

Patterns start with a capital letter that indicates the broad category of the pattern. The primary category 'C' indicates that the stem should be modified before appending the ending, category D indicates the frequency of word forms constructed with the ending. These are all existing categories at the moment. A further category R is planned that restricts the environment to which an ending can be appended.

The category letter is followed by category specific instructions. In our case the 'D' is followed by the word 'rare,' indicating that forms formed with this ending are rare (ex. 1). For category C, in our examples 'C' is followed by "m" and a number (ex. 2), or by "l," a number and one of the characters (a,i,u) (ex. 3). In the first case, the number indicates how many letters to delete from the right of the stem before appending the ending (ex. 4 shows the application of ex. 2). In the second case, the number indicates how many letters to the right of the ending the letter to lengthen is and the character indicates what letter to lengthen before appending the ending. If the letter indicated in the rule matches the letter in the base, the lengthening takes place (ex. 5); otherwise, no lengthening takes place (ex. 6). Category D does not modify the stem and merely adds information about frequency.

(4) bhavaṃ 'sir' → bhav (root) + anto (ex. 2) → bh + anto → bhanto
(5) $\sqrt{pac}$ (root) → paca (base) + mi (ex. 3) → pacā + mi → pacāmi
(6) $\sqrt{kar}$ (root) → karo (base) + mi (ex. 3) → karo + mi → karomi.

4.4   Irregular Word Forms

Changes that affect the morphology in other ways that cannot be encoded in the paradigm are treated differently. For highly irregular morphological forms, we encode the information about the irregular forms in the dictionary. At generation time, the dictionary is consulted, and if any irregular information is found, it is used. The information is encoded as a node of the dictionary entry[1], for example (only the relevant node is shown, surrounding nodes are not shown):

```
{
  "irregular":{
     "numeral":{
        "type":"full",
        "defaultMode":"overwrite",
        "forms":[
           {
              "gender":"masculine",
              "number":"plural",
              "word":"tayo",
              "case":"nominative"
           },
           {
              "gender":"masculine",
              "number":"plural",
              "word":"tiññañ",
              "case":"genitive"
           },
           ...
```

The "irregular" node contains possible word class nodes, since a lemma can belong to more than one word class. The word class nodes contain a type, a default mode and the morphological forms. The "type" information specifies whether the given morphological forms constitute the whole paradigm for the word class node (full), or whether the given information only contains some of the morphological forms (partial). The mode specifies how the morphological forms are treated. The following table illustrates the types and their associated modes.

type	mode
full	overwrite
partial	add
	remove
	overwrite

For the type "full," the only mode is "overwrite." This means that by specifying irregular information as full, the information provided overwrites any applicable paradigm. Hence, all the information specified must be the full paradigm for the word in question.

---

[1] Note: The data structure is specified in JSON format, not XML. This is because our dictionary data is maintained in a NoSQL data base which uses JSON as communication data format.

The type "partial" can have different modes, namely "add," "remove," and "overwrite." We can overwrite specified forms, we can add irregular forms to regularly inflected (generated) forms or we can remove some generated forms. Removal of generated forms is useful for defective paradigms such as TAYO 'three' which has no singular or the defective verb AS 'to be.' Every irregular form can also overwrite the general default mode by specifying another mode.

Depending on the type of the irregular information, other forms are generated, added, removed or no generation takes place at all.

4.5   Dealing with Words of Unknown Word Class

Morphological generation can be used for analysis as well.

If we encounter a word and we want to determine the word class of the word, we could look up the word in the dictionary and retrieve this information. Our dictionary unfortunately is insufficient for this task: we only have sufficient information for roughly 60 % of lemmas in the dictionary [10]. This is due to the fact that so far there does not exist a complete dictionary suitable for computational linguistic tasks.

If we are lucky on a lookup, the dictionary contains word class information for that word. If we are unlucky, the dictionary does not contain information about the word class, or the dictionary does not contain the word at all.

In the latter cases, if we have multiple hypotheses about the word class of a word, we can generate all morphological forms of the word according to these hypotheses. We can then count the number of actually occurring forms for each hypothesis and choose the most probable hypothesis as word class for our word. Previous experiments have shown that this approach yields good results with 76.25 % correct predictions for verb forms to 97.31 % for nouns and adjectives [10].

4.6   Output

Our system returns JSON as output. The following is an excerpt from a successful morphological generation for EKA 'one' (spaces and line breaks inserted for readability):

```
{"lemma":"eka",
 "forms":{
    "numeral":[
    {
    "gender":"masculine",      "number":"singular",
    "word":"eko",              "case":"nominative"
    },
    {
    "gender":"masculine",      "number":"singular",
    "word":"ekassa",           "case":"genitive"
    },
    ...
```

The response is wrapped in a "success" node in case of success. As can be seen, morphological information is encoded as key-value pairs. The user can then, for a given key, decide to consider or ignore certain key-value pairs. For example, rare and poetic forms are marked as being rare; no distinction could be made between rare and poetic, since rare forms often are poetic forms and vice versa. Furthermore, we are not (yet) in possession of qualified information concerning the matter. However, if a user is not interested in rare forms, these can simply be excluded by ignoring forms marked as rare.

Aside from the default JSON output, it is possible to get XML output as well. The desired output format is specified within the request. This way our system is flexible and can adapt to suit the needs of its users.

5   Morphological Analysis in Pali

5.1   Overall Analysis Process

The morphological analysis component produces morphological information about a word. The component can be divided into two distinct sub-components.

The first sub-component performs a look-up in a word table containing irregular forms. If the table contains the word in question, information from the table is returned. Otherwise, the second sub-component is used.

The second sub-component analyzes a word using a rule based approach. Information taken from the paradigms is used to split the word into possible stem–ending elements. Based on these stems and the word class, word class specific lemmata are derived. The morphological analysis corresponds to the morphological information attached to the identified ending element. These analyses are then returned.

5.2   Lookup-Based Approach

The lookup-based approach performs a lookup of the word form to analyze in a a word form table. This table contains all irregular forms and provides exhaustive and valid information for a correct word form analysis. This data can be computed in advance and/or provided manually.

5.3   Heuristic Approach

For a given word, the analyzer matches the word's ending against all paradigms. If a match is found, the information from the paradigm containing the ending is added to the analyses. Based on the identified ending, the word to analyze is split into a stem and an ending.

5.4   Word Class Guesser

Based on the heuristic approach, the word class guesser derives word class hypotheses from morphological information. Hypotheses are weighted based on the ending, the common frequency and the ending's length.

5.5 Output

As with the generation, the output is JSON. The analyses are grouped by calculated lemma. The forms are then grouped by word class. For each word class, the word is shown split into identified stem and ending if applicable. Then, morphological information is listed as key-value pairs[2]. The analysis of "eka" 'one' yields:

```
{"analyses":[
  {"lemma":"eka",
   "forms":{
   "numeral":[
     {"word":"eka",
      "grammar":
         {"gender":"masculine",
          "number":"singular",
          "case":"vocative"
         }
     }]}},
  {"lemma":"eka",
   "forms":
    {"noun":[
      {"word":"ek_a",
       "grammar":
          {"gender":"feminine",
           "number":"singular",
           "case":"vocative",
           "declension":"a"
          }
      }]}},
  ...
```

5.6 Problems

The morphological analyzer does considerably better if a word class can be specified along with the word to analyze. However, such information is not always accessible at the moment of analysis.

The analysis also overgenerates; often, many different and possible analyses are returned. This is due to some morphological forms having identical surface forms, especially verb forms. Another reason for the overanalysis is that we cannot determine which of the possible analyses is the correct analysis. Finally, discriminating between adjectives and nouns is nearly impossible, since their paradigms are very similar. Moreover, many words in Pali can be used both as nouns and as adjectives.

---

[2] For reasons of easy interoperability with all system components we primarily focus on JSON as output format. As mentioned above the programming interface allows retrieval of XML output as well, which then contains the same data as the JSON data structure above.

As we cannot rely on one or more good dictionaries, as in Sanskrit for example, we have to rely more strongly on the morphological analysis and generation. With this information in mind, our dictionary is being completed both manually and computationally at the moment of writing. Nevertheless, as Pali is a dead language about 2500 years old, this is not an easy task. Therefore, we expect that some more research about specific words and word forms will be done in the future.

6 Sandhi in Pali

6.1 Explanation

Sandhi are phonological sound changes that occur when two sounds meet [6]. These phonological changes are also reflected in writing.

There are two types of sandhi: internal and external sandhi [8]. Internal sandhi concerns sound changes within one word that take place when a word takes an inflectional ending or when a verbal root is converted to a verbal stem [8]. External sandhi occurs between two words next to each other [6,8]; external sandhi can lead to two words being combined into one surface form (ex. 7).

Also, when a compound is formed, sandhi can occur (ex. 8). Compounding is frequent and complex in Pali, thus this is important not only if we want our system to be able to generate correct compounds, but even more so if we want to split compounds. Addressing this is relevant for real world applications, whenever someone wants to deal with words from the existing Pali texts.

(7) evaṃ ca → evañca 'and thus'
(8) ajja uposatho → ajjupposatho 'the day of fasting'

Our system can generate compounds according to the rules of sandhi, but splitting of compounds that result from internal sandhi is still future work.

6.2 General Letter-Based Approaches

The problem with sandhi resolution is that we cannot say if and where sandhi took place by looking at a morphological form. In general additional information is needed which increases the complexity of tasks addressing sandhi. We tried multiple approaches and found exclusive letter based approaches to fail due to lack of precision: our approaches led to massive overgeneration during splitting.

For example, one rule states that when two vowels meet, the first vowel may be elided. Another rule states that when two vowels meet, the second one may be elided. When looking at a vowel, we cannot however determine whether one of these rules was applied or not. Using only these two rules, if we have a Pali word with n vowels, and knowing that Pali has 8 vowels [6], the number of possible splits N is

$$N = (1 + (2 * 8))^n \tag{1}$$

Indeed, we can choose not to split the word, or we can split the word in 8 different ways with 2 rules, for each vowel. For $n = 1$, we have 17 possibilities. For $n = 2$ we already have 289 possibilities. The number of possible splits grows exponentially. The full ruleset generates even more possible splits [2].

6.3   Corpus-Based Resolution with Regular Expressions

Due to the massive overgeneration of the first approach, we have opted for a different aproach. Because of the limited amount of Pali text in existence, we use a case based resolution. The external-sandhi splitter we have built operates on the basis of regular expression rules which have been manually compiled from examples occurring in the corpus.

7   Results and Conclusion

In this paper we have shown methods and software components to analyse Pali as well as generate word forms. We found that this is possible to a good extent though Pali is a low resource language and no sufficiently good dictionary is available.

Nevertheless the problem with our approach of word for generation is overgeneration and variable generation quality depending on the word. This is due to the fact that we have to include rare and poetic forms; furthermore, we don't have sufficient information in the dictionary. Still, we have chosen this rule based approach because words in Pali mostly follow a regular inflectional paradigm. Resulting quality issues must be addressed in the future especially by an enhanced version of a Pali dictionary which is currently not yet available.

We also discussed word form analysis including external sandhi splitting. Though there is no sufficiently complete dictionary available right now our approach leads to very valuable results for other scientific projects as it has turned out in the context of our work, and as recent contacting attempts by other researchers have shown. As shown in our paper, sometimes even a pragmatic approach to certain problems can yield surprisingly good results: though of course such an approach has to be selected very carefully, performing splitting of external sandhi in our case of the low resource language Pali led to good results.

We provide our software components and technical infrastructure and (aim to provide) the current version of the Pali dictionary enhanced by our team as a helpful basis for future researchers.

References

1. Aikhenvald, A.Y.: Typological distinctions in word-formation. Lang. Typology Syntactic Description **3**, 1–65 (2007)
2. Alfter, D.: Morphological Analyzer and Generator for Pali. Bachelor's thesis, Universität Trier (2014)

3. Bloch, J.: The Formation of the Marathi Language. Motilal Banarsidass, Delhi (1970)
4. Burrow, T.: The Sanskrit Language. Motilal Banarsidass, Delhi (2001)
5. Davids, T.R., Stede, W.: Pali-English dictionary. Motilal Banarsidass, Delhi (1993)
6. Duroiselle, C.: A Practical grammar of the Pali language. 4th edn. (2007). http://www.pratyeka.org/duroiselle/
7. Hellwig, O.: SanskritTagger: a stochastic lexical and POS tagger for sanskrit. In: Huet, G., Kulkarni, A., Scharf, P. (eds.) Sanskrit Computational Linguistics. LNCS, vol. 5402, pp. 266–277. Springer, Heidelberg (2009)
8. Huet, G.: Formal structure of sanskrit text: requirements analysis for a mechanical sanskrit processor. In: Huet, G., Kulkarni, A., Scharf, P. (eds.) Sanskrit Computational Linguistics. LNCS, vol. 5402, pp. 162–199. Springer, Heidelberg (2009)
9. Huet, G.: Sanskrit segmentation. In: XXVIIIth South Asian Languages Analysis Roundtable, University of Denton, Texas (2009). http://yquem.inria.fr/huet/PUBLIC/SALA.pdf
10. Knauth, J., Alfter, D.: A dictionary data processing environment and its application in algorithmic processing of Pali dictionary data for future NLP tasks. In: Proceedings of the 5th Workshop on South and Southeast Asian NLP, 25th International Conference on Computational Linguistics, pp. 65–73 (2014). http://www.aclweb.org/anthology/W14-5509
11. Kulkarni, A., Paul, S., Kulkarni, M., Kumar, A., Surtani, N.: Semantic processing of compounds in Indian languages. In: Proceedings of COLING 2012: Technical Papers, pp. 1489–1502 (2012). http://www.aclweb.org/anthology/C12-1091
12. Kulkarni, A., Shukl, D.: Sanskrit morphological analyser: some issues. Indian Linguist. **70**(1–4), 169–177 (2009)
13. Kumar, A., Mittal, V., Kulkarni, A.: Sanskrit compound processor. In: Jha, G.N. (ed.) Sanskrit Computational Linguistics. LNCS, vol. 6465, pp. 57–69. Springer, Heidelberg (2010)
14. Vipassana Research Institute: The Pali Tipitaka (2012). www.tipitaka.org

A Universal Feature Schema for Rich Morphological Annotation and Fine-Grained Cross-Lingual Part-of-Speech Tagging

John Sylak-Glassman[1]([⊠]), Christo Kirov[1], Matt Post[2,3], Roger Que[3], and David Yarowsky[3]

[1] Center for Language and Speech Processing, Johns Hopkins University, Baltimore, MD 21218, USA
jcsg@jhu.edu, ckirov@gmail.com
[2] Human Language Technology Center of Excellence, Johns Hopkins University, Baltimore, MD 21218, USA
post@cs.jhu.edu
[3] Department of Computer Science, Johns Hopkins University, Baltimore, MD 21218, USA
{query,yarowsky}@jhu.edu

Abstract. Semantically detailed and typologically-informed morphological analysis that is broadly applicable cross-linguistically has the potential to improve many NLP applications, including machine translation, n-gram language models, information extraction, and co-reference resolution. In this paper, we present a universal morphological feature schema, which is a set of features that represent the finest distinctions in meaning that are expressed by inflectional morphology across languages. We first present the schema's guiding theoretical principles, construction methodology, and contents. We then present a method of measuring cross-linguistic variability in the semantic distinctions conveyed by inflectional morphology along the multiple dimensions spanned by the schema. This method relies on representing inflected wordforms from many languages in our universal feature space, and then testing for agreement across multiple aligned translations of pivot words in a parallel corpus (the Bible). The results of this method are used to assess the effectiveness of cross-linguistic projection of a multilingual consensus of these fine-grained morphological features, both within and across language families. We find high cross-linguistic agreement for a diverse range of semantic dimensions expressed by inflectional morphology.

Keywords: Inflectional morphology · Linguistic typology · Universal schema · Cross-linguistic projection

1 Introduction

Semantically detailed and typologically-informed morphological analysis that is broadly applicable cross-linguistically has the potential to improve many NLP

The first two authors contributed equally to this paper.

© Springer International Publishing Switzerland 2015
C. Mahlow and M. Piotrowski (Eds.): SFCM 2015, CCIS 537, pp. 72–93, 2015.
DOI: 10.1007/978-3-319-23980-4_5

applications, including machine translation (particularly of morphologically rich languages), n-gram language models, information extraction (particularly event extraction), and co-reference resolution.

In this paper, we first present a novel universal morphological feature schema. This schema is a set of features that represent the finest distinctions in meaning that are expressed by inflectional morphology across languages. The purpose of the proposed universal morphological feature schema is to allow any given overt, affixal (non-root) inflectional morpheme in any language to be given a precise, language-independent, semantically accurate definition.

As a demonstration of the utility and consistency of our universal schema, we show how it can enable cross-linguistic projection-based approaches to detailed semantic tagging. We measure the cross-linguistic variability in the semantic distinctions conveyed by inflectional morphology along multiple dimensions captured by our schema. This method relies on representing inflected wordforms from many languages in our universal feature space, and then testing for feature agreement across multiple translations of pivot words chosen from a parallel text (e.g., the Bible). We find high cross-linguistic agreement for a diverse range of semantic dimensions expressed by inflectional morphology, both within and across language families. This is true even in some cases where we expect languages to diverge due to non-semantic or arbitrary divisions of the semantic space (e.g., when assigning grammatical gender to inanimate objects).

2   A Universal Morphological Feature Schema

This section describes the principles that inform the composition of the schema, the methodology used to construct it, and its contents. See Table 1 for a summary of the full schema that includes both the dimensions of meaning and their respective features.

2.1   Guiding Theoretical Principles

The purpose of the universal morphological feature schema is to allow any given overt, affixal (non-root) inflectional morpheme in any language to be given a precise, language-independent, semantically accurate definition. This influences the overall architecture of the schema in two significant ways.

First, the schema is responsible for capturing only the meanings of overt, non-root, affixal inflectional morphemes, which considerably limits the semantic-conceptual space that must be formally described using these features. This significant limitation of the range of data that must be modeled makes an interlingual approach to the construction of the schema feasible (as also noted by Sagot and Walther [43]).

Second, the schema is sensitive only to semantic content, not to overt surface form. This follows the insight in linguistic typology that "crosslinguistic comparison [...] cannot be based on formal patterns (because these are too diverse), but [must] be based primarily on universal conceptual-semantic concepts" [26,

Table 1. Dimensions of meaning and their features, both sorted alphabetically

Dimension	Features
Aktionsart	ACCMP, ACH, ACTY, ATEL, DUR, DYN, PCT, SEMEL, STAT, TEL
Animacy	ANIM, HUM, INAN, NHUM
Aspect	HAB, IPFV, ITER, PFV, PRF, PROG, PROSP
Case	ABL, ABS, ACC, ALL, ANTE, APPRX, APUD, AT, AVR, BEN, CIRC, COM, COMPV, DAT, EQU, ERG, ESS, FRML, GEN, IN, INS, INTER, NOM, NOMS, ON, ONHR, ONVR, POST, PRIV, PROL, PROPR, PROX, PRP, PRT, REM, SUB, TERM, VERS, VOC
Comparison	AB, CMPR, EQT, RL, SPRL
Definiteness	DEF, INDEF, NSPEC, SPEC
Deixis	ABV, BEL, DIST, EVEN, MED, NVIS, PROX, REF1, REF2, REM, VIS
Evidentiality	ASSUM, AUD, DRCT, FH, HRSY, INFER, NFH, NVSEN, QUOT, RPRT, SEN
Finiteness	FIN, NFIN
Gender	BANTU1-23, FEM, MASC, NAKH1-8, NEUT
Information structure	FOC, TOP
Interrogativity	DECL, INT
Mood	ADM, AUNPRP, AUPRP, COND, DEB, IMP, IND, INTEN, IRR, LKLY, OBLIG, OPT, PERM, POT, PURP, REAL, SBJV, SIM
Number	DU, GPAUC, GRPL, INVN, PAUC, PL, SG, TRI
Parts of speech	ADJ, ADP, ADV, ART, AUX, CLF, COMP, CONJ, DET, INTJ, N, NUM, PART, PRO, V, V.CVB, V.MSDR, V.PTCP
Person	0, 1, 2, 3, 4, EXCL, INCL, OBV, PRX
Polarity	NEG, POS
Politeness	AVOID, COL, FOREG, FORM, FORM.ELEV, FORM.HUMB, HIGH, HIGH.ELEV, HIGH.SUPR, INFM, LIT, LOW, POL
Possession	ALN, NALN, PSSD, PSSPNO
Switch-reference	CN_R_MN, DS, DSADV, LOG, OR, SEQMA, SIMMA, SS, SSADV
Tense	1DAY, FUT, HOD, IMMED, PRS, PST, RCT, RMT
Valency	DITR, IMPRS, INTR, TR
Voice	ACFOC, ACT, AGFOC, ANTIP, APPL, BFOC, CAUS, CFOC, DIR, IFOC, INV, LFOC, MID, PASS, PFOC, RECP, REFL

p. 665, and references therein]. Due to the semantic focus of the schema, it contains no features for indicating the form that a morpheme takes. Instead, the schema's features can be integrated into existing frameworks that can indicate the form of morphemes, such as Sagot and Walther [43] for NLP and the Leipzig Glossing Rules for theoretical and descriptive linguistics [12].

The universal morphological feature schema is composed of a set of features that represent semantic "atoms" that are never decomposed into more fine-grained meanings in any natural language. This ensures that the meanings of all morphemes are able to be represented either through single features or through multiple features in combination.

The purpose of the universal morphological feature schema strongly influences its relationship to linguistic theory. The features instantiated in the schema occupy an intermediate position between being universal categories and comparative concepts, in the terminology coined by Haspelmath [26, pp. 663–667]. Haspelmath defines a universal category as one that is universally available for any language, may be psychologically 'real,' and is used for both description/analysis and comparison while a comparative concept is explicitly defined by typologists, is not claimed to be 'real' to speakers in any sense, and is used only for the purpose of language comparison.

Because the purpose of the schema is to allow broad cross-linguistic morphological analysis that ensures semantic equality between morphemes in one language and morphemes, wordforms, or phrases in another, its features are assumed to be possibly applicable to any language. In this sense, features are universal categories. However, like comparative concepts, the features of the universal schema are not presumed to be 'real' to speakers in any sense.

Like both universal categories and comparative concepts, each feature retains a consistent meaning across languages such that every time a feature is associated with a morpheme, that morpheme necessarily bears the meaning captured by that feature (even though that morpheme may bear other meanings and serve other functions as well). This emphasis on semantic consistency across languages prevents categories from being mistakenly equated, as in the dative case example in Haspelmath [26, p. 665], which highlights the problems with establishing cross-linguistic equivalence on the basis of terminology alone.

2.2 Constructing the Schema

The first step in constructing the universal feature schema was to identify the dimensions of meaning (e.g., case, number, tense, mood, etc.) that are expressed by overt, affixal inflectional morphology in the world's languages. These were identified by surveying the linguistic typology literature on parts of speech and then identifying the kinds of inflectional morphology that are typically associated with each part of speech. In total, 23 dimensions of meaning were identified.

For each dimension, we determined the finest-grained distinctions in meaning that were made within that dimension by a natural language by surveying the literature in linguistic typology. That is, we identified which meanings were "atomic" and were never further decomposed in any language. The reduction of the feature set in the universal schema to only those features whose meanings are as basic as possible minimizes the number of features and allows more complex meanings to be represented by combining features from the same dimension.

In addition to these basic features, some higher-level features that represented common cross-linguistic groupings were also included. For example, features such as indicative (IND) and subjunctive (SBJV) represent groupings of multiple basic modality features which nevertheless seem to occur in multiple languages and show very similar usage patterns across those languages [37]. These can be viewed as 'cover features' in which backing off to more basic features remains an option.

Each dimension has an underlying semantic basis that is used to define the features subsumed by that dimension. To determine the underlying semantic basis for each dimension, the linguistic typology and descriptive linguistic theory literature were surveyed for explanations that were descriptively-oriented and offered precise definitions for observed basic distinctions. A simple example is the dimension of number, whose eight features are defined according to a straightforward quantificational scale of the number of entities. The following section presents the schema in detail, describing the semantic basis of each dimension and listing its features.

Because this is the first instantiation of this particular schema, it is likely not yet fully exhaustive and the authors invite input on dimensions or features that should be considered for inclusion. Future work will focus on the possible inclusion of additional features, especially from other known frameworks such as GOLD [24]. Many of the features from the Universal Dependencies Project [47] and the Leipzig Glossing Rules [12] are already integrated into the schema.

2.3   Dimensions of Meaning Encoded by Inflectional Morphology

The semantic bases of the dimensions of meaning that are encoded by inflectional morphology are discussed approximately according to the part of speech with which the dimension is conventionally associated. After the parts of speech themselves, the following dimensions are discussed: (verbs:) Tense, aspect, Aktionsart, mood, voice, evidentiality, switch-reference, person, (nouns:) number, gender, case, animacy, possession, information structure, politeness, (adjectives:) comparison, (pronouns:) deixis. This order is purely expositional: Dimensions of meaning and their features are not formally associated with any particular part of speech.

For reasons of space, we omit discussion of the dimensions of finiteness, interrogativity, and polarity, which exhibit simple binary oppositions, as well as valency and animacy, whose features are typical and defined in the expected way. We also omit discussion of definiteness, which uses features inspired by the the work of Lyons [36, pp. 50,99,278]. These dimensions and their features are included in Table 1.

Parts of Speech. Croft [16, p. 89] defines the conceptual space in Table 2 for parts of speech. It is the cross-product of the concepts of *object*, *property*, and *action* with the functions of *reference*, *modification*, and *predication*. This conceptual space provides definitions for the following cross-linguistically common parts of speech, which are all captured by features in the universal schema: Nouns (N), adpositions (ADP), adjectives (ADJ), verbs (V), masdars (V.MSDR), participles (V.PTCP), converbs (V.CVB), and adverbs (ADV).

Table 2. Functionally-motivated conceptual space defining basic parts of speech, adapted from Croft [16, p. 89]

	Reference	Modification	Predication
Object	object reference: nouns	object modifier: adpositions	object predication: predicate nouns
Property	property reference: substantivized adjectives	property modifier: (attributive) adjectives	property predication: predicate adjectives
Action	action reference: masdars	action modifier: adverbs, participles converbs	action predication: verbs

Masdars, participles, and converbs are distinct parts of speech which are nonfinite and derived productively from verbs [25, pp. 4–5]. Masdars (verbal nouns) refer to the action of a verb, such as *running* in *the running of the race*. Participles can be property modifiers when they function like adjectives, and action modifiers when they function like adverbs. Both adverbs and converbs (i.e., verbal adverbs) modify the action expressed by the verb.

In addition to these parts of speech, the following parts of speech are included based on their use in the Universal Dependencies Project [47], which provides an annotation system for approximately 30 languages: Pronoun (PRO), determiner (DET), auxiliary (AUX), conjunction (CONJ), numeral (NUM), particle (PART), and interjection (INTJ). In addition to these, articles (ART), classifiers (CLF), and complementizers (COMP) were given features based on their inclusion in the Leipzig Glossing Rules [12].

Tense. Tense and aspect are defined according to the framework in [30], which uses the concepts of Time of Utterance (TU, '|'), Topic Time (TT, '[ ]'), and Situation Time (TSit, '{ }') to define tense and aspect categories. Topic Time (TT) and Situation Time (TSit) are conceived as spans while Time of Utterance (TU) is a single point. By defining tense and aspect categories solely in terms of the ordering of these spans and TU, tense and aspect categories can be defined in a language-independent way that facilitates cross-linguistic comparison.

TU is the time at which a speaker makes an utterance, and topic time is the time about which the claim in the utterance is meant to hold true. TSit is the time in which the state of affairs described by the speaker actually holds true. Tense is the relationship of TU to TT while aspect is the relationship of TT to TSit. The three core tenses are defined schematically in (1–3). To simplify the examples of tense, imperfective aspect is always used (i.e., TT is within TSit).

(1) Past tense (PST): TT precedes TU

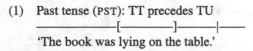

    'The book was lying on the table.'

(2) Present tense (PRS): TU is within TT

    'The book is lying on the table.'

(3) Future tense (FUT): TU precedes TT

    'The book will be lying on the table.'

Some languages further distinguish tense categories by morphologically marking the temporal distance between TU and TT. For example, Bamileke-Ngyemboon (Bantu) distinguishes four levels of temporal distance symmetrically in the past and future, such that for the past there is hodiernal (earlier today; HOD), hesternal (yesterday; 1DAY), recent past (in the last few days; RCT), and remote (RMT) past while for the future there is later today, tomorrow, within the next few days (recent future), and farther ahead yet (remote future) [10, p. 96]. Bamileke-Dschang (Bantu) also has a symmetrical system, but adds an 'immediate' step (IMMED) indicating 'just now' or 'coming up in a moment' [10, p. 97].

Aspect. Aspect indicates the relationship between the time for which a claim is made (TT) and the time for which a situation was objectively true (TSit). The aspects that can be defined by relating TSit and TT are: Imperfective (IPFV), perfective (PFV), perfect (PRF), progressive (PROG), and prospective (PROSP). The iterative (ITER) and habitual (HAB) aspects, sometimes categorized as Aktionsarten, can also be defined this way, but require more than one TSit.

Before defining each category, it is necessary to differentiate 1-state and 2-state verbs. A 1-state verb is a verb like 'sleep,' which lexically encodes only one state (symbolized as '——'). In a 2-state verb, the verb lexically encodes a source state (SS, symbolized as '————') and a target state (TS, symbolized as '++++++'). The verb 'leave' is a 2-state verb, since it is impossible to leave without going through a transition of being somewhere (the source state) and then being gone from that place (the target state).

In the schematic definitions of aspect categories that follow, time of utterance is fixed in the diagrams at a point toward the end of the target state such that all examples are past tense. Note that English does not clearly morphologically distinguish perfective, perfect, and prospective aspects. This complicates translation of the diagrams, but demonstrates their utility in establishing language-independent definitions of these categories.

(4) Imperfective aspect: TT fully within TSit

————————{—[—++]++}+++++++++|++

'She was leaving.'

(5) Progressive aspect: TT is located only within the source state of TSit

————————{—[——]+++++++}++++++|++

'She was leaving.'

(6) Perfective aspect: Partial TT overlap with source state or target state

————————[—{—]—++++}+++++++++|++

'She was about to leave.' (source state overlap)

————————{———++[++}++]++++++|++

'She had left.' (target state overlap)

(7) Perfect aspect: TT is located exclusively within the target state of TSit

————————{———++[++++]}+++++++|++

'She left. / She has left.'

(8) Prospective aspect: TT is located before TSit

————[———]—{———++++++}++++++|++

'She was going to leave. / She was about to leave.'

(9) Iterative aspect: Multiple instances of the same TSit occur fully within a bounded TT

......[......{—+++}$_1$......{—+++}$_2$......{—+++}$_n$......]......|......

'He used to leave often.'

(10) Habitual aspect: Infinite instances of the same TSit occur fully within an unbounded TT

[∞....{—+++}$_n$......{—+++}$_{n+1}$......|......{—+++}$_{n+∞}$....∞]

'He (always) leaves early every morning.'

Aktionsart. Aktionsart refers to the "inherent temporal features" of a verb [30, pp. 29–31], and is a grammatical means of encoding how the action described by a verb unfolds in reality. We include the distinctions defined by Cable [6], Comrie [8], and Vendler [48]. The features that apply to verbs are Stative (STAT), Eventive/Dynamic (DYN), Telic (TEL), Achievement (ACH), Punctual (PCT), Accomplishment (ACCMP), Durative (DUR), Atelic (ATEL), Semelfactive (SEMEL), and Activity (ACTY).

Mood. Grammatical mood is the morphological marking of modality, which "is concerned with the status of the proposition that describes the event" [37, p. 1]. The morphological marking of modality tends to group primary categories of modality into larger superordinate categories. The indicative (IND) and subjunctive (SBJV), realis (REAL) and irrealis (IRR), and Australian non-purposive (AUNPRP) and purposive (AUPRP) moods are superordinate groupings of primary modalities. Each pairs of groupings has a set of core uses that can be reduced to an opposition between indicating information that is asserted as truth and indicating information that is not asserted as truth [37, p. 3]. These superordinate categories are encoded as features for the reasons stated in Sect. 2.2.

Basic modality categories that are typically captured by overt morphology include, first, the imperative-jussive modality (IMP). Imperative-jussive statements express a command for an actor to do something. Imperatives typically refer to commands to a second person actor while jussives command a first person plural or third person actor [37, p. 81]. No case was found in which imperative and jussive modalities were contrasted overtly on the same person. Other basic modality categories express varying speculative attitudes, including likely (LKLY), potential (POT), and unlikely or surprising. The Papuan language Dani contrasts the realis, likely, and potential moods overtly [37, p. 162]. Related to the potential mood is the permissive (PERM) mood, which indicates 'may' in the sense of having permission. A number of Balkan languages, including Bulgarian, mark the admirative modality (ADM), which expresses surprise, doubt, or irony [p. 11]. The North American isolate Tonkawa explicitly marks the opposite of speculative, the intentive (INTEN), which expressed "(definitely) will, going to" [p. 82]. Languages such as Tiwi (isolate; Australia) mark the obligative (OBLIG) modality overtly to indicate "must, have to" [p. 75]. Similar to the obligative, the debitive modality (DEB), "ought to, should," is marked overtly in Tamil [p. 27]. The general purposive (PURP) modality indicates 'in order to, for the purpose of.' The conditional mood, familiar from Spanish, expresses "would (if certain conditions held)," and the simulative, which occurs in Caddo, expresses hypothetical action in the sense of "as if X-ing" [37, p. 178]. Finally, the optative or desiderative modality (OPT) marks that an actor wants an action to occur.

Voice. Voice is the dimension of meaning that "expresses relations between a predicate [typically a verb] and a set of nominal positions - or their referents - in a clause or other structure" [29]. Klaiman [p. 2] defines three types of grammatical voice: Derived, basic, and pragmatic voice systems.

Derived voice includes two voice categories familiar from Indo-European languages, active (ACT) and passive (PASS). In ergative-absolutive languages, an ergative subject is demoted to an absolutive subject in what is termed an antipassive (ANTIP) construction [29, p. 230]. Derived voice can also include middle voice (MID) in languages like Sanskrit, but middle voice is more often part of basic voice systems (as in Modern Fula), in which voice is captured by lexical items, which have an inherent voice associated with them [29, p. 26].

Pragmatic voice systems include what have been called direct-inverse systems, common in North American languages, as well as complex voicing systems in Austronesian languages. In languages with direct-inverse voice systems (e.g., Plains Cree), arguments are ranked according to a salience hierarchy, such as $1 > 2 > 3 >$ non-human animate $>$ inanimate. When the most "salient" argument of the verb functions as the subject, the verb may be marked with a direct voice (DIR) morpheme [29, p. 230]. The inverse voice (INV) marks the argument of the verb that is lower in the hierarchy when it functions as the subject. When the arguments of the verb are at equal ranks, they are marked as either proximate or obviative, as described in Sect. 2.3 (Person).

In Austronesian voice systems, a different voice is used to focus nouns occupying different semantic roles [29, p. 247]. A voice marker that simultaneously marks the semantic role of the focused noun is used on the verb and the overt marker of the semantic role is replaced by a morpheme that marks both the semantic role and its status as focused. The Austronesian language that makes the most distinctions in semantic role marking in its voice system is Iloko (Ilocano). The semantic roles it marks are given dedicated features in the universal schema since they are used by other Austronesian languages. Those roles are: Agent (AGFOC), patient (PFOC), location (LFOC), beneficiary (BFOC), accompanier (ACFOC), instrument (IFOC), and conveyed (CFOC; either by actual motion or in a linguistic sense, as by a speech act) [41, pp. 336–338].

Finally, valency-changing morphology is categorized with voice because it alters the argument structure of a sentence. Reflexives (REFL) direct action back onto a subject, while reciprocals (RECP) indicate that with a plural subject, nonidentical participants perform the action of the verb on each other. Causatives (CAUS) indicate that an action was forced to occur, and may introduce an argument indicating the actant that was forced to perform the action. Applicative morphemes (APPL) increase the number of oblique arguments (that is, arguments other than the subject or object) that are selected by the predicate [38].

Evidentiality. Evidentiality is the morphological marking of a speaker's source of information [1]. The universal morphological feature schema follows Aikhenvald [1] in viewing evidentiality as a separate category from mood and modality. Although categories of evidentiality may entail certain modalities (such as hearsay or reported information evidentials entailing irrealis or subjunctive moods), evidentiality is a distinct category that encodes only the source of the information that a speaker is conveying in a proposition.

The unique evidential categories proposed as features here are based on Aikhenvald's typology [1, pp. 26–60]. Those features are, in approximate order of directness of evidence: Firsthand (FH), direct (DRCT), sensory (SEN), nonvisual sensory (NVSEN), auditory (AUD), non-firsthand (NFH), quotative (QUOT), reported (RPRT), hearsay (HRSY), inferred (INFER), and assumed (ASSUM). The degree to which these categories could be reduced using a deeper featural analysis requires further research.

Switch-Reference. Switch-reference is an anaphoric linkage between clauses that disambiguates the reference of subjects and other NPs [44, p. 1]. Switch-reference is a fully grammaticalized phenomenon in some languages and can occur when the reference of subjects or other NPs is already fully disambiguated. Switch-reference marking is concentrated in languages of North America (notably in the Southwest, Great Basin, and coastal Northern California), Australia, Papua New Guinea, and the Bantu languages of Africa [44, p. 5].

A basic overt distinction in many switch-reference systems is between same subject (SS) and different subject (DS) [44, pp. 3–4]. In addition to this basic distinction, a third underspecified category, open reference (OR) marking, which signals "indifference as to the referential relation between the two [NPs] rather than specified non-identity" [44, p. 34]. In addition, some West African languages have what have been called "logophoric" systems in which pronouns are explicitly coreferential (or logophoric; LOG) with a pronoun in a previous clause [44, pp. 50–56].

More complex switch-reference systems necessitate additional features, which, due to space limitations, are not described here, but are included in the summary of the schema. Note that CN_R_MN is a feature template used to signal switch-reference marking between NPs in any argument position (as must be used for, e.g., Warlpiri) [44, p. 25]. When expanded, these template features bring the total feature count above 212.

Person. The conventional person categories that are encoded on verbs in most languages include first person (1), second person (2), and third person (3). Apart from these common distinctions, some languages also distinguish other categories of person, including zero (0) and fourth person (4), and each conventional person category is sometimes subdivided further. The Santa Ana dialect of Keres distinguishes all four of these categories [20, pp. 75–76].

Zero person, which occurs in Finnish, describes an underspecified third person, as with English 'one,' that refers to any human actor [31, p. 209]. Fourth person is used to describe an otherwise third-person referent that is distinguished via switch-reference (e.g., in Navajo "disjoint reference across clauses" [52, p. 108]) or obviation status [7, pp. 306–307].

The first person plural ('we') is divided into inclusive (INCL), i.e., including the addressee, or exclusive (EXCL), i.e., excluding the addressee. When two or more third person arguments are at the same level of the salience hierarchy in a language with a direct-inverse voice system, one argument is usually overtly marked as proximate (PRX) and the other as obviative (OBV).

Number. The dimension of number is relevant for multiple parts of speech and is one of the most frequent agreement features. Each feature is defined with respect to a quantificational scale of the number of entities indicated. The range of number distinctions on nouns is most extensive, with less common categories like "greater paucal" expressed in a small number of languages on nouns, but never on verbs.

The number categories found on nouns include singular (SG), plural (PL), dual (DU), trial (TRI), paucal (PAUC), greater paucal (GPAUC), and so-called inverse number (INVN) [14]. Sursurunga (Austronesian) contrasts all these, except inverse, on nouns [14, pp. 25–30].

In inverse number systems, such as that of Kiowa [14, pp. 159–161], nouns have a default number that indicates the number with which they are "expected" to occur. For example, if 'child' is by default singular and 'tree' is by default plural, then inverse number marking would make 'child' plural and 'tree' singular, inverting the number value of the noun.

Gender. Gender is a grammatical category that includes both conventional gender from European languages like Spanish and German, and systems with more than three categories that are typically described as noun class systems.

Because gender can be assigned according to semantic, morphological, phonological, or lexical criteria, creating an underlying conceptual-semantic space for defining gender features is of limited utility. In addition, gender categories rarely map neatly across languages, with differences in gender assignment even where semantic criteria primarily determine gender. This schema therefore treats gender as an open-class feature. The working strategy for limiting feature proliferation is to encode features for gender categories that are shared across languages within a linguistic family or stock in order to capture identical gender category definitions and gender assignments that result from common ancestry. Results presented in Table 3a offer evidence that this is an effective strategy, given the level of agreement in gender features within a family. The features masculine (MASC), feminine (FEM), and neuter (NEUT) are motivated by many Indo-European languages. To capture the eight possible Nakh-Daghestanian noun classes, the features NAKH1, NAKH2, etc. are used, and to capture the Bantu noun classes, of which 25 are estimated to have existed in Proto-Bantu [21, p. 272], the features BANTU1, BANTU1A, BANTU2, etc. are used.

Case. "Case is a system of marking dependent nouns for the type of relationship they bear to their heads" [3, p. 1]. The types of overt case that are encountered in the world's languages can be divided into three types: (1) core case, (2) local case, and (3) other types of case [3].

Core case is also known as 'non-local,' 'nuclear,' or 'grammatical' case [3,13], and indicates the role of a syntactic argument as subject, object, or indirect object. The specific core cases vary according to the syntactic alignment that a given language uses and can be defined in terms of three standard "meta-arguments," S (subject of an intransitive verb), A (subject of a transitive verb), and P (object of a transitive verb). Nominative-accusative languages use the nominative case (NOM) to mark S and A and the accuative (ACC) to indicate P. Ergative-absolutive languages use the ergative case (ERG) to indicate A and absolutive (ABS) to indicate S and P. In 'tripartite' languages that fully differentiate S, A, and P, the S-only nominative (NOMS) indicates only S.

Non-core, non-local cases (type 3) express non-core argument relations and non-spatial relations. The dative case (DAT) marks the indirect object, and its functions are sometimes divided into two distinct cases, the benefactive (BEN) for marking the beneficiary of an action and the purposive (PRP) for marking the reason or purpose for an action [3, pp. 144–145]. The genitive (GEN) and relative (REL) cases both mark a possessor, with relative also marking the core A role [p. 151]. The partitive case (PRT) marks a noun as partially affected by an action [p. 153]. The instrumental case (INS) marks the means by which an action is done, and sometimes marks accompaniment, which can be marked distinctly with the comitative case (COM) [p. 156]. The vocative case (VOC) marks direct address [pp. 4–5]. In comparative constructions, the standard of comparison (e.g. 'taller *than X'*) can be explicitly marked with the comparative case (COMPV) when the comparison is unequal and with the equative case (EQTV; e.g., 'as much as *X'*) when the comparison is equal. The formal case (FRML) marks "in the capacity of, as," and the aversive case (AVR), common in Australian languages, indicates something that is to be feared or avoided. Also common in Australian languages are the privative/"abessive" case (PRIV) indicating without or a lack or something and its counterpart, the proprietive case (PROPR), which indicates the quality of having something [3, p. 156].

The local cases express spatial relationships that are typically expressed by adpositions in English (and in the majority of the world's languages) [40, p. 24]. The types of local case morphemes include place, distal, motion, and 'aspect' morphemes, as shown by Radkevich [40].[1] The place morphemes indicate orientation to a very precise degree [p. 29]. The Nakh-Daghestanian languages Tabassaran and Tsez contain the largest number of place morphemes, which include separate morphemes, encoded in the schema as features, for "among (INTER), at (AT), behind (POST), in (IN), near (CIRC), near/in front of (ANTE), next to (APUD), on (ON), on (horizontal; ONHR), on (vertical; ONVR)," and "under (SUB)" [13,40]. Only one morpheme (and feature) indicates distal (REM). The motion category is composed of only three possible parameters, namely essive (static location; ESS), allative (motion toward; ALL), and ablative (motion away; ABL) [40, pp. 34–36]. The 'aspect' category is an elaboration of the motion category, and includes four parameters, namely approximative (APPRX), terminative (TERM), prolative/translative (PROL), and versative (VERS) [pp. 37, 53–55]. The approximative indicates motion toward, but not reaching, a goal, while the terminative indicates that motion "as far as," or "up to" the goal. The versative indicates motion in the direction of a goal, without indication of whether it is reached, and the prolative/translative indicates motion "along, across," or "through" something.

Animacy. To the extent that animacy is a grammatically separate category from person, individuation, and agency, it encompasses only four principal categories: Human (HUM), non-human (NHUM), animate (ANIM), and inanimate (INAN) [11, p. 185]. Animacy is not encoded by dedicated overt morphemes in any language, but can still be isolated as an independent parameter that has overt morphological effects. Animacy conditions the realization of accusative case in Russian, with animate masculine nouns taking a form identical to the genitive and inanimate masculine nouns taking a form identical to the nominative [54, p. 48].

Possession. Some languages, including Turkish and certain Quechua languages, use overt affixal morphology to mark characteristics of the possessor directly on a possessed noun or to encode the type of possession. The simplest type of

---

[1] The local case morphemes can be organized within each category through the use of abstract features that are more general than the feature labels employed in the schema.

marking on the possessed noun marks no characteristics of the possessor, but simply encodes the quality of being possessed (PSSD). This feature occurs in Hausa, Wolof, and in the construct state in Semitic languages [15].

The grammatical characteristics of the possessor that are marked in languages of the world include person, clusivity, number, gender, and politeness. For example, Huallaga Quechua marks person, clusivity, and number [49, pp. 54–55]. Turkish marks person, number, and formality [23, p. 66], and Arabic marks person, number (including dual), and gender (masculine and feminine) [42, p. 301]. The features used to capture these morphemes contain the prefix PSS-, followed by a number indicating person (1–3), S, D, or P for number, I or E for clusivity, M or F for gender, and INFM or FORM for politeness. For example, possession by a second person singular masculine possessor is marked with the feature PSS2SM. This feature is schematized as PSSPNO ('possession-person-number-other').

Finally, many languages (such as Kpelle [Mande]), distinguish alienable possession (ALN), in which ownership can change, from inalienable possession (NALN), in which ownhership is considered to be inherent. For example, Kpelle marks possession by a first person singular possessor distinctly in 'my house' (ŋa pɛrɛi) from 'my arm' (m-pôlu) [50, p. 279].

Information Structure. Information structure is a component of grammar that formally expresses "the pragmatic structuring of a proposition in a discourse" [32, p. 5]. More concretely, information structure directly encodes which parts of a proposition are asserted by the speaker (the focus; FOC) and which are presupposed or otherwise not asserted (the topic; TOP; ibid., pp. 5–6).

The topic signals what the sentence is about. Lambrecht [32, p. 131] defines the topic more specifically as "expressing information which is relevant to [a referent in the proposition] and which increases the addressee's knowledge of this referent." The focus signals information that is not presupposed by the addressee [32, p. 213]. The information marked by the focus forms the core of the proposition's assertion, and typically includes the part of the proposition that is unpredictable or new to the listener (ibid.).

Politeness. Politeness is the dimension of meaning that expresses social status relationships between the speaker, addressee, third parties, or the setting in which a speech act occurs [5,9]. Politeness/honorific systems can indicate relationships along four axes: (1) The speaker-referent axis, (2) the speaker-addressee axis, (3) the speaker-bystander axis, and (4) the speaker-setting axis [5,9].

Levinson [33, p. 90] writes that with honorifics along the speaker-referent axis, "respect can only be conveyed by referring to the 'target' of the respect" and that "the familiar *tu/vous* type of distinction in singular pronouns of address ... is really a referent honorific system, where the referent happens to be the addressee." The T-V distinction encodes the informal (INFM) and formal (FORM) distinction. Data from Japanese motivate positing two sublevels of the formal level. Japanese uses one set of referent honorifics in a speech style called *sonkeigo* to elevate the referent (FORM.ELEV) and a distinct set of referent honorific forms in a speech style called *kenjōgo* to lower the speaker's status (FORM.HUMB), thereby raising the referent's status by comparison [51, pp. 41–43].

In speaker-addressee honorific systems, politeness is conveyed by word choice itself, not just by terms that refer to the addressee. Japanese and Javanese use these systems, and in each, the distinction is between a polite form (POL) that conveys respect and a plain form that does not.

Features are defined for speaker-bystander honorific systems, as occur in Dyirbal (Pama-Nyungan) and Pohnpeian (Austronesian) [33, pp. 90–91], for example, and for the speaker-setting axis (or register), but are not described here due to space limitations.

Comparison. Comparison and gradation can be expressed through overt affixal morphology [18]. The comparative (CMPR), such as English *-er*, relates two objects such that one exceeds the other in exhibiting some quality (ibid.). The superlative (SPRL) relates any number of objects such that one exceeds all the others. This is specifically the relative (RL) superlative, such as that expressed by English *-est*. Another type of superlative, the absolute (AB) superlative, expresses a meaning like "very" or "to a great extent," and is used in Latin, for example [18]. Equative constructions are comparative constructions in which the compared entities exhibit a quality to an equal extent. The adjective itself can be marked as conveying equality (EQT), as in Estonian and Indonesian [18].

Deixis. Deictic features, primarily spatial, are used to differentiate third-person pronouns and demonstrative pronouns, especially in languages where these categories overlap [2, pp. 134–135]. Contrasts can be established according to distance, verticality, reference point, and visibility. The maximal distance distinction occurs in Basque, which contrasts proximate (PROX), medial (MED), and remote (REMT) entities [27, pp. 123,150]. The maximal number of verticality distinctions occurred in the original Lak (Nakh-Daghestanian) pronoun system, which contrasted remote pronouns that encoded being below (BEL), at the same level as (EVEN), or above (ABV) the speaker [22, p. 304]. The maximal reference point distinction occurs in Hausa, which contrasts a pronoun with proximity to the first person (speaker; REF1), to the second person (addressee; REF2), and to neither ('distal'; NOREF) [2, p. 145]. Finally, the maximal visibility distinction occurs in Yupik (Eskimo-Aleut), which distinguishes visible (VIS) from invisible (NVIS), and further subdivides visible elements into those that are 'extended,' i.e., spread out and moving (e.g., the ocean), and those that are 'restricted,' i.e., in sight and stationary [4]. More research into distinctions in the visibility domain is required before positing features beyond VIS and NVIS.

3   Enabling Projection-Based Approaches to Fine-Grained Morphological Tagging

A primary motivation for richly annotating inflectional morphology in a consistent, universally-applicable way is that it enables direct comparison (and even translation) across languages. In this section, we examine variability in the use of inflectional morphological features across languages. Understanding this variability is central to evaluating the viability of simple projection-based approaches (such as those developed by [19,28,46,53]) to fine-grained part-of-speech tagging (i.e., morphological tagging), particularly of underspecified languages.

Some languages, such as English, lack significant surface morphology, so many semantic distinctions must be discovered through contextual analysis. For example, English lacks overt indicators of politeness on verbs, whereas many other languages (e.g., Japanese, Spanish) express it directly through inflectional morphology. If we align the underspecified English word to its foreign counterparts (using standard tools from machine translation), they could provide a consensus label for unspecified semantic values. These consensus-derived labels could be used to generate training data for monolingual semantic tagging algorithms, without the need for costly human annotation effort. The quality of the labels would depend on the tendency of foreign languages to consistently realize inflectional features.

The following sections present a method of measuring cross-linguistic variability in inflectional morphology in order to assess the validity of projection-based approaches to tagging.

3.1   Bible Alignments

We examined cross-linguistic variability in inflectional morphology by comparing which morphological features were expressed across multiple translations of the same meaning. First, we use a set of locations in the New Testament portion of the New International Version (NIV) of the English Bible as 'pivots.' A location is described by a (verse, position) pair and constitutes a context-specific word-meaning combination. All (and only) nominal and verbal words in the NIV New Testament were used as pivots.

For each pivot, we found all single-word foreign translations using verse-level alignments obtained from the Berkeley aligner [35] on the 1169 Bibles from the Parallel Bible Corpus[2]. It was possible for a given pivot to be translated into the same foreign language multiple times, if multiple versions of the Bible were available in that language.

Foreign words were then linked to universal morphological feature representations in our schema via lookup in a database of richly annotated data from Wiktionary.[3] The database contained inflected wordforms from 1,078,020 unique lemmas across the 179 languages represented in Wiktionary's English edition. For further details on the extraction of Wiktionary data and mapping those data to features in the universal morphological feature schema, see Sylak-Glassman, Kirov, Yarowsky, and Que [45].

To avoid ambiguity, only words with a single unique feature vector were used. A total of 1,683,086 translations were able to be mapped this way. Overall, these

---

[2] http://paralleltext.info/data/all/.

[3] http://www.wiktionary.org.

covered 47 unique languages across 18 language families (e.g., Romance, Celtic, Slavic, Germanic, Uralic, Quechuan, etc.). Family affiliation was determined by manually correcting output from Ethnologue [34]. These mappings made it possible to quantify the level of agreement in feature value for each dimension of meaning across different translations of the same pivot. See Fig. 1 for an example in which pairwise agreement may be measured between a Spanish and Russian translation of the same English pivot word. This example also shows how an underspecified English wordform can be labeled with additional morphological features via consensus of its non-English counterparts.

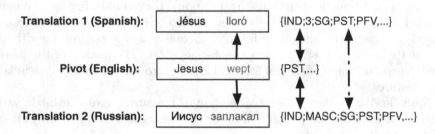

Fig. 1. Pairwise agreement of multiple translations (Spanish and Russian) of the same (English) pivot location. Note that the pivot word in this case, *wept*, only has the PST (past tense) feature overtly specified in English. However, we can assign it other labels including SG and PFV through a consensus of the available translations.

3.2   Results and Discussion

As an indicator of cross-linguistic consistency, Table 3a describes the average percentage of translation pairs (e.g., see Fig. 1) that agree on a particular feature across available pivots.[4] For a particular dimension, only pairs of translations that both specify a non-null feature value were ever compared. The table shows the average pairwise agreement for each dimension across all translations, the average when comparisons are limited to translations from *different* language families, the average when comparisons are limited to the same language family, and the average when comparisons are limited to the same language (i.e., only between different Bible versions).

The results indicate that within-language variability is very low. This is an upper bound measuring variability due to translators' linguistic choices, rather than true differences in cross-language feature realization. There is more variability within language families, but the overall drop in agreement is small. This suggests that consensus-based labeling of a target language would be very effective if parallel data from genealogically-related languages were available. Surprisingly,

---

[4] Some disagreement in the data will be due to errors in our Wiktionary data, or the automated Bible alignment. We do not discuss these sources of noise in this paper, but they should affect all measurements in a uniform way, and thus do not preclude the comparisons we make.

Table 3. Table (a) summarizes cross-linguistic agreement for each feature dimension. The 'overall' results correspond to pairwise agreement across all available translations. The 'different family' column shows pairwise agreement among only translations from different language families. The 'same family' and 'same language' columns show pairwise agreement only between translations from the same family, and the same language, respectively. Table (b) summarizes cross-linguistic projection accuracy for each feature dimension. The 'held-out' column indicates the probability that a held-out translation for an English pivot will match the consensus of the remaining translations. The Albanian and Latin columns indicate the accuracy of consensus compared to gold-standard Albanian and Latin feature labels provided by automatic feature-extraction from Wiktionary.

	Dimension	Overall	Different Family	Same Family	Same Language
	Case	0.45	0.23	0.77	0.91
	Gender	0.75	0.39	0.87	0.96
	Mood	0.89	0.82	0.95	0.99
	Number	0.79	0.74	0.88	0.96
(a)	Part of Speech	0.74	0.73	0.85	0.94
	Person	0.87	0.82	0.93	0.97
	Politeness	0.98	0.84	0.99	1.00
	Tense	0.73	0.66	0.82	0.95
	Voice	0.95	0.83	0.99	0.99
	Average	0.79	0.67	0.89	0.96

	Dimension	Held-Out	Albanian	Latin
	Case	0.50	0.57	0.81
	Gender	0.76	0.74	0.44
	Mood	0.91	N/A	0.96
(b)	Number	0.83	0.83	0.85
	Part of Speech	0.83	0.86	0.59
	Tense	0.79	0.84	0.65
	Voice	0.95	N/A	0.84
	Average	0.80	0.77	0.73

this is true for gender, which, aside from animate nouns with natural masculine or feminine gender, is often assumed to be assigned arbitrarily or according to non-semantic principles [17]. Our data indicate that gender assignment tends to be preserved as related languages diverge from a common proto-language.

Even if we only have parallel text from a set of mutually unrelated languages, the different families column in Table 3a suggests that we may still rely on a solid consensus for many features. Gender, and presumably other arbitrarily-assigned features do show significant drop in agreement across unrelated languages.

Nominal case shows especially poor agreement cross-linguistically. There are a number of possible reasons for this. First, no core case features will agree between languages with different syntactic alignment systems. Second, languages sometimes assign morphological case in idiosyncratic ways. For example, Russian uses instrumental case not only to denote an implement, but also to mark the time of day and season of the year that an action takes place [39]. These linguistic sources of disagreement, combined with a larger overall set of possible labels for the case feature, predict a lower base rate of agreement.

While pairwise agreement statistics provide a general idea of the feasibility of cross-linguistic projection depending on the similarity of available translation languages to the target, they are not a direct evaluation of the accuracy of consensus-based labels. Since we do not currently have hand-labeled gold-standard data with which to perform such an evaluation, we offer three approximations, shown in Table 3b. The held-out column shows the probability that, across all translations of a given pivot, the feature values of a single held-out translation match the consensus values from the remaining translations (i.e., each held-out translation acts as proxy for a gold-standard). The rows in the Albanian and Latin columns show the result of using Albanian and Latin Bibles as a source of pivot locations, and treating our automatically-derived Wiktionary data for these languages as a gold-standard.[5] Albanian is an especially interesting case. Because it is an isolate within the larger Indo-European family, no highly genealogically similar languages were available in our dataset. This simulates the labeling of an unknown new language.

Overall, the results indicate that an approach based on consensus would be effective for assigning feature labels to wordforms. This is especially true if data from languages within the same family are available. For many feature dimensions, even cross-family labels would be useful, especially in low-resource environments where a large gold-standard training set is otherwise unavailable. The high levels of cross-linguistic agreement, particularly for non-arbitrary semantic distinctions, would not be possible if our feature schema could not be consistently applied to multiple, potentially unrelated languages.

4   Conclusion

The universal morphological feature schema presented here incorporates findings from linguistic typology to provide a cross-linguistically applicable method of describing inflectional features in a universalized framework. It greatly expands the coverage of inflectional morphological features beyond previous frameworks and at the same time offers a substantive hypothesis on the dimensions of meaning and which distinctions within them are encoded by inflectional morphology in the world's languages.

The schema offers many potential benefits for NLP and machine translation by facilitating direct meaning-to-meaning translations across language pairs, regardless of form-related differences. We demonstrated that Wiktionary forms, when annotated according to our schema, were very likely to agree along the

---

[5] When comparing Albanian and Latin pivots to the consensus of their translations, no Albanian and Latin translations were used. Using only cross-language consensus prevents unfair advantage from self-similarity.

dimensions of meaning expressed by inflectional morphology when they were aligned to the same pivot words by automatic machine translation tools. This cross-linguistic consistency supports the viability of consensus-based multilingual projection of fine-grained morphological features to an underspecified target language (e.g., tagging formality levels in English even though they are not expressed by the native inflectional system) when parallel text is available.

References

1. Aikhenvald, A.Y.: Evidentiality. Oxford University Press, Oxford (2004)
2. Bhat, D.N.S.: Pronouns. Oxford University Press, Oxford (2004)
3. Blake, B.J.: Case. Cambridge University Press, Cambridge (2001)
4. Bliss, H., Ritter, E.: Developing a database of personal and demonstrative pronoun paradigms: Conceptual and technical challenges. In: Proceedings of the IRCS Workshop on Linguistic Databases. IRCS, Philadelphia (2001)
5. Brown, P., Levinson, S.C.: Politeness: Some Universals in Language Usage. Cambridge University Press, Cambridge (1987)
6. Cable, S.: Tense, Aspect and Aktionsart. http://people.umass.edu/scable/PNWSeminar/handouts/Tense/Tense-Background.pdf
7. Chelliah, S.L., de Reuse, W.J.: Handbook of Descriptive Linguistic Fieldwork. Springer, Dordrecht (2011)
8. Comrie, B.: Aspect: An Introduction to the Study of Verbal Aspect and Related Problems. Cambridge University Press, Cambridge (1976)
9. Comrie, B.: Linguistic Politeness Axes: Speaker-Addressee, Speaker-Referent, Speaker-Bystander. In: Pragmatics Microfiche 1.7 (1976)
10. Comrie, B.: Tense. Cambridge University Press, Cambridge (1985)
11. Comrie, B.: Language Universals and Linguistic Typology. Basil Blackwell, Oxford (1989)
12. Comrie, B., Haspelmath, M., Bickel, B.: Leipzig Glossing Rules. https://www.eva.mpg.de/lingua/resources/glossing-rules.php
13. Comrie, B., Polinsky, M.: The great Daghestanian case hoax. In: Siewierska, A., Song, J.J. (eds.) Case, Typology, and Grammar: In Honor of Barry J. Blake, pp. 95–114. John Benjamins, Amsterdam (1998)
14. Corbett, G.: Number. Cambridge University Press, Cambridge (2000)
15. Creissels, D.: Construct forms of nouns in African languages. In: Proceedings of the Conference on Language Documentation and Linguistic Theory 2, pp. 73–82. SOAS, London (2009)
16. Croft, W.: Parts of speech as language universals and as language-particular categories. In: Vogel, P.M., Comrie, B. (eds.) Approaches to the Typology of Word Classes, pp. 65–102. Mouton de Gruyter, New York (2000)
17. Cucerzan, S., Yarowsky, D.: Minimally supervised induction of grammatical gender. In: Proceedings of HLT-NAACL 2003, pp. 40–47. ACL, Stroudsburg, PA (2003)
18. Cuzzolin, P., Lehmann, C.: Comparison and Gradation. In: Booij, G.E., Lehmann, C., Mugdan, J., Skopeteas, S. (eds.) Morphologie: Ein internationales Handbuch zur Flexion und Wortbildung/An International Handbook on Inflection and Word-Formation, pp. 1212–1220. Mouton de Gruyter, Berlin (2004)
19. Das, D., Petrov, S.: Unsupervised part-of-speech tagging with bilingual graph-based projections. In: Proceedings of ACL 2011, pp. 600–609. ACL, Stroudsburg, PA (2011)

20. Davis, I.: The language of Santa Ana Pueblo. In: Anthropological Papers, Numbers 68–74, Bureau of American Ethnology, Bulletin 191, pp. 53–190. Smithsonian Institution, Washington, DC (1964)
21. Demuth, K.: Bantu noun classes: loanword and acquisition evidence of semantic productivity. In: Senft, G. (ed.) Classification Systems, pp. 270–292. Cambridge University Press, Cambridge (2000)
22. Friedman, V.: Lak. In: Brown, K. (ed.) Encyclopedia of Language and Linguistics, pp. 303–305. Elsevier, Oxford (2006)
23. Göksel, A., Kerslake, C.: Turkish: A Comprehensive Grammar. Routledge, London (2005)
24. General Ontology for Linguistic Description (GOLD). http://linguistics-ontology.org/
25. Haspelmath, M.: The converb as a cross-linguistically valid category. In: Haspelmath, M., König, E. (eds.) Converbs in Cross-Linguistic Perspective, pp. 1–56. Mouton de Gruyter, Berlin (1995)
26. Haspelmath, M.: Comparative concepts and descriptive categories in crosslinguistic studies. Language 8(3), 663–687 (2010)
27. Hualde, J.I., Ortiz de Urbina, J.: A Grammar of Basque. Mouton de Gruyter, Berlin (2003)
28. Hwa, R., Resnik, P., Weinberg, A., Cabezas, C., Kolak, O.: Bootstrapping parsers via syntactic projection across parallel texts. Nat. Lang. Eng. 11, 311–325 (2005)
29. Klaiman, M.H.: Grammatical Voice. Cambridge University Press, Cambridge (1991)
30. Klein, W.: Time in Language. Routledge, New York (1994)
31. Laitinen, L.: Zero person in Finnish: a grammatical resource for construing human reference. In: Helasvuo, M.-L., Campbell, L. (eds.) Grammar from the Human Perspective: Case, Space and Person in Finnish, pp. 209–232. John Benjamins, Amsterdam (2006)
32. Lambrecht, K.: Information Structure and Sentence Form. Cambridge University Press, Cambridge (1994)
33. Levinson, S.C.: Pragmatics. Cambridge University Press, Cambridge (1983)
34. Lewis, M.P., Simons, G.F., Fennig, C.D.: Ethnologue: Languages of the World, 18th edn. SIL International, Dallas (2015). http://www.ethnologue.com
35. Liang, P., Taskar, B., Klein, D.: Alignment by agreement. In: Proceedings of HLT-NAACL 2006, pp. 104–111. ACL, Stroudsburg, PA (2006)
36. Lyons, C.: Definiteness. Cambridge University Press, Cambridge (1999)
37. Palmer, F.R.: Mood and Modality. Cambridge University Press, Cambridge (2001)
38. Polinsky, M.: Applicative Constructions. http://wals.info/chapter/109
39. Pulkina, I., Zaxava-Nekrasova, E.: Russian: A Practical Grammar with Exercises. Russky Yazyk Publishers, Moscow (1992)
40. Radkevich, N.: On Location: The Structure of Case and Adpositions. University of Connecticut, Storrs (2010)
41. Rubino, C.: Iloko. In: Adelaar, A., Himmelmann, N.P. (eds.) The Austronesian Languages of Asia and Madagascar, pp. 326–349. Routledge, London (2005)
42. Ryding, K.C.: A Reference Grammar of Modern Standard Arabic. Cambridge University Press, Cambridge (2005)
43. Sagot, B., Walther, G.: Implementing a formal model of inflectional morphology. In: Mahlow, C., Piotrowski, M. (eds.) SFCM 2013. CCIS, vol. 380, pp. 115–134. Springer, Heidelberg (2013)
44. Stirling, L.: Switch-Reference and Discourse Representation. Cambridge University Press, Cambridge (1993)

45. Sylak-Glassman, J., Kirov, C., Yarowsky, D., Que, R.: A language-independent feature schema for inflectional morphology. In: Proceedings of the 53rd Annual Meeting of the Association for Computational Linguistics and the 7th International Joint Conference on Natural Language Processing (Short Papers), pp. 674-680. Association for Computational Linguistics, Beijing (2015)
46. Täckström, O., Das, D., Petrov, S., McDonald, R., Nivre, J.: Token and type constraints for cross-lingual part-of-speech tagging. Trans. Assoc. Comput. Linguist. **1**, 1–12 (2013)
47. Universal Dependencies. http://universaldependencies.github.io/docs/
48. Vendler, Z.: Verbs and times. Philos. Rev. **66**, 143–160 (1957)
49. Weber, D.J.: A Grammar of Huallaga (Huanuco) Quechua. University of California Press, Berkeley (1989)
50. Welmers, W.E.: African Language Structures. University of California Press, Berkeley (1973)
51. Wenger, J.R.: Some Universals of Honorific Language with Special Reference to Japanese. University of Arizona, Tucson (1982)
52. Willie, M.: Navajo Pronouns and Obviation. University of Arizona, Tucson (1991)
53. Yarowsky, D., Ngai, G., Wicentowski, R.: Inducing multilingual text analysis tools via robust projection across aligned corpora. In: Proceedings of the First International Conference on Human Language Technology Research, pp. 1–8. ACL, Stroudsburg, PA (2001)
54. Yamamoto, M.: Animacy and Reference. John Benjamins, Amsterdam (1999)

Dsolve—Morphological Segmentation for German Using Conditional Random Fields

Kay-Michael Würzner[(✉)] and Bryan Jurish

Berlin-Brandenburg Academy of Sciences and Humanities, Berlin, Germany
wuerzner@bbaw.de

Abstract. We describe Dsolve, a system for the segmentation of morphologically complex German words into their constituent morphs. Our approach treats morphological segmentation as a classification task, in which the locations and types of morph boundaries are predicted by a Conditional Random Field model trained from manually annotated data. The prediction of morph-boundary types in addition to their locations distinguishes Dsolve from similar approaches previously suggested in the literature. We show that the use of boundary types provides a (somewhat counter-intuitive) performance boost with respect to the simpler task of predicting only segment locations.

1 Introduction

The goal of the morphological segmentation of words is their decomposition into *morphemes* (lexical level) or *morphs* (text level), each of which may be associated with a lexical meaning and/or a grammatical function. The segmentation of a word into morphemes is often referred to as *deep* segmentation, and is contrasted to *surface-level* segmentation into morphs (e.g., [5]). Given the segmentation of the German compound *Ärztekammern* (engl. "medical associations") into *Ärzt-e-Kammer-n*, the difference between the deep and the surface levels is observable in the segment *Ärzt*, which is a variant of the noun *Arzt* (engl. "doctor") which may only be realized in the plural. *Arzt* and *Ärzt* are distinct surface realizations—called *allomorphs*—of the morpheme {Arzt}. The task of surface-level morphological segmentation of a word can be viewed as identification on the one hand of the word formation operations which contribute to the word's construction (i.e., *compounding, derivation, inflection*) and of the morphs which constitute the operands of these operations on the other.

Morphological segmentations have many applications in (computational) linguistics, including information retrieval [19], language learning [2], and letter-to-sound conversion [6]. In the following, we present Dsolve, a system for surface-level segmentation of words based on supervised training of a conditional random field model (CRF) [17]. In order to classify our approach, we first give an overview of the related literature. We then describe Dsolve in more detail, evaluate its performance on a modest set of manually annotated German words, and conclude with some insights and loose ends.

© Springer International Publishing Switzerland 2015
C. Mahlow and M. Piotrowski (Eds.): SFCM 2015, CCIS 537, pp. 94–103, 2015.
DOI: 10.1007/978-3-319-23980-4_6

2   Related Work

Approaches to automatic morphological segmentation can be classified based on two characteristics. The first of these is the distinction between methods which rely on the manual specification of potential morph(eme) combinations—typically using some grammar formalism—and those which automatically induce such knowledge from un-annotated language data using distributional inference. The second characteristic is whether the approach in question makes use of some list or lexicon of (free) morphemes or not. Such a list can substantially increase quality of the results, but is often associated with a great deal of manual effort.

Traditional finite-state or two-level approaches [1] use manually constructed rules together with an extensive lexicon. The initial cost of creating a reliable system is thus quite high. The scope of finite-state morphologies usually includes other applications such as base-form reduction, word categorization, or lexical-semantic analysis. This broad scope often implies the inclusion of morphologically complex forms into the underlying lexica, which adversely affects their performance on the task of morphological segmentation. For German, the most prominent systems are GERTWOL [12], SMOR [28], and TAGH [9], which are either closed-source commercial products (GERTWOL and TAGH) or suffer from the aforementioned over-lexicalization issue (SMOR and TAGH).

A great number of proposals have been made to reduce the effort involved in the creation of morphological analysis systems. One class of proposals makes use of the fact that the number of affixes is much smaller than the number of free morphemes. Such *affix removal stemmers* [8] successively remove known affixes from words under the assumption that the remaining string is the word stem [22,24].

In statistical methods, linguistic knowledge is represented as a probability distribution over some atomic unit which is inferred from language data. In unsupervised settings (sometimes called *morphology induction*), these data are raw (i.e., unannotated) texts. Important works in this category include [3,4,7,10]. All of these approaches have in common that they aim at constructing lists of possible morph(eme)s using a set of pre-defined heuristics. The identification of morph(eme)s occurs by means of reference to character or string frequencies. In [10] for example, an underlying word structure $prefix?\ stem\ suffix*$ is assumed in order to identify so-called *signatures*, classes of stems which occur with common affixes. The performance of systems trained in an unsupervised manner is surprisingly high (compare, for example, the results of *Morpho Challenge* [16]), but still insufficient for productive applications.

The inclusion of manually segmented words in the training process (so called semi-supervised settings) can improve the performance of statistical methods dramatically [15]. An early instance of a data-driven approach which is trained in a completely supervised manner is MOSES [14]. For each bigram of adjacent characters in a word, the most likely intervening boundary type is selected on the basis of the boundary type distributions in the training material. Following this idea, there have been a number of proposals which focus on modeling the relation between local substrings and morph(eme) boundaries. Dsolve itself falls into this category, and we elaborate on the precise nature of the relation to be modeled below.

CRFs have previously been applied to word segmentation in Chinese in [30]. Studies on morphological segmentation of languages with alphabetic writing systems were carried out on Arabic [11,26], English [2,26,27], Finnish [26,27], Hebrew [26] and Turkish [26,27].

3   Morphological Segmentation as Sequence Classification

Sequence classification is a popular technique in natural language processing, already having been used successfully, e.g., for tokenization, part-of-speech tagging, and named entity recognition. At its core, the sequence classification task is defined in terms of a given set of symbols O and a set of classes C, and maps each symbol $o_i \in O$ in an observation string $o = o_1 \ldots o_n$ onto a class $c_i \in C$ by determining the most probable string of classes $c = c_1 \ldots c_n$ associated with o by an underlying stochastic model. Individual statistical models differ in the manner in which the most probable classes are calculated. Hidden Markov models for example optimize the joint probability $P(o, c)$ [23], while CRFs optimize the conditional probability $P(c|o)$ [31].[1]

For the task of morphological segmentation, the set of symbols is simply the surface character alphabet itself (or the set of character N-grams over this alphabet [14]). The set of target classes is usually two-valued (e.g., $C = \{0, 1\}$), leading to a classifier which predicts for every position i whether or not there is a segment boundary following (rsp. preceding) the observed symbol at position i of the input word, as illustrated in Fig. 1a.

$$\text{G e f o l g s l e u t e n}$$

(a)   0 1 0 0 0 1 1 0 0 0 0 1 0

(b)   0 + 0 0 0 ˜ # 0 0 0 0 ˜ 0

Fig. 1. The German noun compound *Gefolgsleuten* (engl. "henchmen[DATIVE]") boundary classified using (a) a binary classification scheme and (b) a type-sensitive classification scheme.

Some approaches (e.g., [14,26]) use more complex classification schemes in order to define morph(eme)s as *spans* in words (e.g., $C = \{B, I, E, S\}$ with B indicating the initial character of a multi-character morph, I a character inside a multi-character morph, E the final character of a multi-character morph, and S a single-character morph. Since such a span-based classification may result in inconsistent predictions, further disambiguation heuristics are required to interpret the classification results.

---

[1] Although as correctly noted in [23], any class-string c which maximizes $P(c, o)$ will also maximize $P(c|o)$ if the observation string o is held fixed.

The mere detection of boundaries is itself however insufficient for some applications. Consider for example the task of syllabification which in most languages follows the maximum onset principle [29]. In German, the morphological structure of words overrides this principle in cases of prefixion and compounding. Dsolve attempts to accommodate such phenomena by using a type-sensitive classification scheme: $C_{\text{Dsolve}} = \{+, \#, \sim, 0\}$, where '+' indicates that a prefix morph ends at the current position, '#' indicates that a free morph starts with the following position, '$\sim$' indicates that a suffix morph starts with the following position, and 0 indicates that there is no morph boundary after the current position. An example using this classification scheme is given in Fig. 1b.

We chose CRFs as the computational framework for the classification task. CRFs are a class of stochastic models using chain-structured undirected graphs to encode the dependencies between observations and output labels (i.e., classes). These dependencies are expressed in terms of feature functions representing salient properties of the input. Feature functions depending on external data sources, distributional properties such as "successor frequency" [13] as extracted from a large corpus of (un-annotated) data [27], or the distinction between vowels and consonants [2] have also been proposed for the current task.

In the case of Dsolve, we defined a simple feature inventory using only unigram features based on local string context. Each position i in the input string $o = o_1 \ldots o_n$ is assigned a feature for each substring of o of length $m \leq N$ within a context window of $N - 1$ characters relative to position i (including implicit word boundary symbols with pseudo-indices 0 and $n + 1$). Formally, a Dsolve model of "order"[2] N has $2N^2 - \sum_{m=1}^{N} m$ distinct feature functions f_j^k, where $-N < j \leq k < N$ and $k - j < N$, with $f_j^k(o_i) = o_{i+j}o_{i+j+1} \cdots o_{i+k-1}o_{i+k}$. A model with $N = 3$ for example has 12 distinct feature functions. If $o = sport$, then o_3 has the non-zero features $\{f_{-2}^{-2} = `s`, f_{-2}^{-1} = `sp`, f_{-2}^{0} = `spo`, f_{-1}^{-1} = `p`, f_{-1}^{0} = `po`, f_{-1}^{1} = `por`, f_0^0 = `o`, f_0^1 = `or`, f_0^2 = `ort`, f_1^1 = `r`, f_1^2 = `rt`, f_2^2 = `t`\}$. During model training, the influence of each feature expressed as a real-valued weight is optimized with respect to a manually classified training set. For the current experiments, optimization was performed by means of the L-BGFS algorithm [20].

4   Evaluation

In this section, we investigate the influence of model order on the tasks of boundary detection and optional classification of word-internal morph boundaries. We report model performance in terms of *string accuracy* (acc), *precision* (pr), *recall* (rc), and the and unweighted precision-recall harmonic average F [25]. For evaluation purposes, given a finite set W of annotated words and a finite set C of boundary classes with $0 \in C$ the designated non-boundary class, we associate

---

[2] Note that our use of "model order" in this paper refers only to the context window size used to define the feature function inventory, and is unrelated to the order of linear-chain feature dependencies in the underlying CRF models.

Table 1. Comparison of two independent manual segmentations of a sample of Dsolve's training materials.

Boundary symbol	pr%	rc%	F%	acc%
+	92.05	97.20	94.56	n/a
#	96.01	93.28	94.63	n/a
~	93.28	92.66	92.97	n/a
TOTAL [+types]	93.74	93.74	93.74	87.40
TOTAL [−types]	96.20	96.20	96.20	87.40

with each word $w = w_1w_2\ldots w_m \in W$ a partial *relevant* boundary-placement function $B_{\text{relevant},w} : \mathbb{N} \rightarrow C \backslash \{0\}$ such that $B_{\text{relevant},w}(i) = c$ if and only if there exists a manually annotated morph boundary of type $c \in C$ in the word w between the characters w_{i-1} and w_i, $1 < i \leq m$. The *retrieved* morph-boundary placement function $B_{\text{retrieved},w}$ is defined analogously based on the output of the CRF labeling. The evaluation quantities for the detection and classification task can then be defined in the usual manner:

$$\text{pr} = |\text{relevant} \cap \text{retrieved}| \ / \ |\text{retrieved}| \qquad (1)$$

$$\text{rc} = |\text{relevant} \cap \text{retrieved}| \ / \ |\text{relevant}| \qquad (2)$$

$$\text{F} = (2 \cdot \text{pr} \cdot \text{rc}) \ / \ (\text{pr} + \text{rc}) \qquad (3)$$

$$\text{acc} = |\{w \in W \mid B_{\text{retrieved},w} = B_{\text{relevant},w}\}| \ / \ |W| \qquad (4)$$

where:

$$\text{relevant} = \bigcup_{w \in W} \{w\} \times B_{\text{relevant},w} \ = \ \{(w,i,c) \mid (i \mapsto c) \in B_{\text{relevant},w}\} \qquad (5)$$

$$\text{retrieved} = \bigcup_{w \in W} \{w\} \times B_{\text{retrieved},w} \ = \ \{(w,i,c) \mid (i \mapsto c) \in B_{\text{retrieved},w}\} \qquad (6)$$

Evaluators for the detection-only task can be defined identically, after mapping all boundary types $c \in C \backslash \{0\}$ to a single, shared value.

4.1 Materials

We created a list of 15,522 distinct German word-forms and manually annotated types and locations of all word-internal morph boundaries. In unclear cases, we consulted `canoo.net` and/or the *Etymologisches Wörterbuch des Deutschen* [21]. If multiple correct segmentations were applicable, we randomly selected one of them. Candidate word-forms were selected from various corpora in the collection of the *Zentrum Sprache* at the Berlin-Brandenburg Academy of Sciences and Humanities[3]. A total of 21,068 word-internal morph boundaries were annotated in this fashion. In the interest of providing an accurate approximation of the morph boundary distribution in German and to guard against false-positive

---

[3] http://www.bbaw.de.

Table 2. Evaluation results for Dsolve on the combined boundary-detection and classification task for [+types] model variants.

N	pr%	rc%	F%	acc%
1	27.27	0.01	0.03	22.84
2	70.84	60.92	65.51	47.29
3	85.23	82.64	83.91	70.60
4	91.39	88.77	90.07	80.50
5	93.46	90.67	92.04	83.50

Table 3. Detailed results for Dsolve boundary classification by boundary type.

	Prefix-stem (+)			Stem-stem (#)			Stem-suffix (∼)		
N	pr%	rc%	F%	pr%	rc%	F%	pr%	rc%	F%
1	–	0.00	–	27.27	0.05	0.10	–	0.00	–
2	63.97	50.25	56.28	71.47	51.27	59.71	72.65	69.83	71.21
3	83.62	85.65	84.63	87.27	77.31	81.99	84.89	84.31	84.60
4	92.44	92.35	92.39	93.04	86.07	89.42	90.21	88.87	89.54
5	95.57	94.68	95.12	95.01	88.83	91.81	91.92	90.16	91.03

boundary predictions, 3,555 monomorphemic words were also included in the list. The complete list is published under the terms of the CC BY-SA 3.0 license, and is available for download.[4] In order to provide an assessment of the plausibility of our segmentations, we created explicit written annotation guidelines and asked a professional linguist of our acquaintance to edit a sample of 1,000 words accordingly. The results of a comparison to our segmentation is shown in Table 1, where our segmentations as above are interpreted as "relevant" boundaries, and the independent third-party segmentations provide the "retrieved" boundaries. Training and run-time application of CRFs were performed with the wapiti toolkit [18].

4.2   Method

The evaluation data was randomly partitioned into ten chunks of approximately equal size and evaluated by 10-fold cross-validation. For each of the ten training subsets and for each model order N with $1 \leq N \leq 5$, we trained two CRF model variants using a context window of N characters for CRF model features as described in Sect. 3. The first model variant, which we designate with the subscript [+types] predicts both boundary location and type by internal use of 3 distinct boundary labels for prefix-, stem-, and suffix-boundaries, respectively, in addition to a designated label for non-boundaries. The second model variant, indicated by the subscript [−types], uses only two labels indicating the presence or absence of a morph boundary, regardless of its type. For purposes of

---

[4] http://kaskade.dwds.de/~moocow/gramophone/de-dlexdb.data.txt.

Table 4. Evaluation results on the boundary-detection task for Dsolve variants both with (+types]) and without (−types) model-internal use of distinct boundary classes.

Method	Variant	N	pr%	rc%	F%	acc%
FlatCat	–	–	79.18	89.48	84.01	75.27
spanCRF	–	1	40.33	9.57	15.47	24.13
spanCRF	–	2	77.35	71.80	74.47	55.04
spanCRF	–	3	88.43	87.52	87.97	74.49
spanCRF	–	4	92.83	91.33	92.08	82.57
spanCRF	–	5	93.56	92.29	92.92	84.45
Dsolve	+types	1	36.36	0.02	0.04	22.84
Dsolve	+types	2	79.45	68.32	73.47	53.16
Dsolve	+types	3	89.36	86.64	87.98	74.35
Dsolve	+types	4	93.49	90.81	92.13	82.55
Dsolve	+types	5	94.46	91.63	93.02	84.36
Dsolve	−types	1	56.34	0.72	1.42	23.03
Dsolve	−types	2	77.53	69.61	73.36	52.94
Dsolve	−types	3	88.81	86.58	87.68	73.70
Dsolve	−types	4	92.93	90.78	91.85	81.92
Dsolve	−types	5	93.89	91.73	92.80	83.98

comparison, we also included results on the boundary detection task for both Morfessor FlatCat[5] as well as a `wapiti` re-implementation of the span-based CRF model described in [26] as methods "FlatCat" and "spanCRF," respectively. Each trained model was applied to the respective disjoint test subset, and the evaluation quantities defined above were computed for the concatenation of all test subsets.

4.3　Results and Discussion

Evaluation results for the joint task of boundary detection and classification are given in Tables 2 and 3, and results for the boundary detection task modulo classification are given in Table 4. Note that since the [−types] model variants were incapable of predicting boundary classes, they were not considered for the joint detection and classification task.

　　The most prominent effect observable in the data is the fact that all evaluation quantities increase monotonically as model order grows. Such a tendency is common for n-gram models of natural language phenomena, and can be interpreted in the current case as a lexicalization effect: as model order grows,

---

[5] http://www.cis.hut.fi/projects/morpho/morfessorflatcat.shtml; FlatCat models were trained with perplexity threshold 10.0 using annotated corpus data in semi-supervised mode.

the induced models are able to incorporate information on the distributions of increasingly long whole morphs. This hypothesis is supported on the one hand by the data from Table 3, indicating that the induced models performed most poorly for strong (#) morph boundaries—which necessarily occur between comparatively long stem morphs—and on the other hand by the disproportionate performance gain of the models with orders 2 and 3 with respect to their predecessors, since most German prefixes and suffixes are of length 2 or 3.

Unsurprisingly, comparing the quantities for the [+types] model variants from Tables 2 and 4 shows that the task of morph boundary detection is in some sense easier than the joint task of boundary detection and classification. Since both the models and data-set partitions used for evaluation were identical, the observed differences are clearly due to the fact that some "errors" in the joint task arose from incorrect predictions of boundary types, albeit at the correct positions: $B_{\mathrm{relevant},w}(i) = c \neq c' = B_{\mathrm{retrieved},w}(i)$.

Both of the Dsolve model variants as well as the spanCRF models substantially outperformed the Morfessor FlatCat baseline for all model orders $N > 3$. The Dsolve[+types] model variants performed quite similarly to the closely related spanCRF models. For $N > 1$, the Dsolve[+types] models were slightly more precise than the spanCRF models of the same order, while the latter achieved slightly higher recall rates. Since the Dsolve[+types] errors were more uniformly distributed between false positives and false negatives for $N > 3$, these achieved a higher harmonic average F than their spanCRF counterparts, although the latter were slightly more successful in terms string accuracy. Due to the limited size of the test corpus, differences on the order of magnitude observed between the Dsolve[+types] and spanCRF models must be viewed with a modicum of skepticism: the differences for $N = 5$ for example stem from a total of only 136 boundary errors and 13 string errors.

Despite the simplicity of the detection-only task, the Dsolve[+types] model variants making use of distinct boundary classes consistently outperformed the [−types] variants using a only binary label set for all model orders $N > 1$ in terms of both precision and string accuracy, leading to a relative error reduction of 9.33 % for precision at model order $N = 5$. While the [−types] variants displayed a slightly improved recall in some cases, the effect was not sufficient to outperform the [+types] models on either of the "top-level" evaluation quantities F or string accuracy for nontrivial model orders $N > 1$. This somewhat counterintuitive effect can only be attributed to the use of multiple boundary classes in the [+types] variants: since the underlying CRF models allow not only the *presence* of a boundary but also its *class* to influence the conditional path probability, these models are capable of capturing distributional regularities beyond those available to the [−types] models, which only encode boundaries' presence or absence. Postulation of a prefix-boundary for example allows a [+types] model to abstract over the lexical content of the prefix in question when estimating subsequent path probabilities, whereas a [−types] model would require additional surface context in order to identify the prefix morph as such and adjust its predictions accordingly.

5 Conclusion and Outlook

We have presented a system for the surface segmentation of morphologically complex words. Treating segmentation as a classification task, our approach uses a Conditional Random Field model trained on a modest set of manually annotated data to predict both the locations and the respective types of morph boundaries for each new input word. Evaluation by cross-validation on a list of 15,522 manually annotated German word-forms showed promising results, with a model using a context window of $N = 5$ input characters achieving a total precision-harmonic average $F \approx 93\%$ on a joint boundary detection and classification task. Somewhat surprisingly, the incorporation of multiple distinct boundary classes into the CRF model was shown to provide a performance gain on a boundary detection task when compared to an otherwise equivalent model encoding only boundary presence or absence. We attribute this effect to the classification models' greater ability to represent linguistically salient distributional regularities.

We are interested in applying our approach to other languages and data-sets, and in extending the approach as presented above by the optional inclusion of user-supplied lexical data (e.g., lists of known prefixes, stems, and/or suffixes). Future work should also investigate to what degree if any the model training phase can be augmented by semi-supervised learning techniques [15] using a large corpus of un-annotated data.

References

1. Beesley, K.R., Karttunen, L.: Finite State Morphology. CSLI, Stanford (2003)
2. Chang, J.Z., Chang, J.S.: Word root finder: a morphological segmentor based on CRF. In: Proceedings of COLING 2012: Demonstration Papers, pp. 51–58 (2012)
3. Creutz, M., Lagus, K.: Unsupervised discovery of morphemes. In: Proceedings of the ACL 2002 Workshop on Morphological and Phonological Learning, pp. 21–30 (2002)
4. Creutz, M., Lagus, K.: Unsupervised models for morpheme segmentation and morphology learning. ACM Trans. Speech Lang. Process. 4(1), 3:1–3:34 (2007)
5. Creutz, M., Lindén, K.: Morpheme segmentation gold standards for Finnish and English. Technical report A77, Helsinki University of Technology (2004)
6. Daelemans, W.: Grafon: a grapheme-to-phoneme conversion system for Dutch. In: Proceedings of COLING 1988, pp. 133–138 (1988)
7. Déjean, H.: Morphemes as necessary concept for structures discovery from untagged corpora. In: Proceedings of the Joint Conferences on New Methods in Language Processing and Computational Natural Language Learning, pp. 295–298 (1998)
8. Frakes, W.B.: Stemming algorithms. In: Frakes, W.B., Baeza-Yates, R. (eds.) Information Retrieval, pp. 131–160. Prentice-Hall, Upper Saddle River (1992)
9. Geyken, A., Hanneforth, T.: TAGH: a complete morphology for German based on weighted finite state automata. In: Yli-Jyrä, A., Karttunen, L., Karhumäki, J. (eds.) FSMNLP 2005. LNCS (LNAI), vol. 4002, pp. 55–66. Springer, Heidelberg (2006)

10. Goldsmith, J.: Unsupervised learning of the morphology of a natural language. Comput. Linguist. **27**(2), 153–198 (2001)
11. Green, S., DeNero, J.: A class-based agreement model for generating accurately inflected translations. In: Proceedings of ACL 2012, pp. 146–155 (2012)
12. Haapalainen, M., Ari, M.: GERTWOL und morphologische Disambiguierung für das Deutsche. In: Proceedings of the 10th Nordic Conference of Computational Linguistics. University of Helsinki, Department of General Linguistics (1995)
13. Harris, Z.: From phoneme to morpheme. Language **31**, 190–222 (1955)
14. Klenk, U., Langer, H.: Morphological segmentation without a lexicon. Literary Linguist. Comput. **4**(4), 247–253 (1989)
15. Kohonen, O., Virpioja, S., Lagus, K.: Semi-supervised learning of concatenative morphology. In: Proceedings of SIGMORPHON 2010, pp. 78–86 (2010)
16. Kurimo, M., Virpioja, S., Turunen, V., Lagus, K.: Morpho challenge competition 2005–2010: evaluations and results. Proceedings of SIGMORPHON 2010, pp. 87–95 (2010)
17. Lafferty, J.D., McCallum, A., Pereira, F.C.N.: Conditional random fields: probabilistic models for segmenting and labeling sequence data. In: Proceedings of the Eighteenth International Conference on Machine Learning, pp. 282–289. Morgan Kaufmann (2001)
18. Lavergne, T., Cappé, O., Yvon, F.: Practical very large scale CRFs. In: Proceedings of ACL 2010, pp. 504–513 (2010)
19. Müller, C., Gurevych, I.: Semantically enhanced term frequency. In: Gurrin, C., He, Y., Kazai, G., Kruschwitz, U., Little, S., Roelleke, T., Rüger, S., van Rijsbergen, K. (eds.) ECIR 2010. LNCS, vol. 5993, pp. 598–601. Springer, Heidelberg (2010)
20. Nocedal, J., Wright, S.J.: Numerical Optimization. Springer, Berlin (1999)
21. Pfeifer, W.: Etymologisches Wörterbuch des Deutschen, 2nd edn. Akademie-Verlag, Berlin (1993)
22. Porter, M.F.: An algorithm for suffix stripping. Electron. Libr. Inf. Syst. **14**(3), 130–137 (1980)
23. Rabiner, L.R.: A tutorial on hidden Markov models and selected applications in speech recognition. Proc. IEEE **77**(2), 257–285 (1989)
24. Reichel, U.D., Weilhammer, K.: Automated morphological segmentation and evaluation. In: Proceedings of LREC, pp. 503–506 (2004)
25. van Rijsbergen, C.J.: Information Retrieval. Butterworth-Heinemann, Newton (1979)
26. Ruokolainen, T., Kohonen, O., Virpioja, S., Kurimo, M.: Supervised morphological segmentation in a low-resource learning setting using conditional random fields. In: Proceedings of the Seventeenth Conference on Computational Natural Language Learning, pp. 29–37 (2013)
27. Ruokolainen, T., Kohonen, O., Virpioja, S., Kurimo, M.: Painless semi-supervised morphological segmentation using conditional random fields. In: Proceedings of EACL 2014, pp. 84–89 (2014)
28. Schmid, H., Fitschen, A., Heid, U.: SMOR: a German computational morphology covering derivation, composition and inflection. In: Proceedings of LREC (2004)
29. Selkirk, E.O.: On the nature of phonological representation. In: Myers, T., Laver, J., Anderson, J. (eds.) The Cognitive Representation of Speech, pp. 379–388. North-Holland Publishing Company, Dordrecht (1981)
30. Tseng, H., Chang, P., Andrew, G., Jurafsky, D., Manning, C.: A conditional random field word segmenter for SIGHAN bakeoff 2005. In: Proceedings of the Fourth SIGHAN Workshop on Chinese Language Processing (2005)
31. Wallach, H.M.: Conditional random fields: an introduction. Technical report MS-CIS-04-21, University of Pennsylvania, Department of Computer and Information Science (2004)

A Multi-purpose Bayesian Model
for Word-Based Morphology

Maciej Janicki[(✉)]

Institute of Computer Science, University of Leipzig,
Augustusplatz 10, 04109 Leipzig, Germany
janicki@informatik.uni-leipzig.de

Abstract. This paper introduces a probabilistic model of morphology based on a word-based morphological theory. Morphology is understood here as a system of rules that describe systematic correspondences between full word forms, without decomposing words into any smaller units. The model is formulated in the Bayesian learning framework and can be trained in both supervised and unsupervised setting. Evaluation is performed on tasks of generating unseen words, lemmatization and inflected form production.

Keywords: Word-based morphology · Machine learning · Generative model · Inflection · Lemmatization · Lexicon expansion

1   Introduction

Morphological analysis is an indispensable element of the NLP pipeline for many languages. Lemmatization or stemming is essential for virtually every semantic processing and information retrieval task, whereas syntactic processing, like parsing or chunking, usually requires Part-of-Speech tags and inflectional features, e.g., case or gender. As a rich inflectional system is typically able to generate hundreds of word forms for a single lemma, storing all those information in a lexicon is highly inefficient. In addition to inflection, also derivational morphology (especially compounding is some languages, e.g., German) often employs highly productive and regularized processes, which can result in a potentially unlimited number of lemmas. Therefore, systems for automatic morphological processing are a topic of ongoing research.

Despite the importance of morphological analysis, up to now no clear task definition has been established. The output of tools ranges from morpheme segmentation and labeling to just inflectional analysis (lemma + tag). Although the segmentation-based approach provides more detailed information, some non-straightforward tasks are often left to the user, like distinguishing between inflectional and derivational affixes, reconstructing the lemma or deriving the properties of the word from the properties of its morphemes. Also the handling of non-concatenative morphological phenomena varies from tool to tool. The reasons for those problems lie already in the underlying morphological theory, which requires

© Springer International Publishing Switzerland 2015
C. Mahlow and M. Piotrowski (Eds.): SFCM 2015, CCIS 537, pp. 104–123, 2015.
DOI: 10.1007/978-3-319-23980-4_7

all word formation processes to be expressed in terms of morphemes. Therefore, we introduce alternative theories, in particular *Whole Word Morphology*, in Sect. 3.

In addition to morphological analysis, there are also other NLP tasks, which require the knowledge of a language's morphology. *Inflected form generation*, understood as producing an inflected word form from a lemma and a set of desired inflectional features, is needed in machine translation, among others. Another morphology-related task is *lexicon expansion*, i.e., anticipating morphologically motivated, but unseen words.

The goal of the present work is a generative probabilistic model of the lexicon, that accounts for morphological relations between words. It can be trained either in an unsupervised or a supervised setting, and, once trained, it is capable of solving various morphology-related tasks, including the above-mentioned. Relying on a relational description of morphology, it does not suffer from the limitations of the segmentation-based approaches.

The rest of this paper is structured as follows: Sect. 2 provides an overview of the state-of-the-art in machine learning of morphology. Section 3 introduces linguistic theories, on which the present work is based. The generative model is described in Sect. 4 and the algorithms for training and applying it are sketched in Sect. 5. Section 6 describes evaluation of the model on practical NLP tasks. Topics for further research are described in Sect. 7. Section 8 summarizes the opportunities and advantages of the present work.

2   Related Work

2.1   Morpheme Segmentation

Automatic morpheme segmentation, especially unsupervised, has been a topic of active research for at least the last two decades [10]. The probably most known state-of-the-art tool is Morfessor [23]. It is based on the Minimum Description Length principle, which in this case is strongly connected to Bayesian learning. Other approaches based on probabilistic models include the work of Poon et al. [16] (log-linear models) and Can [5] (chap. 5, probabilistic hierarchical clustering).

Another group of approaches seeks to first group morphologically similar words together. The words belonging to the same cluster are then aligned in order to extract morphemes. Especially context similarity is typically used for this purpose, sometimes along with ortographical similarity. This group includes the approaches of Can [5] (chap. 4) and Kirschenbaum [12], among others.

Many further approaches have been submitted to MorphoChallenge [13], which offered standarized task formulation and datasets for morpheme segmentation. This yearly competition took place from 2005 to 2010.

Supervised learning of morphological segmentation is significantly less common. A method using Conditional Random Fields has been presented recently by Ruokolainen et al. [19]. Moreover, some models developed for unsupervised learning can also be trained in a supervised setting, like Morfessor [23] or the log-linear model of Poon et al. [16].

2.2 Lemmatization and Learning Inflectional Paradigms

Another branch of research considering automatic learning of morphology targets especially inflectional morphology. The task is then defined as either aligning an inflected word form to its root or lemma, or clustering the inflected forms of same lemma together. Many approaches exploit the high mutual dependency of inflectional processes, expressed in *paradigms*, which is a characteristic feature of inflection.

Yarowsky and Wicentowski [26], followed by Wicentowski [25], present a model of inflection, which can account for some non-concatenative phenomena, like root vowel change. The supervised approach employs a trie-based classifier, whereas the unsupervised performs the matching between an inflected word form and lemma based on a combination of various features: ortographical similarity, context similarity, and frequency ratio. The paradigm-oriented approaches include Chan [6], who uses Latent Dirichlet Allocation to group suffixes into paradigms, and Durrett and DeNero [8]. Unsupervised clustering of inflected word forms into lexemes has been approached by Janicki [11].

2.3 Tagging Unknown Words

A slightly different approach to morphological analysis is found in handling unknown words in the task of stochastic PoS-tagging. In this case, the goal is to predict the tag and sometimes the lemma of an unknown word in a given context. The tagging is thus token-based, rather than type-based. In addition to context features, which are the main component of such taggers, morphological features like prefix and suffix n-grams are sometimes incorporated in order to improve the tagging. The examples of such approaches include Mikheev [14], Tseng et al. [22] and Chrupała et al. [7], among others.

2.4 Lexicon Expansion

Compared to the above topics, the prediction of morphologically motivated unseen words is relatively little explored. Rasooli et al. [18] have shown in a recent paper, how the segmentation produced by Morfessor can be used for generation of new words. Their approach is to generate all possible sequences of morphemes with a finite-state automaton and to apply additional reranking steps based on letter trigram probabilities. On the other hand, Neuvel and Fulop [15] define the whole task of morphology learning as learning to produce new words using morphological mechanisms. The approach is inspired by the theory of Whole Word Morphology [9] and bears many similarities to the present work. However, it does not use probability or any kind of scoring, the discovered rules are applied wherever possible, which may lead to overgeneration, especially when learning from noisy data.

3   Word-Based Morphology

The notion of *word-based morphology* has been introduced by Aronoff [2] with the claim that "all regular word-formation processes are word-based," i.e., they apply to whole existing words, rather than some abstract structural elements. While Aronoff only took derivational morphology into account, the claim was further extended by Anderson [1]. In the latter theory, both inflection and derivation consists of word-formation rules, which operate on *stems* (defined as "word minus inflectional material") without creating any internal word structure. The difference is that inflectional rules derive surface words out of stems, while derivational rules derive new stems.

A theory that rejects any abstract elements of word structure, called *Whole Word Morphology* (henceforth WWM), has been proposed by Ford et al. [9]. A lot of criticism is devoted to the notion of "morpheme" there: first of all, it does not account for non-concatenative morphological phenomena. Also, the definition of morpheme as "the minimal element of language having a meaning or function" is troublesome, since some units participating in word-formation processes do not have a meaning on their own, while some functions are realized not by addition, but rather by absence or even truncation of phonological material. An example would be French adjective inflection, where the masculine form is formed from the feminine by truncation of the last consonant. Finally, the distinction between inflection and derivation is rejected as unmotivated.

In WWM, the minimal meaningful elements of language are words themselves. Morphology, on the other hand, describes the frequently recurring formal similarity patterns between words in terms of rules, called *morphological strategies*. Those rules always relate full lexical representations (phonological, syntactic, and semantic) of two words to each other and are not decomposable. An example of a rule for English plural formation would be $/X/_{\text{N.SG}} \leftrightarrow /Xs/_{\text{N.PL}}$. X is here a variable element, that can be instantiated with any string of phonemes. The two-sided arrow indicates, that the rule is bidirectional: no direction is privileged and no word is said to be morphologically "more complex" than the other. The atomicity of the rule means that no direct link is established between the -*s*-ending and the PL feature. In other words, there is no "plural morpheme," there is just a systematic correspondence between many plural nouns and their singular counterparts. While such interpretation may seem awkward in this case, it allows to treat all morphological phenomena uniformly, including the above mentioned non-concatenative and truncation cases, among others.

Finally, WWM does not distinguish "compounds" as words derived from more than one other word. It is pointed out, that only one part is always responsible for the base meaning and grammatical properties of a compound, while the other part is merely an "affix," the similarity of which to an existing word being irrelevant for the morphology. Compounds can thus also be explained with regular morphological strategies: for example the German word *Arbeitsmarkt* is linked to *Markt* via the rule: $/X/_{\text{N}} \leftrightarrow /arbeitsX/_{\text{N}}$. Doubtful cases between derivation and compounding, like the German rule $/X/_{\text{ADJ.PRED}} \leftrightarrow /Xerweise/_{\text{ADV}}$, speak in favour of this unification.

4   The Model

4.1   Lexicon as Directed Graph

The model of morphology introduced in this paper adopts many of the ideas from the WWM theory. The morphological structure of a language is understood as a graph of words, with morphological rules as edges. However, the bidirectionality of the rules is not preserved, because it would lead to many redundant edges. Instead, every word can only be derived from a single base word, i.e., every node can have at most one ingoing edge.

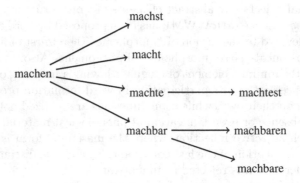

Fig. 1. A sample tree from a German lexicon.

Figure 1 presents a sample graph for German lemmas *machen* 'to do' and *machbar* 'feasible' with a couple of inflected forms. Note that if we used bidirectional rules, an edge would have to be drawn between every pair of the shown words, also pairs like (*machtest, machbaren*). Such a multitude of redundant rules can hardly correspond to a language speaker's competence. Therefore, we are rather looking for a spanning tree of the full morphological graph, which contains for each word a single base word, from which it is "really" derived.

In Fig. 1, the edges are drawn according to the usual morphological theory: inflected forms are derived from lemmas (possibly through other inflected forms, like *machtest* from the "imperfect stem" *machte*), while derivational rules derive "more complex" lemmas from "simpler" ones. Such behavior might be desirable for solving some specific tasks, like lemmatization, and can be controlled by training data and model parameters. However, from the point of view of model architecture, *any* trees of words are allowed, regardless of whether they make sense for the linguistic theory. Especially in the unsupervised learning task, where the graph structure emerges from the data through optimization, the regularities in word shape can be captured in quite different ways than traditional grammatical description (see also introduction to Sect. 6).

4.2   Model Formulation

A Bayesian model with parameter θ consists of two probability distributions: the *prior probability* $P(\theta)$, which expresses a-priori beliefs about the possible parameter values, and the *likelihood function* $P(D|\theta)$, which expresses the compatibility of the data D with the model parametrized by θ. The goal of the learning task is to find the most likely model given the observed data, i.e., the parameter value θ^* which maximizes the *posterior probability* $P(\theta|D)$. The latter can be transformed using the Bayes' theorem:

$$\theta^* = \arg\max_{\theta} P(\theta|D) = \arg\max_{\theta} \frac{P(\theta) \cdot P(D|\theta)}{P(D)} = \arg\max_{\theta} P(\theta) \cdot P(D|\theta) \quad (1)$$

The last equality follows because $P(D)$ does not depend on θ. Instead of computing the likelihood directly, the *log-likelihood* is often used, because it is easier to manipulate numerically. As logarithm is an increasing function, the maximization of those two is equivalent.

In our model of morphology, the observed data is the *lexicon* L: a directed acyclic graph, in which every node has at most one ingoing edge. The nodes of the lexicon contain words, while the edges correspond to morphological rules. The parameter of the model is the set R of morphological rules. In the following, we will define the distributions $P(R)$ and $P(L|R)$.

In order to define $P(L|R)$, we will decompose L into layers: $L_0, L_1, \ldots$ as follows: let L_0 contain all the nodes, that have no ingoing edge. Such nodes will be called *roots*.[1] Then, each L_{i+1} contains the nodes, that are derived from a node from L_i. Let rt be a probability distribution (called *root probability distribution*) over the set of all strings using letters from the target language's alphabet. For example, rt can be based on letter frequencies. Then we define:

$$P(L_0) := P(|L_0|) \cdot |L_0|! \cdot \prod_{w \in L_0} rt(w) \quad (2)$$

First, we draw the length of L_0 from some distribution. Then, each of the elements of L_0 is drawn independently from the root distribution. As the ordering of the elements is irrelevant, the result is multiplied by the number of possible orderings. Note that $P(L_0)$ does not depend on R and that rt is not a model parameter (i.e., it is fixed). We can get rid of the factorial term by using Poisson[2] distribution with parameter λ_L for $P(|L_0|)$, which yields:

$$P(L_0) := e^{-\lambda_L} \lambda_L^{|L_0|} \prod_{w \in L_0} rt(w) \quad (3)$$

---

[1] The notion of *root* used here has nothing to do with the definition typically used in morphology. It is meant as a root of a derivational tree, like the one shown in Fig. 1, which principally can be any word.

[2] The distribution of set length has negligible influence on the behavior of the model and is included only for formal completeness. Poisson distribution is chosen because of mathematical simplicity.

Next, we will define the probability $P(L_{i+1}|L_i, R)$ of deriving the layer L_{i+1} from L_i using the rules from set R. For each rule r, let π_r denote a probability, called *productivity* of r. Further, let $r(w)$ denote the (possibly empty) set of words resulting from applying the rule r to w.[3] Finally, let E_L denote the set of edges of L. Then:

$$P(L_{i+1}|L_i, R) := \prod_{w \in L_i} \prod_{r \in R} \prod_{w' \in r(w)} \begin{cases} \pi_r & \text{if } (w, w') \in E_L \\ 1 - \pi_r & \text{if } (w, w') \notin E_L \end{cases} \tag{4}$$

In other words, for each word from the layer L_i, each rule can apply with its inherent probability π_r. The latter corresponds to the definition of *productivity* mentioned by Aronoff [2, p. 36]. The lexicon also contains information about cases where a rule *does not* apply, the probability of which equals $1 - \pi_r$.

Finally, we can define the complete likelihood function:

$$P(L|R) := P(L_0) \cdot \prod_{i=0}^{\infty} P(L_{i+1}|L_i, R) \tag{5}$$

The product going to infinity can be justified as follows: once there is a $L_k = \emptyset$, then all further layers must also be empty and (4) yields $P(\emptyset|\emptyset, R) = 1$.

The rule set prior $P(R)$ is defined similarly to $P(L_0)$: first, we introduce a distribution $P(r)$ over single rules. For this purpose, we decompose a rule into a sequence of elementary edit operations (insertion or deletion of a character). We also introduce a third operation *COPY* (c), which leaves an arbitrary number of characters unchanged. For example, the German rule $/Xen/_{\text{V.INF}} \to /geXt/_{\text{V.PP}}$ would be expressed as the sequence:

$$(i('\text{g}'), i('\text{e}'), c, d('\text{e}'), d('\text{n}'), i('\text{t}'), d(\text{V.INF}), i(\text{V.PP}))$$

The distribution $P(r)$ is obtained by assigning (fixed) weights to each of the three operations and taking a probability distribution over letters and tags (e.g., according to their corpus frequency).

The next step is specifying a prior distribution for rule productivities. It is easy to check that the rule frequency in the lexicon follows a binomial distribution. Therefore, we use a standard non-informative prior $\text{BETA}(1, 1)$ for productivity. Finally, as we did with L_0, also here we use a Poisson distribution with parameter λ_R for $|R|$. Then we obtain:

$$P(R) := e^{-\lambda_R} \lambda_R^{|R|} \prod_{r \in R} P(r)P(\pi_r) \tag{6}$$

---

[3] In our formalism, rules are functions mapping words to *sets* of words. The set is empty if the constraints on the left-hand side of the rule are not met. Otherwise, typically a single word is produced, but cases with more than one result are also possible.

4.3   Extension with Features

The model sketched above can be further extended to include arbitrary features, like word frequency, semantic vectors, inflectional classes, etc. In this case, the graph nodes contain feature vectors and the rules are conditional distributions on feature values.

As an example, consider the PoS-tag of a word. In the model presented in the previous section, it was treated like a part of the word's string representation. Instead, we can define it as a separate feature t. Then, the nodes of the lexicon are pairs (w, t), while the rules additionally contain a probability distribution (called *transformational distribution*) $\tau_r(t'|t)$ of the tag of the resulting word, given the tag of the base word. For the above-mentioned rule for German past participle formation, $\tau_r(t'|\text{V.INF})$ would equal 1 for $t' = \text{V.PP}$ and 0 otherwise. For $t \neq \text{V.INF}$, $\tau_r(t'|t)$ can be left undefined, because the rule does not produce any results.

Equations (3), (4) and (6) become then:

$$P(L_0) := e^{-\lambda_L} \lambda_L^{|L_0|} \prod_{(w,t) \in L_0} rt(w) P(t|w) \tag{7}$$

$$P(L_{i+1}|L_i, R) := \prod_{(w,t) \in L_i} \prod_{r \in R} \prod_{w' \in r(w)} \begin{cases} \pi_r \tau_r(t'|t) & \text{if } \exists_{t'}((w,t),(w',t')) \in E_L \\ 1 - \pi_r & \text{otherwise} \end{cases} \tag{8}$$

$$P(R) := e^{-\lambda_R} \lambda_R^{|R|} \prod_{r \in R} P(r) P(\pi_r) P(\tau_r) \tag{9}$$

In addition, we need the distribution on root tags (possibly conditioned on the string form of the word) $P(t|w)$ and the prior distribution on τ, $P(\tau)$. In this example, the former can just be based on the frequencies of the tags in training data, while the latter can be a uniform distribution on all possible tag pairs (only degenerate τ, that equal 1 for exactly one resulting tag, are taken into account).

While the above example may look overcomplicated, this formalism allows us to incorporate a large variety of features into the model. Let us consider another example: the *frequency class* of a word, defined as $f_w = \lfloor \log_2 \frac{\max_{w' \in L} freq(w')}{freq(w)} \rfloor$, where $freq$ is the corpus frequency. There are reasons to assume, that morphological rules add a roughly constant factor to the word's frequency class. Consider Fig. 2, which shows the differences in frequency class between German word pairs conforming to the rule $/X/ \rightarrow /Xs/$, in the absence of PoS-tags. The histogram forms a bell-shaped curve with mean approximately 2. Moreover, the cases near the mean correspond to regular morphological phenomena, while the tails contain mostly pairs of unrelated words, which happen to fit the pattern, like *hau*, the imperative of *hauen* ('to hit', 'to chop') and *Haus* 'house'. Assuming a Gaussian distribution of this quantity allows us to filter out much of the noise. Thus, we introduce a feature f corresponding to the frequency class of a word. Its corresponding transformational distribution $\phi_r(f'|f)$ is a Gaussian distribution with some mean μ_{ϕ_r} (being a model parameter for each rule) and unit variance. The priors $P(f|w)$ and $P(\mu_\phi)$ can be skipped at this moment for the sake of simplicity, since they have little influence on the likelihood function. Note that the frequency classes are integers, so $\phi_r(f'|f)$ is in fact an integral of the Gaussian distribution on a unit interval. The means μ_ϕ are also limited to integers so that the prior can assign non-zero probabilities to concrete values.

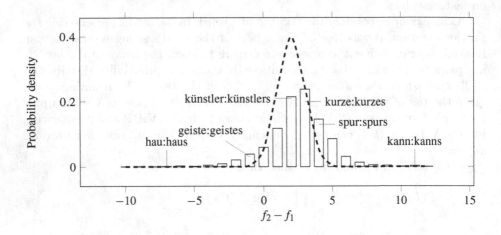

Fig. 2. Difference of frequency classes of various pairs following the rule $/X/ \rightarrow /Xs/$. The dashed line is Gaussian probability density with $\mu = 2$ and $\sigma^2 = 1$.

4.4   Local Properties

In this section, we will present some local properties of the model based on the global formulae introduced above. For the sake of simplicity, we will use the basic model without features.

Edge Score. Let's consider the contribution to the overall log-likelihood of drawing a new edge $w_1 \overset{r}{\rightarrow} w_2$, compared to a situation, where w_2 is a root. If L' denotes the lexicon with the considered edge, and L the lexicon without it, the score is given by:

$$\ln P(L'|R) - \ln P(L|R) = \ln \frac{\pi_r}{(1 - \pi_r)\lambda_L rt(w_2)} \tag{10}$$

Note that this score depends on nothing else than w_2 and π_r. This fact will play an important role in the unsupervised training algorithm.

Rule Contribution. Let ν_r denote the frequency of rule r in lexicon and μ_r the number of words, to which r could be applied, but is not. The contribution of r, together with all its corresponding edges, to the overall log-likelihood is given by:

$$-\ln(\lambda_R P(r)\pi_r^{\nu_r}(1 - \pi_r)^{\mu_r}) = -\ln \lambda_R - \ln P(r) - \nu_r \ln \pi_r - \mu_r \ln(1 - \pi_r) \tag{11}$$

Using the above formula, we can also easily derive the optimal productivity as:

$$\pi_r^* = \frac{\nu_r}{\nu_r + \mu_r} \tag{12}$$

Word Cost. When a new word is inserted into the lexicon, it can either be attached to an existing node, or left as a root.[4] The cost of insertion is thus:

$$cost(w) = -\max(\ln rt(w), \max_{\substack{r \in R \\ L \cap r^{-1}(w) \neq \emptyset}} \ln \frac{\pi_r}{1 - \pi_r}) \tag{13}$$

As the contribution to the log-likelihood is typically negative, it is plausible to call the opposite of this quantity the "cost".

Back-Formation. In some cases, adding a word as a root may seem implausible even though we do not see any possible base word. Let's consider the case of inserting *understandable*$_{\text{ADJ}}$, when *understand*$_\text{V}$ is not contained in the lexicon, but the rule $/X/_\text{V} \rightarrow /Xable/_{\text{ADJ}}$ is known and highly productive. If the root distribution *rt* has bias towards shorter words (which is the case for example for N-gram-based distributions), it may turn out, that inserting *understand* and an edge *understand* → *understandable* may yield lower cost than inserting *understandable* directly as a root. The model is thus capable of back-formation.

5   Algorithms

5.1   Preprocessing

In both unsupervised and supervised setting, the input data must be adjusted to the right format, before the actual training can start. The training data for supervised learning consist of a list of word pairs, for which the second word is known to be derived from the first. In order to convert it to a proper lexicon, a rule has to be extracted from each pair. This is done with the same algorithm as in unsupervised learning (see below).

The unsupervised learning task requires a couple more preprocessing steps. The training data consist of a list of words, with optional features (like frequency class or PoS-tag). First of all, pairs of words with sufficient string similarity are found using the FastSS algorithm [3]. The algorithm is modified in order to find morphologically related pairs: a difference of up to 5 characters at the beginning and at the end of words is allowed, as well as up to 3 characters in a single slot inside the word. While those constants can be configured arbitrarily, this setting fits to morphological rules of many languages.

Once the pairs of similar words are found, a rule is extracted from each pair. For this purpose, the Wagner-Fischer algorithm for computing string edit distance [24] is used to compute the optimal *alignment* between words. The alignment is then transformed into prefix, suffix, and internal change, plus optionally PoS-tag change if tags are used.

---

[4] For simplicity, it is assumed here that the newly inserted word does not take over any child nodes from other words.

Finally, the frequency of rules is counted and only the top-N frequent rules are preserved. This filtering step has little influence on the correctness of the results and is done for performance reasons: most extracted rules are accidental similarities between unrelated words, which typically have low frequency. Filtering them out speeds up the further processing greatly. By setting N to 10000 we can be almost sure, that all real morphological rules are preserved.

5.2 Training

Problem Formulation. In the supervised learning task, we now have a full lexicon available. It remains to find a plausible rule set, which can be done in a single Maximum Likelihood estimation step. In the unsupervised setting, the graph resulting from the preprocessing steps contains all possible edges, but the subset of those, that corresponds to the lexicon structure, still has to be found. In this case, we treat the lexicon structure as a hidden variable and apply the "hard Expectation-Maximization" algorithm, as described by Samdani et al. [20], which consists of alternating Maximum Likelihood estimations of lexicon given rule set and rule set given lexicon.

Rule Optimization. Before the ML estimation steps are carried out, an additional step is performed in both unsupervised and supervised task. At the point of rule extraction, the rules were made as general as possible: only the segments that change are recorded. For example, the rule extracted from the German pair (*achten, achtung*) would be $/XeY/ \rightarrow /XuYg/$, although the more specific pattern $/Xen/ \rightarrow /Xung/$ is definitely more appropriate. The current step fixes this problem with the help of likelihood: for each pair of words (w_1, w_2) following a rule r, we extract *all* possible rules that describe the transformation from w_1 to w_2. Then we calculate the contribution of each rule to the overall log-likelihood using (11). Finally, we choose the set of rules that minimizes the costs.

In the above example, the original rule $r : /XeY/ \rightarrow /XuYg/$ is splitted into $r_1 : /Xen/ \rightarrow /Xung/$ and $r_2 : /XeY/ \rightarrow /XuYg/$. r_1 covers the most cases, so $\nu_{r_1} \approx \nu_r$, but $\mu_{r_1} < \mu_r$, because the constraint on the left side is stronger. Thus, the last term of (11) is weakened. Also, $\pi_{r_1} > \pi_r$, which decreases the cost further. The remaining cases, like for example the accidental similarity (*ber, burg*)[5], are covered by r_2. Here, $\mu_{r_2} = \mu_r + \nu_{r_1}$, but ν_{r_2} and π_{r_2} are very small. In conclusion, the following inequality is fulfilled:

$$P(r)\pi_r^{\nu_r}(1 - \pi_r)^{\mu_r} < \lambda_R P(r_1)\pi_{r_1}^{\nu_{r_1}}(1 - \pi_{r_1})^{\mu_{r_1}} P(r_2)\pi_{r_2}^{\nu_{r_2}}(1 - \pi_{r_2})^{\mu_{r_2}} \qquad (14)$$

This justifies the splitting of r into r_1 and r_2. In unsupervised learning, this step is performed only once, before running the EM algorithm.

---

[5] Although *ber* is not a valid German word, it may happen to occur in the data, for example as an abbreviation or a foreign word.

Estimating Rules Given Lexicon. In this step, the productivity of each rule is set to the optimal value given by (12). Once it falls to 0, the rule is deleted. If the model uses frequency class as a feature, also the means μ_{ϕ_r} have to be estimated for each rule. This is done by setting each mean to the rounded average difference of frequency classes for the pairs of words following the rule.

Estimating Lexicon Given Rules. While searching for an optimal lexicon, we consider the edges obtained in the preprocessing steps and look for a subset of those, in which every node has at most one ingoing edge. This problem is known as *optimal branching* of a graph and can be solved with Chu-Liu-Edmonds' algorithm [21]. As weight of the edges, we use the contribution of an edge to the log-likelihood given by (10). The property, that this weight depends on nothing else than the pair of nodes between which the edge is drawn, is crucial at this point. It allows the weights to stay constant as the structure of the graph is manipulated.

Checking Rules. This additional step, performed after each iteration of the EM algorithm in unsupervised training, allows for easier elimination of "weak rules." The contribution of each rule to the log-likelihood (the "cost" of the rule), given by (11), is compared to the "gain," which is achieved by using this rule to derive words. In order to compute the gain of rule r, for each word w derived by r, we count the minimum cost of deriving w by another rule, or the cost of introducing w as a root if no other rule is possible. The sum of those costs constitutes the gain of r:

$$gain(r) := - \sum_{w:\xrightarrow{r}w} \max(\ln rt(w), \max_{\substack{r'\in R\setminus\{r\}\\w\in rng(r')}} \ln \frac{\pi_{r'}}{1-\pi_{r'}}) \qquad (15)$$

The notation $\xrightarrow{r} w$ means summing over all w that are derived by r in the present lexicon and $rng(r')$ means the set of words that can be derived by r'. Thus, words that contribute a lot to the gain of r are those, for which r has no good replacement. The rules, for which the cost exceeds the gain, are deleted.

5.3   Lexicon Search

Word Insertion. An insertion of a new word into the lexicon requires finding a position, at which the optimal cost, given by (13), is achieved. This is done by iterating over rules, in the order of decreasing productivity. For each rule r, it is assumed that the word w in consideration is derived by r. The corresponding base word w' is computed. If w' is not contained in the lexicon, back-formation is attempted, i.e., the recursively computed cost of inserting w' into the lexicon is added. The algorithm terminates if some rule r would yield bigger costs, than the previously considered rules, even in the "optimistic case," i.e., if the postulated base word was found in the lexicon. As the rules are sorted according to decreasing productivity, further search would yield even bigger costs. In this case, the best solution found so far is returned. The depth of the recursion of back-formation is typically restricted to some small number (like 1 or 2) for performance reasons.

If the model uses PoS-tags as a feature and the new word w is given without tag, this algorithm is also able to find the optimal tag. In this case, each time w is matched against a rule r, the tag standing on the right-hand side of r is used.

Lexicon Expansion. This algorithm finds morphologically motivated, but unknown words, which can be inserted into the lexicon with low cost. As the previous algorithm, the present one also considers rules in the order of decreasing productivity. For each rule r, words in lexicon are found, to which it could be applied, but is not. The results of applying r to those words are added to the list of newly generated words. Note that in this case, the cost of the newly generated word depends only on the productivity of the rule, since the base word is always contained in the lexicon. The algorithm terminates as the cost achieves some predefined threshold.

Note that the cost of adding a word may be negative ($\frac{\pi_r}{1-\pi_r} > 1$). In this case, the word is so strongly motivated, that the lexicon containing it is more likely than the one without it. Thus, even setting the cost threshold to 0 can result in generating new words.

6   Experiments

A full morphological analysis under the presented model would mean producing a graph akin to the one shown in Fig. 1, or equivalently, providing a derivation sequence for each word. This task is not yet approached. On one hand, evaluation and supervised learning would be difficult because of the lack of appropriate datasets (to our knowledge). On the other hand, first experiments with unsupervised learning produced results, that are not directly usable. For example, German prefixed verbs, like *erheben, beheben, anheben,* etc. are analyzed as a "chain" of derivations (*erheben → beheben → anheben,* etc.) instead of all being derived directly from a common base *heben*. This behaviour is understandable: a rule like */erX/ → /beX/* has much higher productivity than */X/ → /beX/*, because the former applies to a more restricted set of words. Also, no property of the model punishes long chains. Such analysis might even correspond to the speaker's competence, since the knowledge, that a stem occurs with prefix *er-* makes its occurrence with prefix *be-* more likely and the whole process could also take place in the absence of *heben*. However, a method of obtaining a grammatically meaningful and practically usable analysis in the unsupervised setting still has to be found.

Nevertheless, some more specific tasks have been approached with good results, demonstrating the usefulness of the model. The following sections describe its performance in predicting unseen words, lemmatization, and inflected form generation.

6.1   Lexicon Expansion

This experiment measures the capability of the model to generate new words using morphological rules. The model has been trained in the unsupervised setting on top-50k untagged wordlists obtained from the corpora of the Wortschatz Project[6] for German and Polish. All words have been lowercased; words containing characters from outside the language's alphabet were removed. Then, the lexicon expansion algorithm is used with the cost threshold of 5.0. For each language, two models were trained: with and without frequency class as a feature. The root distribution $rt(\cdot)$ is based on letter unigrams.

The precision of the results has been evaluated by matching them against lexical resources: the *list of inflected words* of the *Dictionary of the Polish Language*[7] and the German morphological analyzer Morphisto [27], respectively. An appropriate recall measure seems impossible to calculate: we would need to know *all* words, that can be predicted given the input. Instead, we plot the precision against the number of words generated.

The results are shown in Fig. 3. For both languages, the benefit of using frequency class as a feature is clearly visible, especially when generating a small number of words. At 50k words – the amount that corresponds to doubling the size of the lexicon – the precision is still around 60 %. It is important to point out, that those results may be slightly lowered, because the resources used for evaluation are not perfect. In particular, the worse results on German dataset can be due to the errors of Morphisto, which fails to recognize some existing words, e.g., *Tschetschene* or *korrelieren.*

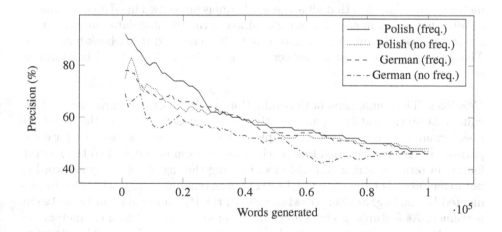

Fig. 3. Results of the unsupervised lexicon expansion task.

---

[6] http://corpora.uni-leipzig.de.
[7] http://sjp.pl/slownik/odmiany/.

6.2   Lemmatization and Tagging

The model can also be used for inflectional analysis of unknown words. In this case, the lexicon is a bipartite graph: the L_0 layer contains lemmas, and L_1 contains inflected forms. The analysis of a new word is computed by the word insertion algorithm described in Sect. 5.3. For the evaluation, we used wordlists extracted from the following tagged corpora: TIGER [4] for German and KIPI-PAN [17] for Polish. Only open lexical classes (nouns, verbs, adjectives and adverbs) were used. The only preprocessing was removing circular lemmatizations, e.g., between *Aufsichtsratsvorsitzende* and *Aufsichtsratsvorsitzender* in TIGER, which are obvious errors. In the supervised learning task, both wordlists have been divided into a training set of around 30k words and a testing set of around 10k words. Both frequency class and a full inflectional tag (containing information like case, number, gender, etc. in addition to the part of speech) were used as features. The root distribution $rt(\cdot)$ is based on letter trigrams and the tag distribution $P(t|w)$ is conditioned on the last three letters of the word. Such choices account for some morphological knowledge, which improves generating unknown lemmas through back-formation.

In the *unsupervised* learning task, the input data are a list of inflected forms and a (separate) list of lemmas. The unsupervised training algorithm has been slightly modified to incorporate the knowledge of the list of lemmas: after the full graph is generated in the preprocessing step, it is filtered so that only edges connecting a lemma to an inflected form are left.

For each language and each learning task (unsupervised/supervised), four experiments have been conducted, depending on two parameters. The **Lem** parameter set to '+' means, that all necessary lemmas are known in advance, while '–' means, that only lemmas, that are contained in the training data, are known. In the latter case, the missing lemmas have to be generated using back-formation. The **Tags** parameter states whether the tag of the analyzed word is known in advance.

Baselines. The comparison of the evaluation results to other approaches is difficult, because the results depend greatly on the datasets used and the details of task formulation. Instead, we use simple ad-hoc approaches as baselines for comparison. In the unsupervised task, each inflected form is matched to the nearest lemma in terms of string edit distance. Finding the tag of the analyzed word is not attempted. For the supervised setting, a maximum-entropy classifier implemented by the `LogisticRegression` class of the Python module `scikit-learn` is trained. As features, prefixes and suffixes of length from 1 to 3 characters are used, along with the tag, provided that **Tags** parameter is set. The classifier outputs the postulated lemmatizing rule (an idea borrowed from [7]).

Results. Table 1 shows results for the unsupervised task. The three results given for each experiment correspond to the number of words, that were correctly lemmatized, correctly tagged, and both. The string edit distance-based baseline is outperformed in all experiments. Especially the discrepancy between the baseline and the model in the case, where not all lemmas are known in advance, shows, that the model is successful in generating unknown lemmas through back-formation. The performance of tag guessing is rather poor. This is not surprising, because the correct tagging often requires knowledge of the context and should be token-based, rather than type-based. However, the model could be used as a lexical predictor for a stochastic tagger.

The results for the supervised task are given in Table 2. Also here the baseline is clearly outperformed. The top-3 experiments for both languages display very good lemmatization correctness of around 90 %, which means, that only the simultaneous absence of tags *and* lemmas poses a major problem for the model, while absence of only one of those is handled well. The baseline classifier on the other hand displays a sharp drop of performance in the absence of tags and cannot benefit from knowing the lemmas in advance (its results do not depend on **Lem** parameter at all).

Table 1. Results for unsupervised lemmatization and tagging.

	Data		Results			Baseline		
Language	Lem	Tags	Lem	Tags	Lem+Tags	Lem	Tags	Lem+Tags
German	+	+	93%	100%	93%	84%	–	–
	+	–	80%	46%	45%	76%	–	–
	–	+	76%	100%	76%	44%	–	–
	–	–	61%	34%	28%	43%	–	–
Polish	+	+	84%	100%	84%	80%	–	–
	+	–	80%	61%	59%	67%	–	–
	–	+	80%	100%	80%	41%	–	–
	–	–	79%	61%	55%	40%	–	–

Table 2. Results for supervised lemmatization and tagging.

	Data		Results			Baseline		
Language	Lem	Tags	Lem	Tags	Lem+Tags	Lem	Tags	Lem+Tags
German	+	+	97%	100%	97%	89%	97%	89%
	+	–	92%	38%	38%	19%	20%	19%
	–	+	90%	100%	90%	89%	97%	89%
	–	–	57%	20%	19%	19%	20%	19%
Polish	+	+	94%	100%	94%	83%	94%	83%
	+	–	93%	56%	56%	33%	36%	33%
	–	+	88%	100%	88%	83%	94%	83%
	–	–	68%	40%	38%	33%	36%	33%

6.3 Inflected Form Generation

Another experiment concerning inflectional morphology is generating an inflected word form given the lemma and the tag of the target form. For this purpose, the supervised models and datasets from the previous section were used. The baseline is a similar classifier as in the previous experiments: it also uses prefixes and suffixes of length from 1 to 3 as features, in addition to the lemma tag and the target tag. The resulting class is the rule that produces the inflected form. The results are given in Table 3. The baseline is slightly outperformed by our model.

Table 3. Results for supervised inflected form generation.

Language	Result	Baseline
German	84 %	83 %
Polish	86 %	84 %

7 Further Work

Compounds. Conforming to the WWM theory, the model treats compounding rules as simple derivational rules, with one of the parts fixed. However, a generalization which would allow to create new compounds, in which neither part has previously been seen as a part of a compound, would be desirable. It is planned to introduce "meta-rules" (or "second-order rules") into the model: a kind of rules that would apply to *words* and produce *rules*. For example, a meta-rule $/X/ \rightarrow (/Y/ \rightarrow /XsY/)$ would apply to the word *Arbeit* to create $/Y/ \rightarrow /arbeitsY/$, which could be futher applied to *Markt* to derive *Arbeitsmarkt*. In this fashion, the analysis of compounding postulated by WWM would be maintained and the productivity of this phenomenon would be fully accounted for. However, a serious unsolved problem is that it would make the rule set depend on the lexicon, which means, that the dependency between those two would become circular.

Learning Paradigms. The notion of *paradigm* could be understood in our model as "a group of rules that frequently occur together". Those could be incorporated into the model by using a paradigm ID in the same way as a PoS tag. Knowing the paradigm IDs of words would greatly increase the productivity of rules by decreasing the μ_r-values (see (12)), because each rule could only apply to words following a certain paradigm. The paradigm IDs could thus be assigned automatically, in a fashion that maximizes the log-likelihood.

Segmentation. Although not all morphological phenomena can be described in terms of morphemes, word segmentation remains a useful description in many cases. The relational description produced by our model identifies groups of related words. Such groups can be used for segmentation into morphemes, for example with multiple sequence alignment methods explored by Kirschenbaum [12]. This additional output would make it easier to compare our model to other tools and help make it available for users, who are not convinced by the WWM theory.

Token-Based Tagging. As pointed out in Sect. 6.2, finding the right tag of an unknown word requires knowledge of the context, in addition to morphological criteria. Therefore, integrating the model with a stochastic tagger (e.g., HMM-based) will be attempted.

8 Conclusion

We have presented a probabilistic model based on the Whole Word Morphology theory. The model is an alternative to the widely used segmentation-oriented approaches. It employs a relational description of morphology, without attempting to decompose words into smaller structural units. In this way, both concatenative and non-concatenative morphological phenomena can be described in a unified way. The underlying linguistic theory is minimalistic and the behaviour of the model can be controlled by training data and prior distributions, which makes it appliable for many languages and use cases. Contrary to many machine learning approaches, the trained model, which consists of a lexicon and a set of rules with assigned probabilities, is easily interpretable and can be edited by a human expert.

The generative model contains broad knowledge, which can be attributed to "morphological competence." By manipulating its probability distributions, a single trained model can be applied to various tasks, like for instance lemmatizing unknown words, producing inflected forms, or anticipating unknown vocabulary. It is also flexible with respect to the data employed in solving those tasks: features like PoS-tag and word frequency (and possibly others) are optional, as well as labeled training data.

In addition to its machine learning capabilities, the model could perhaps also contribute to empirical linguistic studies. The definition of "productivity" as the probability of applying a rule, when the necessary conditions for applying it are met, seems reasonable from a linguistic point of view. The model accounts for phenomena like back-formation or analogy, the latter being justified in reducing the number of rules and the preference of more productive rules over less productive. As the lexicon is a part of the model and its content affects the probabilities assigned to words, the differences in morphological competence between various speakers of a language could be modeled through the differences in the content of their lexica, whereas the rules tend to be a property of the language and thus same for every speaker.

References

1. Anderson, S.R.: A-Morphous Morphology, Cambridge Studies in Linguistics, vol. 62. Cambridge University Press, New York (1992)
2. Aronoff, M.: Word Formation in Generative Grammar. The MIT Press, Cambridge (1976)
3. Bocek, T., Hunt, E., Stiller, B.: Fast Similarity Search in Large Dictionaries. Technical report, University of Zurich (2007)
4. Brants, S., Dipper, S., Eisenberg, P., Hansen, S., König, E., Lezius, W., Rohrer, C., Smith, G., Uszkoreit, H.: TIGER: linguistic interpretation of a German corpus. J. Lang. Comput. **2**, 597–620 (2004)
5. Can, B.: Statistical Models for Unsupervised Learning of Morphology and POS Tagging. Ph.D. thesis, University of York (2011)
6. Chan, E.: Learning probabilistic paradigms for morphology. In: Proceedings of the Eighth Meeting of the ACL Special Interest Group on Computational Phonology at HLT-NAACL, pp. 69–78 (2006)
7. Chrupała, G., Dinu, G., van Genabith, J.: Learning morphology with morfette. In: Proceedings of the 6th International Conference on Language Resources and Evaluation, LREC 2008, pp. 2362–2367 (2008)
8. Durrett, G., DeNero, J.: Supervised learning of complete morphological paradigms. In: Proceedings of the 2013 Conference of the North American Chapter of the Association for Computational Linguistics: Human Language Technologies, pp. 1185–1195 (2013)
9. Ford, A., Singh, R., Martohardjono, G.: Pace Pini: towards a word-based theory of morphology. American University Studies. Series XIII, Linguistics, vol. 34. Peter Lang Publishing Incorporated (1997)
10. Hammarström, H., Borin, L.: Unsupervised learning of morphology. Comput. Linguist. **37**(2), 309–350 (2011)
11. Janicki, M.: Unsupervised learning of a-morphous inflection with graph clustering. In: Proceedings of the Student Research Workshop associated with RANLP 2013, Hissar, Bulgaria, pp. 93–99 (2013)
12. Kirschenbaum, A.: Unsupervised segmentation for different types of morphological processes using multiple sequence alignment. In: Dediu, A.-H., Martín-Vide, C., Mitkov, R., Truthe, B. (eds.) SLSP 2013. LNCS, vol. 7978, pp. 152–163. Springer, Heidelberg (2013)
13. Kurimo, M., Virpioja, S., Turunen, V., Lagus, K.: Morpho challenge 2005–2010: evaluations and results. In: Proceedings of the 11th Meeting of the ACL-SIGMORPHON, ACL 2010, pp. 87–95, July 2010
14. Mikheev, A.: Automatic rule induction for unknown word guessing. Comput. Linguist. **23**, 405–423 (1997)
15. Neuvel, S., Fulop, S.A.: Unsupervised learning of morphology without morphemes. In: Proceedings of the 6th Workshop of the ACL Special Interest Group in Computational Phonology (SIGPHON), pp. 31–40 (2002)
16. Poon, H., Cherry, C., Toutanova, K.: Unsupervised morphological segmentation with log-linear models. In: Proceedings of Human Language Technologies The 2009 Annual Conference of the North American Chapter of the Association for Computational Linguistics on NAACL 2009, pp. 209–217 (2009)
17. Przepiórkowski, A.: The IPI PAN Corpus: Preliminary Version. Institute of Computer Science, Polish Academy of Sciences, Warsaw (2004)

18. Rasooli, M.S., Lippincott, T., Habash, N., Rambow, O.: Unsupervised morphology-based vocabulary expansion. In: ACL, pp. 1349–1359 (2014)
19. Ruokolainen, T., Kohonen, O., Virpioja, S., Kurimo, M.: Supervised morphological segmentation in a low-resource learning setting using conditional random fields. In: Proceedings of the Seventeenth Conference on Computational Natural Language Learning (CoNLL), Sofia, Bulgaria, pp. 29–37 (2013)
20. Samdani, R., Chang, M.W., Roth, D.: Unified expectation maximization. In: 2012 Conference of the North American Chapter of the Association for Computational Linguistics: Human Language Technologies, pp. 688–698 (2012)
21. Tarjan, R.E.: Finding optimum branchings. Networks **7**, 25–35 (1977)
22. Tseng, H., Jurafsky, D., Manning, C.: Morphological features help POS tagging of unknown words across language varieties. In: Proceedings of the Fourth SIGHAN Workshop on Chinese Language Processing, pp. 32–39 (2005)
23. Virpioja, S., Smit, P., Grönroos, S.A., Kurimo, M.: Morfessor 2.0: Python Implementation and Extensions for Morfessor Baseline. Technical report, Aalto University, Helsinki (2013)
24. Wagner, R.A., Fischer, M.J.: The string-to-string correction problem. J. ACM **21**(1), 168–173 (1974)
25. Wicentowski, R.H.: Modeling and Learning Multilingual Inflectional Morphology in a Minimally Supervised Framework. Ph.D. thesis, Johns Hopkins University (2002)
26. Yarowsky, D., Wicentowski, R.: Minimally supervised morphological analysis by multimodal alignment. In: ACL 2000, pp. 207–216 (2000)
27. Zielinski, A., Simon, C.: morphisto - an open source morphological analyzer for German. In: 7th International Workshop on Finite-State Methods and Natural Language Processing, FSMNLP 2008, pp. 224–231. Ispra, Italy (2008)

Using HFST—Helsinki Finite-State Technology for Recognizing Semantic Frames

Krister Lindén[✉], Sam Hardwick, Miikka Silfverberg, and Erik Axelson

University of Helsinki, Helsinki, Finland
{krister.linden,sam.hardwick,miikka.silfverberg,
erik.axelson}@helsinki.fi

Abstract. To recognize semantic frames in languages with a rich morphology, we need computational morphology. In this paper, we look at one particular framework, HFST–Helsinki Finite-State Technology, and how to use it for recognizing semantic frames in context. HFST enables tokenization, morphological analysis, tagging, and frame annotation in one single framework.

1 Introduction

Language technology enables text mining, e.g., by recognizing semantic frames. In this paper we will look at one particular framework, HFST–Helsinki Finite-State Technology, and its use in processing text from tokenization to recognizing semantic frames in context.

HFST–Helsinki Finite Technology is a framework for building morphologies including morphological lexicons [13–15]. We present how HFST *identifies semantic frames in context*. To do so, we first present how HFST supports building tokenizers and taggers, which is the minimum requirement for recognizing semantic frames in languages with a rich morphology. In Sect. 2, we give an overview of the HFST p-match syntax and some examples of how to develop a tokenizer based on a lexicon containing multi-word expressions. In Sect. 3, we give an introduction to building morphological taggers with HFST using machine learning. In Sect. 4, we give an introduction to semantic frame recognition with HFST. In Sect. 5, we give a brief evaluation of developing a rule set for semantic frame annotation. In Sect. 6, we discuss our results compared with other approaches to semantic frame annotation.

2 Tokenization Using `hfst-pmatch`

Tokenization is a necessary first step in most text-based natural language processing tasks. For some languages, e.g., English, it is often considered to be a mechanical preprocessing task without linguistic importance, whereas for others, e.g., Chinese, it is an intricate task called segmentation. However, even in languages that generally insert spaces between words, there are issues that influence the quality or feasibility of tools down the pipeline. We may, for example,

© Springer International Publishing Switzerland 2015
C. Mahlow and M. Piotrowski (Eds.): SFCM 2015, CCIS 537, pp. 124–136, 2015.
DOI: 10.1007/978-3-319-23980-4_8

want to be able to identify multi-word units, identify compound words and mark their internal boundaries, control various dimensions of normalization, or produce possible part-of-speech tags or deeper morphological analyses. We describe a general approach to these issues based on morphological transducers, regular expressions and the pattern matching operation pmatch [10].

2.1 A Short Introduction to pmatch

pmatch [13] is a pattern-matching operation for text based on regular expressions. In HFST, it has been further developed from the ideas in Xerox fst. The regular expressions, i.e., *rules*, are named, and are invoked ultimately by a root expression, i.e. the *top level*, which by convention has the name TOP. Expressions may refer to themselves or each other circularly by special arcs which are interpreted at runtime, allowing context-free grammars to be expressed.

Matching operates in a loop, accepting the largest possible amount of input from the current position, possibly modifying it according to the rules and tagging left and right boundaries of sub-rules, and continuing on the the next position in the input. When the rules successfully accept (and possibly transform) some length of input, that is a *match*. When the match has triggered the operation of a tagging directive, e.g., EndTag(TagName) or [].t(TagName), the enclosed length of the input is tagged with *TagName*. For example, here is a very naïve tokenizer for English

```
define TOP [[ ("'") Alpha+ ] | Sigma({,.;!?})]] EndTag(w);
```

where Sigma() is a function that extracts the alphabet of its argument, which in this case is some punctuation marks given as a string denoted by curly braces. When operated on the sentence *"If I am out of my mind, it's all right with me, thought Moses Herzog."*, it produces output that looks like this

```
<w>If</w> <w>I</w> <w>am</w> <w>out</w> <w>of</w> <w>my</w>
<w>mind</w> <w>,</w> <w>it</w> <w>'s</w> <w>all</w> <w>right</w>
<w>with</w> <w>me</w><w>,</w> <w>thought</w> <w>Moses</w>
<w>Herzog</w> <w>.</w>
```

in normal *matching mode*. The runtime operation of matching can be controlled to only output the matched parts, or give positions and lengths of tagged parts in *locate mode* as well as operating as a more conventional tokenizer outputting one token per line in *extract-matches mode*.

2.2 Tokenizing with a Dictionary

A tokenizer consists of the input side of a morphological dictionary. Good coverage in vocabulary and derivation can satisfactorily solve many tokenization headaches on its own. For example, consider the plural possessive of the compound in

(1) The Attorney-Generals' biographies are over there.

To get the tokenization of the example exactly right, a tokenization rule needs to understand that the hyphen is joining parts of a compound word, unlike in e.g., *Borg-McEnroe*, and that the apostrophe is indicating the possessive form, not the end of a quotation. A dictionary can also be augmented to recover from formatting or digitization issues. For example, a text may split words at line boundaries with hyphens, as in

(2) He seemed suddenly to have been endowed with super-human strength

In this example, the correct tokenization is *superhuman* rather than *super* and *human*, but a dictionary would miss this possibility. However, we can use a finite-state operation to allow the string $-\backslash$n (hyphen followed by a newline) to appear anywhere inside the words in the dictionary. In regular expressions this operation is sometimes called *ignoring*.

2.3   Preserving the Parts of a Multi-word Unit

Dictionaries are often equipped with a collection of short idioms, e.g., *in view of*, and other tokens which include whitespace, e.g., *New York*. While these are useful, it may be too early at this stage to fix the tokenization as the longest possible match. A discriminative tagger may not be able to make the correct choice in

(3) The ball was in view of the referee.

if it only sees a tokenization where *in view of* is a single token.

We can extend the dictionary in a simple way to also contain the other possible tokenizations and, in the case of a morphological dictionary, the analyses, as follows

```
define combined_tokens [dict].u .o. [dict | [" " dict]*]
```

where `dict` is our dictionary and `[dict].u` is its input projection. We compose it with arbitrarily many copies of itself, interspersed with space characters. The result contains every multi-word expression both as itself, and as a combination of other words found in the dictionary.

In addition to bare tokens, many downstream tools use analysis cohorts, i.e., the full set of possible base forms and morphological tags for the token in question. The `hfst-pmatch` utility exposes an API that allows retrieval of the position, length, input, output, tag and weight of each of the longest matches, so cohort formatters can be written. For example, suppose our dictionary includes the following entries when tokenizing *in view of*. The combined dictionary will then produce the full set of combinations which may be formatted as follows

in	in AVP	in NN0	in PRP
view	view NN1	view VVB	view VVI
of	of PRF	of PRP	
in view of		in view of PRP	

```
"<in view of>"
  "in view of" PRP
  "in" AVP "view" VVI "of" PRF
  "in" NN0 "view" VVB "of" PRF
  "in" NN0 "view" VVB "of" PRP
  "in" NN0 "view" VVI "of" PRF
  etc.
```

Since in pmatch multiple rules operate on the same input, it is possible to integrate higher-level tokenization, such as chunking, named-entity recognition, grouping tokens into sentences and sentences into paragraphs in the same ruleset.

3 Morphological Tagging using hfst-finnpos

In this section, we describe the morphological tagger hfst-finnpos.

FinnPos [20] is a data driven *morphological tagging* toolkit distributed with the HFST interface. The term morphological tagging [6] refers to assigning one full morphological label, including for example part-of-speech, tense, case, and number, to each word in a text. It can be contrasted with POS tagging where the task is to infer the correct part-of-speech for each word.

The FinnPos toolkit is based on the Conditional Random Field (CRF) framework [12] for data driven learning. Most work on CRF taggers and other discriminative taggers has concentrated on POS tagging for English, which has a very limited selection of productive morphological phenomena. In contrast, FinnPos is especially geared toward morphologically rich languages with large label sets, that cause data sparsity and slow down estimation when using standard solutions. FinnPos gives state-of-the-art results for the morphologically rich language Finnish [20] both with regard to runtime and accuracy. In addition to morphological tagging, FinnPos also performs data driven lemmatization. Moreover, it can be combined with a morphological analyzer to make a data-driven morphological disambiguator. The capability of FinnPos to take advantage of the linguistic choices made by developers of morphological lexicons is the reason for including FinnPos in the HFST tool set.

In this section, we will focus on describing FinnPos from a practical point of view. A more detailed description of the theoretical foundations as well as evaluation can be found in [20].

3.1   FinnPos for Morphologically Rich Languages

In part-of-speech (POS) tagging, the label sets are usually fairly small. For example, the Penn Treebank uses only 45 distinct label types. When tagging morphologically complex languages, where full morphological labels are required, vastly larger label sets are used. Label sets of around 1,000 distinct label types frequently occur.

Large label sets create a data sparsity problem. For example, for a second order language model and a label set of 1,000 distinct label types, an overwhelming majority of the one billion possible $(1,000^3)$ label trigrams are never seen in a training corpus of realistic scope. Even label unigrams may be rare as many label unigrams tyically occur only a couple of times in a training corpus.

Although morphological label sets can be very large, individual labels are usually created by combining smaller sub-units from a relatively small inventory. A typical example of such a structured morphological label is the label Noun|Sg|Nom, which consists of three sub units: the main word class Noun, the singular number Sg and the nominative case Nom. FinnPos utilizes the internal structure of complex labels by extracting features for sub-units as well as for the entire labels [19]. This alleviates the data sparsity problem because features relating to sub-units of entire tags are used as fall-back. Additionally, sub-unit features allow FinnPos to model grammatical generalizations such as case congruence in isolation of the full labels.

In addition to data sparsity, large label sets cause long training times because the complexity of standard CRF training of an nth order model depends on the $(n + 1)$st power of the label set size. To speed up training, FinnPos uses an adaptive beam search and a label guesser [20] during inference and estimation. These substantially reduce run-time.

3.2   Training and Using a Model

FinnPos uses an averaged perceptron algorithm with early stopping for estimation of model parameters. The error-driven perceptron training algorithm iterates through the training corpus one sentence at a time, labels the sentences and adjusts model weights when erroneous labels are detected. Usually the Viterbi algorithm [2] is used for labeling. This, however, is too slow in practice when dealing with large label sets.

Instead of the Viterbi algorithm, FinnPos uses beam search with an adaptive beam width [18]. Additionally FinnPos uses a generative label guesser modeled after the OOV word model used in [1] to restrict label candidates during training. Because of inexact inference during the training phase, FinnPos additionally uses violation fixing [8].

3.3   FinnPos and Morphological Analyzers

FinnPos benefits from a morphological analyzer for morphological disambiguation. The analyzer can be used in two ways: to provide label candidates for words and as a generator of features. For words not recognized by the analyzer,

FinnPos will use a data-driven suffix-based guesser to generate label candidates. In addition to the morpological label, FinnPos also uses the morphological analyzer for determining the lemma of a given word. For words not recognized by the analyzer, a data-driven lemmatizer is used instead. The data-driven components are learned from the training corpora, which means that the FinnPos tagger could be used without a morphological analyzer, but a lexicon with reasonable coverage improves the tagging performance.

4 Semantic Tagging Using `hfst-pmatch`

In this section, we outline a scheme for extracting semantic frames from text using hand-written rules. The rules and approach have been demonstrated in [7]. The current paper is more extensive and includes an evaluation of the rule set. While it does not currently represent a system for extracting a large number of different frames, the `hfst-pmatch` tool has been extensively tested in a full-fledged named-entity recognizer for Swedish [11]. Our motivation here is to present additional capabilities of `hfst-pmatch` as a natural language processing system for extracting factoids from textual data to be used in text and data mining.

4.1 Introduction

A semantic frame [5] is a description of a *type* of event, relation or entity and related participants. For example, in FrameNet, a database of semantic frames, the description of an `Entity` in terms of physical space occupied by it is an instance of the semantic frame `Size`. The frame is evoked by a *lexical unit* (LU), also known as a *frame evoking element* (FEE), which is a word, in this case an adjective, such as *big* or *tiny*, descriptive of the size of the `Entity`. Apart from an `Entity`, which is a core or compulsory element, the frame may identify a `Degree` to which the `Entity` deviates from the norm, e.g., *a **really** big dog*, and a `Standard` with which it is compared, e.g., *tall **for a jockey*** (Tables 1 and 2).

Table 1. The semantic frame *Size*.

Lexical unit (LU)	Adjective describing magnitude (large, tiny, ...)
Entity (E)	That which is being described (house, debt, ...)
Degree (D), optional	Intensity or extent of description (really, quite, ...)
Standard (S), optional	A point of comparison (for a jockey, ...)

For example:

Table 2. A tagged example of *Size*

$$\left[_{\text{Size}} \left[_{\text{E}} \text{He}\right] \text{is} \left[_{\text{D}} \text{quite}\right] \left[_{\text{LU}} \text{tall}\right] \left[_{\text{S}} \text{for a jockey}\right]\right]$$

4.2   A Rule

A simple and common syntactic realization of the Size frame is a single noun phrase containing one of the LUs, such as *the big brown dog that ran away*. Here we would like to identify *big* as LU, *brown dog* as Entity and the combination as Size. Our first rule for identifying this type of construction might be

Table 3. A simplified first rule

```
define LU {small} | {large} | {big} EndTag(LU);
define Size1 LU (Adjective) [Noun EndTag(Entity)].t(Entity);
define TOP Size1 EndTag(Size);
```

This rule set has been simplified for brevity—it only has a few of the permitted LUs, and word boundary issues have not been addressed. The [].t() syntax in the definition of Size1 is a tag delimiter controlling the area tagged as Entity. The extra Adjective is optional, which is conveyed by the surrounding parentheses (Table 3).

We can verify that our rules extract instances of our intended pattern by compiling them with hfst-pmatch2fst and running the compiled result with hfst-pmatch --extract-tags. In the following we have input the text of the King James Bible from Project Gutenberg[1] and allowed some extra characters on both sides for a concordance-like effect:

```
...
there lay a <Size><LU>small</LU> round <Entity>thing</Entity></Size>
...
there was a <Size><LU>great</LU> <Entity>cry</Entity></Size> in Egypt
...
saw that <Size><LU>great</LU> <Entity>work</Entity></Size> which
...
```

A natural next step is to add optional non-core elements, such as an adverb preceding the LU being tagged as Degree and a noun phrase beginning with *for a* following it as Standard (Table 4).

Table 4. Extending the rule with optional elements

```
define Size1 [Adverb].t(Degree) LU (Adjective) [Noun].t(Entity)
             [{for a} NP].t(Standard);
```

and here are some examples this rule finds in the British National Corpus[2]:

----

[1] http://gutenberg.org.
[2] http://www.natcorp.ox.ac.uk/.

```
...
presence of an <Size><Degree>arbitrarily</Degree>
   <LU>small</LU> <Entity>amount</Entity></Size> of dust
...
one <Size><LU>small</LU> <Entity>step</Entity>
   <Standard>for a man</Standard> </Size>
...
```

We can see that in *small amount of dust*, we might want to tag not just the immediate noun as `Entity` but the entire noun phrase which could be implemented up to a context-free definition of a noun phrase, and in *one small step for a man* a common indirect use of the `Standard` construction. As well as correct matches, such as *small round thing* in the biblical example, we have metaphorical meanings of `Size`, such as *great cry*. This may or may not be desired—perhaps we wish to do further processing to identify the target domains of such metaphors, or perhaps we wish to be able to annotate physical size, and physical size only.

4.3   Incorporating Semantic Information

Size is a very metaphorical concept, and syntactic rules as above will produce a large amount of matches that relate to such uses, e.g., *a great cry* or *a big deal*. If we wish to refine our rules to detect such uses, there are a few avenues to explore. First of all, some LUs are much more metaphorical than others. A *great man* is almost certainly a metaphorical use, whereas a *tall man* is almost certainly concrete. Accuracy may be improved by requiring *great* to be used together with common nouns meaning several individuals like a *great crowd*. In addition, there are semantic classifications of words, such as WordNet [17]. We may compile the set of hyponyms of *physical entity* and require them to appear as the nouns in our rules as shown in Table 5.

Table 5. Reading an external linguistic resource

```
define phys_entity  @txt"phys_entity.txt";
```

4.4   Incorporating Part-of-Speech Information

We have so far used named rules for matching word classes like `Noun`, without specifying how they are identified. Also our collection of LUs might need some closer attention—for example *little* could be an adverb. Considering that in writing our rules, we are effectively doing shallow syntactic parsing, even a very simple way to identify parts of speech may suffice, e.g., a morphological dictionary. For example, a finite-state transducer representing English morphology may be used to define the class of common nouns as in Table 6. If we have the use of a part-of-speech tagger, we may write our rules to act on its output, as in Table 7 where `W` refers to some word delimiter.

Table 6. Using a dictionary to extract words of a given word-class

```
! The lexicon we want to read
define English @bin"english.hfst";
! We compose it with a noun filter and extract the input side
define Noun  [ English .o. [?+ "<NN1>" | "<NN2>"] ].u;
! (NN1 is singular, NN2 plural)
```

Table 7. Using tags in pre-tagged text

```
define Noun LC(W) Wordchar+ ["<NN1>"|"<NN2>"] RC(W);
```

4.5 Increasing Coverage

Having considered for each rule where **Degree** and **Standard** may occur, coverage may be evaluated by also finding those cases where a LU is used as an adjective but does not match the current rules, for example:

```
define TOP Size1 | Size2 | [LU].t(NonmatchingLU);
```

The valid match is always the longest possible one, so `NonmatchingLU` will be the tag only if no subsuming `SizeN` rule applies. For example in

```
the moving human body is <NonmatchingLU>large</NonmatchingLU>,
obtrusive and highly visible
```

we see another realization of the `Size` frame: the `Entity` is followed by a copula, and the LU appears to the right. We can write a new rule `Size2` to capture this, adding positions for non-core elements either by linguistic reasoning or by searching the corpus.

5   Evaluation

FrameNet has published a tagged extract of the American National Corpus[3,4], consisting of 24 texts. Of these, one uses the `Size` frame 35 times, but the remainder use it only an additional 6 times for a total of 41 times. This is too thin a selection and suggests some inconsistency in the use of this frame vs.some

---

[3] http://www.anc.org.
[4] The FrameNet-annotated texts are at https://framenet.icsi.berkeley.edu/fndrupal/index.php?q=fulltextIndex.

alternative ones such as `Dimension`, and various metaphorical sub-cases of that frame. Evaluating the extraction of the `Size` frame on the basis of this minute corpus was unfeasible, but we used it as a reference when developing our own training and test set.

To develop our rule set, we took 200 sentences of the British National Corpus containing, as a token, one of the LUs, and tagged them by hand. We considered a LU to be any inflected form of a word of the synonyms to *size* given by WordNet including metaphorical meanings of size. The sentences had POS tags from the original material, but punctuation and information about multi-word units was removed before developing the rule set. This corresponds to running surface text through a POS tagger which does not recognize multi-word expressions before running the frame extractor.

We had one person spend a working day developing rules based on our set of training samples, iterating a process of spotting the difference between the hand-tagged samples and the tagging produced by our rules, and modifying the rule set. This resulted in two top-level rules, one corresponding to cases where the LU precedes the `Entity`, and one to cases where it follows as these were the only compulsory elements in the frame. Overall, the rule set was 46 lines long, excluding comments and whitespace.

To get an idea of the quality of the rules, we also hand-tagged another 100 sentences from the same corpus. These do not necessarily contain the `Size` frame to test that the rules do not over-generate. Of these sentences, 81 were tagged completely correctly by the rule set. Results by LU are in Table 8.

Table 8. LU-level semantic tagging performance on the 100 sentence test set

Number of sentences	100
Number of LUs	113
Number of LUs corresponding to a `Size` frame	56
Number thereof matched by the rules	50
Total number of matches made by the rules	54
Coverage	89 %
Accuracy	93 %

In Table 8, a match in the test material is considered correct if the relevant LU is correctly identified. We explore some further details regarding the quality of both correct and incorrect test matches in Table 9.

We note that the test tagging was not independent of us but no other tagging existed and that the overall amount of both training and test material is rather small. We do not think this is a conclusive result, but it is an indication of the semantic tagger that could be developed in a relatively small amount of time with this approach.

Table 9. Quality of matches made by the rules in the test samples

Matches where wrong `Entity` was tagged	4(8 %)
Matches where `Entity` was partially wrongly tagged	8(16 %)
Matches where `Degree` was incorrectly tagged	2(33 % of hand-tagged `Degrees`)
Incorrect tagging due to insufficient rule sophistication	9(53 % of mistakes)
Incorrect tagging due to mistakes in POS tagging	5(29 % of mistakes)
Incorrect tagging due to lacking multi-word unit information	2(12 %)
Incorrect tagging due to lacking multi-word unit information	1(16 %)

6   Discussion

In this section, we contrast HFST with some other semantic frameworks for recognizing semantic frames, i.e., Shalmaneser [4], LTH [9] and SEMAFOR [3].

Shalmanser treats semantic frame extraction as a pipeline of syntactic parsing, frame identification, semantic argument identification and semantic role labeling. Syntactic parsing uses an external toolkit. Note that frame identification precedes role labeling, i.e., they are not done in parallel. However, Erk and Pado [4] claim that this would give very small gains in accuracy while incurring huge CPU cost. Shalmaneser can be trained for any semantic annotation scheme provided appropriate training data exists. Users can replace some components of the system with customized components. Full scale models for English and German are available. Evaluation was done on manually annotated data. FrameNet 1.2 for English and the SALSA corpus for German. Evaluation is with regard to the F1-score on unlabeled argument chunks and labeling accuracy for argument labels. The F1-score for argument chunks was 0.751 for English and 0.6 for German. Argument label accuracy was 0.784 for English and 0.673 for German.

LTH also treats semantic frame extraction as a pipeline of syntactic parsing, frame identification, semantic argument identification, and semantic role labeling. In contrast to many other systems, LTH uses a dependency syntactic parser instead of a constituent parser. Frame identification is accomplished using a classifier based on input words and dependency structure. To aid argument identification, the FrameNet lexical database was extended with WordNet data. A classifier was trained to identify words that were likely to belong to a given semantic frame. Evaluation was with regard to F1-score for frames and frame elements. As training data, FrameNet 1.3 was used; as test data, three manually annotated segments from the American National Corpus were used. The data sets come from the SemEval 2007 joint task on frame semantic structure extraction. The F1-score for English on the test data was 0.621.

The basic architecture of SEMAFOR is similar to Shalmaneser and LTH. The frame parsing task is divided into two sub-tasks: predicate identification and argument identification. SEMAFOR features a latent-variable model, semi-supervised extension of the predicate lexicon and joint identification of the entire argument set of a predicate using linear programming. This allows for integration of linguistic constraints on the argument sets in a principled way. A model for

English is available. The evaluation and data was the same as for LTH. The F1-score on English is 0.645.

In contrast, HFST treats semantic frame extraction as a pipeline in only two stages: morphological tagging and semantic labeling, i.e., frame identification, semantic argument identification, and semantic role labeling are done in parallel. The fact that HFST recognizes the whole frame in one step, means that HFST has access to the whole frame element configuration when making the decision to commit to the frame and the argument labels. In addition, HFST can take linguistic constraints into consideration both in the morphological and the frame and role labeling tasks. This contributes to the high coverage and accuracy in the evaluation which no doubt is still much too limited. When the whole semantic frame and all its argument roles are considered at the same time, HFST removes part of the need for syntactic processing as an intermediate step, but nothing prevents a user from replacing or enriching the morphological tagging with information from a syntactic parser. Future work is a large-scale evaluation of HFST for semantic frame and role labeling of a semantically rich language like Finnish where we will draw on the availability of FinnWordNet [16] to extend the lexical unit coverage.

7   Conclusion

In this paper, we have outlined the steps involved when using HFST–Helsinki Finite-State Technology for recognizing semantic frames in context. A small-scale evaluation indicates that the setup is capable of highly accurate semantic information labeling.

References

1. Brants, T.: TnT: a statistical part-of-speech tagger. In: Proceedings of the Sixth Conference on Applied Natural Language Processing, pp. 224–231 (2000)
2. Collins, M.: Discriminative training methods for hidden markov models: theory and experiments with perceptron algorithms. In: Proceedings of the ACL-02 Conference on Empirical Methods in Natural Language Processing, EMNLP 2002, vol. 10, pp. 1–8. Association for Computational Linguistics, Stroudsburg (2002)
3. Das, D., Chen, D., Martins, A., Schneider, N., Smith, N.: Frame-semantic parsing. Comput. Linguist. **40**(1), 9–56 (2014)
4. Erk, K., Pado, S.: Shalmaneser – a flexible toolbox for semantic role assignment. In: Proceedings of the Fifth International Conference on Language Resources and Evaluation (LREC2006) (2006)
5. Fillmore, C.J.: Frame semantics and the nature of language. Annals New York Acad. Sci.: Conf. Origin Dev. Lang. Speech **280**(1), 20–32 (1976)
6. Grzegorz Chrupala, G.D., van Genabith, J.: Learning morphology with Morfette. In: Proceedings of the Sixth International Conference on Language Resources and Evaluation (LREC 2008). European Language Resources Association (ELRA), Marrakech, May 2008
7. Harwick, S., Silfverberg, M., Lindén, K.: Extracting semantic frames using hfst-pmatch. In: Proceedings from NODALIDA 2015, pp. 305–308. Vilnius, May 2015

8. Huang, L., Fayong, S., Guo, Y.: Structured perceptron with inexact search. In: Proceedings of the 2012 Conference of the North American Chapter of the Association for Computational Linguistics: Human Language Technologies, pp. 142–151 (2012)
9. Johansson, R., Nugues, P.: LTH: semantic structure extraction using non-projective dependency trees. In: Proceedings of SEMEVAL 2007 (2007)
10. Karttunen, L.: Beyond morphology: pattern matching with FST. In: Mahlow, C., Piotrowski, M. (eds.) SFCM 2011. CCIS, vol. 100, pp. 1–13. Springer, Heidelberg (2011)
11. Kokkinakis, D., Niemi, J., Hardwick, S., Lindén, K., Borin, L.: HFST-sweNER - a new NER resource for Swedish. In: Proceedings of the 9th Edition of the Language Resources and Evaluation Conference (LREC 2014), Reykjavik 26–31 May 2014, pp. 2537–2543 (2014)
12. Lafferty, J.D., McCallum, A., Pereira, F.C.N.: Conditional random fields: probabilistic models for segmenting and labeling sequence data. In: Proceedings of the Eighteenth International Conference on Machine Learning, ICML 2001, pp. 282–289. Morgan Kaufmann Publishers Inc., San Francisco (2001)
13. Lindén, K., Axelson, E., Drobac, S., Hardwick, S., Kuokkala, J., Niemi, J., Pirinen, T.A., Silfverberg, M.: HFST — a system for creating NLP tools. In: Mahlow, C., Piotrowski, M. (eds.) SFCM 2013. CCIS, vol. 380, pp. 53–71. Springer, Heidelberg (2013)
14. Lindén, K., Axelson, E., Hardwick, S., Pirinen, T.A., Silfverberg, M.: HFST—framework for compiling and applying morphologies. In: Mahlow, C., Piotrowski, M. (eds.) SFCM 2011. CCIS, vol. 100, pp. 67–85. Springer, Heidelberg (2011)
15. Lindén, K., Silfverberg, M., Pirinen, T.: HFST tools for morphology – an efficient open-source package for construction of morphological analyzers. In: Mahlow, C., Piotrowski, M. (eds.) SFCM 2009. CCIS, vol. 41, pp. 28–47. Springer, Heidelberg (2009)
16. Lindén, K., Carlson, L.: FinnWordNet – WordNet p finska via ttning (in Swedish with an English abstract). LexicoNordica – Nordic J. Lexicogr. 17, 119–140 (2010)
17. Miller, G.A.: Wordnet: a lexical database for English. Commun. ACM 38(11), 39–41 (1995)
18. Pal, C., Sutton, C., McCallum, A.: Sparse forward-backward using minimum divergence beams for fast training of conditional random fields. In: 2006 IEEE International Conference on Acoustics, Speech and Signal Processing, ICASSP 2006 Proceedings, vol. 5, pp. V-581–V-584. IEEE (2006)
19. Silfverberg, M., Ruokolainen, T., Lindén, K., Kurimo, M.: Part-of-speech tagging using conditional random fields: exploiting sub-label dependencies for improved accuracy. In: Proceedings of the 52nd Annual Meeting of the Association for Computational Linguistics (Volume 2: Short Papers), pp. 259–264. Association for Computational Linguistics (2014)
20. Silfverberg, M., Ruokolainen, T., Lindén, K., Kurimo, M.: FinnPos: an open-source morphological tagging and lemmatization toolkit for finnish. In: Language Resources and Evaluation (Forthcoming) (2015)

Developing Morpho-SLaWS: An API for the Morphosyntactic Annotation of the Serbian Language

Toma Tasovac[✉], Saša Rudan, and Siniša Rudan

Belgrade Center for Digital Humanities, Belgrade, Serbia
{ttasovac,sasha.rudan,sinisa.rudan}@humanistika.org

Abstract. Serbian Lexical Web Service (SLaWS) is a resource-oriented web service designed to offer multiple functionalities—including morphosyntactic, lexicographic, and canonical text services—to create the backbone of a digital humanities infrastructure for the Serbian language. In this paper, we describe a key component of this service called Morpho-SLaWS, the atomic morphosyntactic component of the service infrastructure. The goal of Morpho-SLaWs is to offer a reliable, programmatic way of extracting morphosyntactic information about word forms using a revised version of the MULTEXT-East specification. As a service-oriented lexical tool, Morpho-SLaWS can be deployed in a variety of contexts and combined with other linguistic and DH tools.

Keywords: API design · Service architecture · Morphological lexicon · Serbian language · Digital humanities

1 Intro: A Language in Search of an Infrastructure

A recent white paper evaluating the state of the Serbian language technologies has shown that Serbian rates poorly in most categories, including the quantity and availability of lexical resources (Vitas et al. 2012).[1] The lack of easily accessible, open-sourced language resources and ready-made frameworks for quantitative textual analysis that take into consideration the specificities of Serbian morphology and syntax has been a major stumbling block in the development of Serbian Digital Humanities.

Serbian Lexical Web Service (SLaWS) is a resource-oriented web service designed to offer multiple functionalities, including morphosyntactic, lexicographic, and canonical text services that are the backbone of a digital humanities infrastructure for the Serbian language. In this paper, we focus on one key aspect of SLaWS: Morpho-SLaWS, the atomic morphosyntactic component of the service infrastructure and the API for the query-driven extraction of Serbian morphosyntactic data. The web service and the API follow standard practices in the field of web-based language resources, while also making provisions for the peculiarities of contemporary Serbian,

---

[1] At the same time, it is important to keep in mind that Serbian is not the only language suffering from the predicament of underdeveloped resources. "It is estimated that for most European languages, "even the basic resources are not yet available." (Váradi et al. 2008).

© Springer International Publishing Switzerland 2015
C. Mahlow and M. Piotrowski (Eds): SFCM 2015, CCIS 537, pp. 137–147, 2015.
DOI: 10.1007/978-3-319-23980-4_9

such as active Cyrillic/Latin digraphia and substandard Latin orthographic practices in computer-mediated communication.

Morpho-SLaWS is a flexible and easily pluggable Digital Humanities (DH) tool, developed in conjunction with recent developments in language service infrastructures (Ishida 2006; Váradi et al. 2008; Murakami et al. 2010) and the goals of interoperability, collaborative creation, management, and sharing of language resources by means of distributed architectures (Calzolari 2008). For an under-resourced language like Serbian, Morpho-SLaWS (and the SLaWS Framework in general) represents a major departure in the way language resources are conceptualized, developed, and disseminated. We see Morpho-SLaWS as part of a long-term effort to build an infrastructure, which will encourage programmatic accessibility and manipulability of Serbian textual data in various DH contexts, including text annotation, indexing, cross-referencing, text analysis, and visualization.

2 The Infrastructural Turn in Digital Humanities

DH encompass a wide range of scholarly activities ranging from digital philology and creation of digital editions to text mining, distant reading, algorithmic criticism (see Ramsay 2011; Berry 2012; Gold 2012; Liu 2012). As a community of practice, digital humanists deal with electronic text not as a static artifact, but rather as a complex, multi-dimensional and multi-layered datasets that need to be analyzed, annotated, and manipulated in order to produce new knowledge. It should come as no surprise that one of the most important challenges facing Digital Humanities today is how to consolidate and repurpose available tools; how to create reusable but flexible workflows; and, ultimately, how to integrate and disseminate knowledge, instead of merely capturing it and encapsulating it. This technical and intellectual shift is what makes the 'infrastructural turn' in Digital Humanities.

The increasing appeal of web services in the context of this infrastructural turn is both technical and social. On the technical level, web services let heterogeneous agents dynamically access and reuse the same sets of data using application programming interfaces (API) and standardized workflows. On the social level, web services help overcome the problem of "shy data," i.e., data you can "meet in public places but you can't take home with you." (Cooper 2010) Designing DH projects in line with the principles of the service-oriented architecture (SOA) is, therefore, an important step in the creation of open scholarly ecosystems.

A growing number of large-scale, international projects is delineating the contours of the infrastructural turn in digital humanities and related fields, in which web services, APIs, and Open Linked Data play a significant role. Large European consortia such as CLARIN and DARIAH coordinate and direct efforts in the realm of digital research infrastructures for language technologies and digital arts and humanities. Initiatives such as the Open Annotation Collaboration (OAC) and the Web Annotation Working Group are working on data models and interoperability specifications for a distributed Web annotation architecture (Hunter et al. 2010; Haslhofer et al. 2011;

Sanderson et al. 2013). While emerging protocols such as the Canonical Text Services (CTS) identify and retrieve XML-structured textual passages of Classical authors using an URN scheme (Smith 2009; Tiepmar et al. 2014).

The trend of open, shareable, and easily accessible "infrastructuralized" data is catching on in individual DH projects as well: Open Siddur's API (Nosek 2013) retrieves, for instance, Jewish liturgical resources, while Folger Digital Texts offers a simple API to identify and retrieve words, lines, or other segments of Shakespeare plays, concordances as well as the so-called witness scripts for individual characters, i.e., portions of the play that characters witness by virtue of being on stage.[2] The correspSearch API provides access to metadata of diverse scholarly letter editions with regard to senders, addresses, as well as places and time of origin.[3] APIs are nowadays used not only to deliver content but also to document and make easily accessible the encoding choices made in creating digital editions (Holmes 2014).

3 Morphosyntactic Annotation in the Service of Serbian DH

We know from experience that serious textual work in Digital Humanities, especially with highly inflected languages such as Serbian, cannot be imagined without morphosyntactic analysis. Lemmatization, POS-tagging, and removal of function or most frequent words are basic pre-requirements for a variety of DH practices, including, for instance, annotating a scholarly digital edition, performing a quantitative analysis of a collection of electronic texts, or topic modeling.

In view of both the state of the Serbian language technologies and the infrastructural turn in Digital Humanities, we judged it essential to invest both time and effort in developing a web service that would help with some of those tasks.

As a web service compliant with the REpresentational state transfer (REST) architecture (Richardson and Ruby 2007), Morpho-SLaWS provides a framework for query-based extraction of morphosyntactic data over the network. It follows the principles of Resource Oriented Architecture (ROA): it makes the components of the underlying lexical dataset addressable through URIs; it uses the HTTP GET method to retrieve a representation of the resource; and every HTTP request happens in stateless isolation, which makes backend implementation and architectural integration much simpler.

Compared to conventional XML transport mechanisms such as SOAP, RESTful protocol provides a lighter solution, more suitable for an online infrastructure, including light mobile solutions (see Muehlen et al. 2005). These aspects happen to be particularly important for under-resourced languages, where communities of developers and crowdsourced editors can lead to significant improvements in resource availability and quality.

---

[2] http://www.folgerdigitaltexts.org/api.
[3] http://correspsearch.bbaw.de/index.xql?id=api.

4 Morpho-SLaWS

4.1 The Morpho-SLaWS Lexicon

The morphosyntactic dataset that forms the backbone of Morpho-SLaWS was originally developed as part of Transpoetika, a bilingualized, WordNet-based Serbian-English dictionary (Tasovac 2009; Tasovac 2012). It has been extended over time and used internally in various contexts including encoding and indexing of literary texts (Tasovac and Ermolaev 2011a; Тасовац and Јермолаев 2012) as well as dictionary backends (Tasovac and Ermolaev 2011b; Чемерикић 2013).

The Morpho-SLaWS Lexicon (MSL) links individual word forms with their corresponding lemmas and morphosyntactic annotation. The MSL tagset relies on the revision of the MULTEXT-East morphosyntactic specification (Erjavec 2010; Tasovac and Petrović, forthcoming). The specification defines a formal set of feature structures for annotating salient word-level grammatical properties for each of the languages concerned. The specification also provides a mapping between its feature structures and the so-called morphosyntactic descriptions (MSD)—a compact annotation scheme which can be used in a variety of natural language processing tasks. For instance, the MSD `Ncnpg--n` corresponds to the feature structure consisting of attribute-value pairs `Category = Noun`, `Type = common`, `Gender = neuter`, `Number = plural`, `animate = no`.

The full paradigm of the Serbian noun *писмо* (letter) in the Morpho-SLaWS lexicon looks like this:

```
Form       Lemma    MSD
писама     писмо    Ncnpg--n
писма      писмо    Ncnpa--n
писма      писмо    Ncnpn--n
писма      писмо    Ncnpv--n
писма      писмо    Ncnsg--n
писмима    писмо    Ncnpd--n
писмима    писмо    Ncnpi--n
писмима    писмо    Ncnpl--n
писмо      писмо    Ncnsa--n
писмо      писмо    Ncnsn--n
писмо      писмо    Ncnsv--n
писмом     писмо    Ncnsi--n
писму      писмо    Ncnsd--n
писму      писмо    Ncnsl--n
```

The MSL is itself under active development. As of this writing, it consists of 3,948,328 morphological entries for 114,932 lemmas. In comparison, the morphological dictionary of the Serbian language in the LADL/DELA format (Krstev 2008) covers a total of around 4.5 million word forms and 130,000 lemmas (Krstev et al. 2011).

4.2   The Morpho-SLaWS Backend

The Morpho-SLaWS backend is implemented as a JavaScript service running in the NodeJS runtime environment, supported by the light Express web application framework and MongoDB persistent storage. MongoDB is a non-relational (NoSQL), schema-less, document-oriented, persistent storage solution, which offers multiple benefits over conventional storage solutions (Wei-ping 2011), such as architectural design patterns greater scalability and standardized solutions for easier replication scenarios.

4.3   The Morpho-SLaWS API

Query Parameters

Method: GET.

https://api.slaws.info/v1/forms/wordForm?fields=apikey,limit,offset,filter,paradigm, transliterate,strict,created_since,modified_since,form,lemma,ana
The following table outlines a list of possible parameters, indicating whether they are required (y) or not (n), briefly describing their functions, default values and data types (Table 1).

Table 1. Morpho-SlaWS parameters

Parameter	Req.	Function	Data Type
apikey	y	API key	String
limit	n	The maximum number of results to return. Default: 10.	Number
offset	n	The pagination of results to return. Default: 0.	Number
filter	n	Filters results based on the MSD notation. * returns all forms, N* returns all nouns, Nc* all common nouns, Nps* proper nouns in the singular, etc. Default: *.	String
paradigm	n	By default, the system returns the MSD for the queried word form. If `true`, the system returns a full inflectional paradigm of the word form, regardless of whether the requested word form is a lemma or not. /forms/руке?paradigm = false =>руке (gen. sg), руке (nom. pl.), руке (acc. pl.) /forms/руке?paradigm = true =>рука, руке, руци, руку, etc. Default: `false`	Boolean
transliterate	n	Transliterate the requested word form from Latin to Cyrillic. This does not affect the output. Default: `false`.	Boolean
strict	n	If transliterate is set to `true` and strict is set to `false`, the system will try to match and offer results for loose transliteration: /forms/reci?transliterate = true&strict = true =>реци /forms/reci?transliterate = true&strict = false =>реци, рећи, речи. Default: `true`	

(*Continued*)

Table 1. (*Continued*)

Parameter	Req.	Function	Data Type
created_since	n	Either zero or the Unix timestamp. Default: 0. Returns entries created since a given time and date.	Number
modified_since	n	Either zero or the Unix timestamp. Default: 0. Returns entries modified since a given time and date.	Number
form	n	Include the requested word form in the response. Default: `true`.	Boolean
lemma	n	Include the lemma of the requested word form in the response. Default: `true`.	Boolean
msd	n	Include the morphosyntactic analysis of the form in the response. Default: `true`.	Boolean

Most of the parameters and functionalities described in the above table are self-explanatory. Two of them, however, deserve special attention, as they address a peculiarity of contemporary Serbian as an actively digraphic language, which can be natively written in both Cyrillic and Latin alphabets (Magner 2001). The API provides two parameters: `transliterate` and `strict` to accommodate this feature. The former instructs the system to transliterate from Latin to Cyrillic:

`/forms/prisustvo?transliterate=true` =>returns results for присуство
`/forms/čašćavali?transliterate=true` => returns results for чашћавали

etc. Unlike the transliteration from Cyrillic to Latin, which is unambiguous, the transliteration from Latin to Cyrillic poses some additional difficulties. Cyrillic graphemes љ, њ, and џ correspond to Latin digraphs: lj, nj, and dž. Unicode does provide single characters for the Latin digraphs, but they are hardly ever used in word processing and in web content. While in majority of cases, the Latin digraphs can be safely transliterated to their monographic Cyrillic counterparts, there are exceptions that require a digraphic Cyrillic representation: for instance, džak = џак (dž = џ), but nadživeti = надживети (dž = дж).

The system deploys what we call a *maximal transliteration approach*: every Latin-script word is internally transformed into all of its theoretically possible Cyrillic representations: džak => [џ|дж]ак and nadživeti becomes на[џ|дж]ивети; the system then returns the results for all the forms that it has encountered in the lexicon.

A further difficulty for the processing of web-based Serbian texts is that a large portion of Serbian speakers in computer mediated communication employs non-standard orthographic practices, most notably the diacritic-free versions of Latin graphemes č, ć, š, đ, ž, and dž (Брборић 2000; Ivković 2013). Keeping in mind that diacritics in the Serbian Latin alphabet are markers of distinct phonemes rather than accent marks, the substandard orthographic practices can interfere with morphosyntactic annotation.

As we saw above, Morpho-SLaWS can transliterate standard orthographic conventions by employing a maximal approach to compensate for the potential graphemic ambiguities. In cases of non-standard orthographic practices, the API accepts an additional parameter, `strict`, to indicate whether the system should try or not to resolve the potential substandard graphemic alternatives.

```
/forms/reci?transliterate=true&strict=true => реци
/forms/reci?transliterate=true&strict=false=>реци,
рећи, речи
```

Setting the parameter `strict` to `false` will search for all possible substandard transliterations and return those that have an entry in the lexicon: in the case of *reci*, the client will receive MSDs for reci (реци), reći (рећи), and reči (речи):

реци	редак	Ncmpn--n
реци	редак	Ncmpv--n
реци	река	Ncfsd--n
реци	река	Ncfsl--n
реци	рећи	Vmmp2s-an-n---e
речи	реч	Ncfsd--n
речи	реч	Ncfsg--n
речи	реч	Ncfsi--n
речи	реч	Ncfsl--n
речи	реч	Ncfsv--n
рећи	рећи	Vmn----an-n---e

The system accounts for multiple orthographic mappings:

1. the "traditional" non-standard Latin: c => [cčć]; dj => [dj|đ]; s => [sš]; z => [zž]; dz => [dz|dž];
2. the "Anglicized" non-standard Latin: ch => [čć]; cj => ć; zh => ž; sh => š; dzh =>dž;
3. the "telegraphic" non-standard Latin: cc => č; ch =>ć; zz => ž; ss => š; dzz = > dž;

Output Formats. Morpho-SLaWS returns lexicon entries in two formats: as JSON objects and as TEI-XML documents.

JSON notation.
```
{"entry":{
  "form": "учитеља",
  "lemma": "учитељ",
  "msd": [
    "Ncmsg--y",
    "Ncmsa--y",
    "Ncmpg--y"
  ]
}}
```

TEI Notation. Entries from the Morpho-SLaWS Lexicon can also be returned as valid TEI documents, consisting of a `teiHeader` (Fig. 1) and lexicon entries encoded as TEI feature structures. The header, which is a required TEI element, provides basic metadata about the service as well as the full request query (Fig. 2).

```
← → C  🗋 http://api.slaws.dev:8080/forms/учитеља                                          P
```

This XML file does not appear to have any style information associated with it. The document tree is shown below.

```
▼<TEI xmlns="http://www.tei-c.org/ns/1.0">
  ▼<teiHeader>
    ▼<fileDesc>
      ▼<titleStmt>
         <title>Morpho-SLaWS Analysis of word form "учитеља"</title>
        ▼<respStmt>
           <resp>Service Provider:</resp>
           <name>Belgrade Center for Digital Humanities</name>
         </respStmt>
       </titleStmt>
      ▼<publicationStmt>
        ▼<authority>
           <ref target="http://humanistika.org">Belgrade Center for Digital Humantieis</ref>
         </authority>
        ▼<availability>
          ▼<licence>
             <p>CC+BY</p>
           </licence>
         </availability>
       </publicationStmt>
      ▼<sourceDesc>
         <p>Born digital</p>
        ▼<p>
           Your query was:
           <lb/>
           http://api.slaws.dev:8080/forms/учитеља
         </p>
       </sourceDesc>
     </fileDesc>
   </teiHeader>
```

Fig. 1. TEI header response

```
   </teiHeader>
  ▼<text>
    ▼<body>
      ▼<fs>
        ▼<f name="form">
           <string>учитеља</string>
         </f>
        ▼<f name="lemma">
           <string>учитељ</string>
         </f>
        ▼<f name="msd">
           <string>Ncmsg--y</string>
           <string>Ncmsa--y</string>
           <string>Ncmpg--y</string>
         </f>
       </fs>
     </body>
   </text>
 </TEI>
```

Fig. 2. TEI body response

5   Conclusion and Future Work

Currently, Morpho-SLaWS provides atomic access to the morphosyntactic lexicon through the read-only GET interface. It is the first-ever such web service for the Serbian language. It has been successfully tested with ongoing projects at the Belgrade Center for Digital Humanities, including the Transpoetika Dictionary (Tasovac 2012), LitTerra[4], and Bukvik.[5]

Further work on Morpho-SLaWS will continue in two parallel tracks: technically, we will focus on expanding the scope of the service, on the one hand, to cover batch processing of both plain-text and TEI-encoded XML files; and, on the other, to handle creating, updating and deleting resources. At the same, we will pursue the development of API-based applications in the realm of collaborative editing, crowdsourcing and gamification of annotation tasks and morphosyntactic disambiguation.

References

Berry, D.M.: Understanding Digital Humanities. Palgrave Macmillan, Houndmills (2012)

Calzolari, N: Approaches towards a lexical web: the role of interoperability. In: Proceedings of the First International Conference on Global Interoperability for Language Resources, pp. 34–42 (2008)

Cooper, D.: When nice people won't share: shy data, web APIs, and beyond. In: Proceedings of the Second International Conference on Global Interoperability for Language Resources (ICGL 2010) (2010)

Erjavec, T.: MULTEXT-east version 4: multilingual morphosyntactic specifications, lexicons and corpora. In: Proceedings of the Seventh International Conference on Language Resources and Evaluation (LREC 2010), European Language Resources Association (ELRA) (2010)

Gold, M.K. (ed.): Debates in the Digital Humanities. University of Minnesota Press, Minneapolis (2012)

Haslhofer, B., Simon, R., Sanderson, R., Van de Sompel, H.: The open annotation collaboration (OAC) model. In: Cyberpsychology and Behavior: The Impact of the Internet, Multimedia and Virtual Reality on Behavior and Society, pp. 5–9 (2011)

Holmes, M.: CodeSharing: a simple API for disseminating our TEI encoding. In: Jenstad, J. (ed.): The Map of Early Modern London (2014). http://mapoflondon.uvic.ca/BLOG10.htm

Hunter, J., Cole, T., Sanderson, R., Van de Sompel, H.: The open annotation collaboration: a data model to support sharing and interoperability of scholarly annotations. In: Digital Humanities 2010, pp. 175–78 (2010), espace.library.uq.edu.au

Ishida, T.: Language grid: an infrastructure for intercultural collaboration. In: International Symposium on Applications and the Internet, SAINT 2006 (2006)

Ivković, D.: Pragmatics meets ideology: digraphia and non-standard orthographic practices in serbian online news forums. J. Lang. Politics 12(3), 335–356 (2013)

Krstev, C.: Processing of Serbian: Automata, Texts and Electronic Dictionaries. Faculty of Philology, Belgrade (2008)

---

[4] http://litterra.info/.

[5] http://bukvik.litterra.info/.

Krstev, C., Vitas, D., Obradović, I., Utvić, M.: E-Dictionaries and finite-state automata for the recognition of named entities. In: Proceedings of the 9th International Workshop on Finite State Methods and Natural Language Processing, FSMNLP 2011, pp. 48–56. ACL, Stroudsburgh (2011)

Liu, A.: The state of the digital humanities: a report and a critique. Arts Humanit. High. Educ. **11** (1–2), 8–41 (2012)

Magner, T.F.: Digraphia in the territories of the croats and serbs. Int. J. Sociol. Lang. **2001**(150), 11–26 (2001)

Muehlen, M., Nickerson, J.V., Swenson, K.D.: Developing web services choreography standards —the case of REST vs. SOAP. Decis. Support Syst. **40**(1), 9–29 (2005)

Murakami, Y., Lin, D., Tanaka, M., Nakaguchi, T., Ishida, T.: Language service management with the language grid. In: Proceedings of the Seventh International Conference on Language Resources and Evaluation (LREC 2010), European Language Resources Association (ELRA) (2010)

Nosek, J.D.: Open access liturgical resources for judaism. Theological Librarianship: Online J. Am. Theological Library Assoc. **6**(2), 63–66 (2013)

Ramsay, S.: Reading Machines: Toward an Algorithmic Criticism. University of Illinois Press, Urbana (2011)

Richardson, L., Ruby, S.: RESTful Web Services. O'Reilly Media Inc., Sebastopol (2007)

Sanderson, R., Ciccarese, P., Van de Sompel, H.: Open Annotation Data Model. W3C Community Draft 8 (2013)

Smith, N.: Citation in Classical Studies. Digital Humanities Quarterly (2009). http://www.digitalhumanities.org/dhq/vol/3/1/000028/000028.html

Tasovac, T.: More or less than a dictionary? wordnet as a model for Serbian L2 lexicography. Infotheca: J. Inf. Librarinaship **10**(1–2), 13–22 (2009)

Tasovac, T.: Potentials and challenges of WordNet-based pedagogical lexicography: the transpoetika dictionary. In: Granger, S. (ed.) Potentials and Challenges of WordNet-Based Pedagogical Lexicography: The Transpoetika Dictionary. Electronic Lexicography, pp. 237–58. Oxford University Press (2012)

Tasovac, T., Ermolaev, N.: Encoding diachrony: digital editions of serbian 18th-century texts. In: Gradmann, S., Borri, F., Meghini, C., Schuldt, H. (eds.) TPDL 2011. LNCS, vol. 6966, pp. 497–500. Springer, Heidelberg (2011a)

Tasovac, T., Ermolaev, N.: A User-Centered Digital Edition of Vuk Stefanović Karadžić's Lexicon Serbico-Germanico-Latinum. Digital Humanities 2011 (2011b). http://xtf-prod.stanford.edu/xtf/view?docId=tei/ab-297.xml;query=;brand=default

Tasovac, T., Petrović, S.: MULTEXT-East Revisited: Serbian Morphosyntactic Tags in Action (forthcoming)

Tiepmar, J., Teichmann, C., Heyer, G., Berti, M., Crane, G.: A new implementation for canonical text services. In: Proceedings of the 8th Workshop on Language Technology for Cultural Heritage, Social Sciences, and Humanities (LaTeCH). ACL, Stroudsburgh (2014)

Zhu, W.-P., Li M.-X., Huan,C.: Using MongoDB to implement textbook management system instead of MySQL. In: IEEE 3rd International Conference on Communication Software and Networks (ICCSN) (2011)

Vitas, D., Popović, L., Krstev, C., Obradović, I., Pavlović-Lažetić, G., Stanojević, M.: The serbian language in the digital age. In: Rehm, G., Uszkoreit, H. (eds.) META-NET White Paper Series. Springer, Heidelberg (2012)

Váradi, T., Wittenburg, P., Krauwer, S., Wynne, M., Koskenniemi, K.: CLARIN: common language resources and technology infrastructure. In: Proceedings of the Sixth International Conference on Language Resources and Evaluation (LREC 2008), European Language Resources Association (ELRA) (2008)

Брборић, В.: О Језичком расколу. Социолингвистички огледи I. Београд и Нови Сад: ЦПЛ-Прометеј (2000)

Тасовац, Т., Јермолаев, Н.: Дијахронијски приступ дигиталним издањима српских текстова 18. века. In: Вранеш, А. (ed.) Дигитализација културне и научне баштине 71–88. Филолошки факултет, Београд (2012)

Чемерикић, Д.: Збирка речи из Призрена ДимитријаЧемерикића. Центар за дигиталне хуманистичке науке, Препис.орг. Београд (2013)

Morphological Analysis and Generation of Monolingual and Bilingual Medical Lexicons

Annibale Elia, Alessandro Maisto, and Serena Pelosi[✉]

Department of Political, Social, and Communication Sciences,
University of Salerno, Via Giovanni Paolo II, 84084 Fisciano, SA, Italy
{elia,amaisto,spelosi}@unisa.it

Abstract. To efficiently extract and manage extremely large quantities of meaningful data in a delicate sector like healthcare requires sophisticated linguistic strategies and computational solutions. In the research described here we approach the semantic dimension of the formative elements of medical words in monolingual and bilingual environments. The purpose is to automatically build Italian–English medical lexical resources by grounding their analysis and generation on the manipulation of their consituent morphemes. This approach has a significant impact on the automatic analysis of neologisms, typical for the medical domain. We created two electronic dictionaries of morphemes and a morphological finite state transducer, which, together, find all possible combinations of prefixes, confixes, and suffixes, and are able to annotate and translate the terms contained in a medical corpus, according to the meaning of the morphemes that compose these words. In order to enable the machine to "understand" also medical multiword expressions, we designed a syntactic grammar net that includes several paths based on different combinations of nouns, adjectives, and prepositions.

Keywords: Morphosemantics · Machine translation · Dictionary population · Neoclassical formative elements

1 Introduction

In the age of Big Data, which clearly affects also the healthcare sector, one of the most important challenges is the extraction of information from raw data. This implies the automatic detection of significant facts in unstructured texts and their transformation into structured documents, indexable and queryable exactly like databases.

The volume, the variety, the velocity, the verification, and the value of data raise the necessity of managing information with the most sophisticated linguistic and computational architectures, able to approach the semantic dimension of words and sentences.

A satisfying computational treatment of the language, above all in the medical domain, requires a large quantity of lexical resources, accurately described from a linguistic point of view. Unfortunately, not all the languages are provided with

© Springer International Publishing Switzerland 2015
C. Mahlow and M. Piotrowski (Eds.): SFCM 2015, CCIS 537, pp. 148–165, 2015.
DOI: 10.1007/978-3-319-23980-4_10

complete and freely available lexical databases, like the English one. As regards the Italian language, that is the language under examination in this work, in the rare cases in which the lexical resources are accessible for free, they are not as reach as their English counterparts (think of the differences between the Italian and the English version of WordNet, cf. [24]).

Anyway, the manual elaboration of these resources (that can take the shape of monolingual and/or bilingual electronic dictionaries, thesauri, ontologies, etc.) represents a strong time-consuming activity. The human-built databases can not be updated in real time, and, for this reason, they are not so flexible to the proliferation of neologisms, typical of the medical domain.

All that strengths the idea that sometimes the elaboration of strategies and tools for the automatic creation and enlargement of lexical databases is preferable to the (more accurate but slower) manual formalization of them.

The present paper summarizes the techniques used to build Italian medical thesauri and dictionaries in which every lemma is automatically associated with its own terminological and semantic properties. The starting point is a large-sized corpus of medical records, the output, medical thesauri and electronic dictionaries enriched with semantic information, that can be easily used as knowledge base in every clinical decision support system.

Furthermore, we explored the possibility to ground a machine translation task in the medical special language on morphology: starting from the Italian list of medical morphemes, we built an Italian-English multilingual electronic dictionary, which is usable for the generation and the translation of medical words on the base of morphological correspondences.

The whole work is grounded on the productive morphology and on the semantics of the word formation elements. The basic intuition is that, in the special language of the medicine, the meaning of a relatively small number of morphemes can be used to inherit the meaning of the words that are formed with them.

In this research we basically reorganize the information derived from the semantics of the word formation elements, by making the medical words derive the meaning of the morphemes which they are formed with.

The paper is structured as follows. Section 2 recapitulates the state of the art contributions on both the morpheme-based population of linguistic resources and the machine translation based on morphological clues in the medical domain. Section 3 briefly describes the morphosemantic method used in this work. Sections 4 and 5 present, respectively, in more detail the *ad hoc* electronic dictionaries and the morphological and syntactic local grammars created for the automatic annotation of a corpus of 5,000 medical diagnoses and for the generation of English medical words, on the base on the morphological correspondences with the Italian ones. In Sect. 6 we report the results regarding both the realization of medical dictionaries and thesauri, based on the annotations extracted from the medical corpus, and the automatic generation of the Italian-English bilingual medical database.

2   State of the Art

Due to the variety of the topics and tasks faced in the present research, this section will approach every one of them separately. In detail, we will firstly define, from a linguistic point of view, the neoclassical formative elements, on which the entire work has been based. Then, we will briefly present the most important studies on the automatic population of thesauri, with special attention to the ones that exploited a morpho-semantic approach. In the end, we will focus on the researches that exploited morphological rules in machine translation tasks.

2.1   Linguistic Studies on Neoclassical Formative Elements

The *neoclassical formative elements* are those morphological elements that come into being from Latin and Greek words and that are used to form both technical-scientific words and ordinary words. They can combine themselves with other formative elements or with independent words.

Due to their heterogeneous nature, we can notice in literature difficulties in the classification and in the definition of such entities. The denominations they received in the course of time are *prefixoids, suffixoids* [23]; *cultured elements*[6]; *formative elements of Latin and Greek origin* [37]; *semiwords* [33]; *scientific formative elements* [34]; *compound words with "lexical stems" or semiwords* [32]; *confixes* [4, 9, 18, 22, 35]; *neoclassical elements* [38]. For the sake of simplicity, from now on we will use the term "confixes," which has been predominantly used in literature.

The terms that are created with the neoclassical formative elements are called "neoclassical compounds," but actually they do not find a correct definition neither in "compounds" nor in "derivatives" [16].

In this work we will just focus only on the technical-scientific word formation in order to avoid unpredictable and more important ambiguity problems.

2.2   Morphosemantic Approaches for the Automatic Population of Thesauri

Morphosemantic approaches, similar to the one presented here, have been already applied to the medical domain in many languages.

Works that deserve to be mentioned are Pratt [31] on the identification and on the transformation of terminal morphemes in the English medical dictionary; Wolff [42] on the classification of the medical lexicon based on formative elements of Latin and Greek origin; Pacak et al. [30] on the diseases words ending in *-itis*; Norton e Pacak [29] on the surgical operation words ending in *-ectomy* or *-stomy*; Dujols et al. [11] on the suffix *-osis*.

Between the 1990s and the 2000s, many studies were published on the automatic population of thesauri. We recollect among others Lovis et al. [21], who derived the meaning of the words from the morphemes that compose them; Lovis et al. [20], who identified ICD codes in diagnoses written in different languages; Hahn et al. [15], who segmented the subwords in order to recognise and extract medical documents; and Grabar and Zweigenbaum [14], who used machine learning methods on the morphological data of the SNOMED thesaurus (French, Russian, English).

An advantage of the morphosemantic method is that complex linguistic analyses designed for a language can be often transferred to other languages. Delger, Naner, and Zweigenbaum [10], for example, adapted the morphosemantic analyzer DériF [28], designed for the French language, for the automatic analysis of English medical neoclassical compounds.

2.3 Morphem-Based Approaches in Machine Translation Tasks

With regard to the studies which exploited morphological clues in machine translation tasks, we mention the work of Cartoni [3], who implemented lexical morphology principles into an Italian–French machine translation tool, in order to deal with the computational treatment of neologisms. We also consider Toutanove, Suzuki, and Ruopp [39] and Minkov, Toutanova, and Suzuki [25], who proposed models for the prediction of inflected word forms for the generation of morphologically rich languages (e.g., Russian and Arabic) into a machine translation context.

Furthermore, Virpioja et al. [41] exploited the Morfessor algorithm, a method for the unsupervised *morph-tokens* analysis, with the purpose of reducing the size of the lexicon and improving the ability to generalize in machine translation tasks. Their approach, which basically treated morphemes as word-tokens, has been tested on the Danish, Finnish, and Swedish languages.

Daumke, Schulz, and Mark [7] exploited a set of subword (morphologically meaningful units) to automatically translate biomedical terms from German to English, with the purpose to morphologically reduce the number of lexical entries to sufficiently cover a specific domain.

Lee [19] explored a novel morphological analysis technique that involved languages with highly asymmetrical morphological structures (e.g., Arabic and English) in order to improve the results of statistical machine translations.

Finally, Amtrup [1] proposed a method that involved finite state technologies for the morphological analysis and generation tasks compatible with machine translation systems.

3 Methodology

As stated by [2], linguistic sub-codes can be described as varieties of the linguistic code that possess peculiarities that depend on specific knowledge domains. Such sub-codes are provided with special lexicons, thanks to which it is possible to determine concepts that go beyond the common use of the language.

The technical-scientific language of the medicine, endowed with an amount of technical lemmas that is larger than any other sub-code, is a part of the set of sub-codes that are organized in taxonomies and strong notional fields [5].

This large number of terms, besides, occurs in texts with a very low frequency. To accept that a key term could be a "rare event" [26], has clearly a strong impact on the performances of the statistical and the machine learning methods, that hardly take into account these kinds of problems.

In our work we took advantage from a number of Italian and English word-formation strategies for the automatic analysis of Italian words and for the generation of Italian/English bilingual lexicons in the medical sub-code.

The basic hypothesis in that the global meaning of the words is often strongly connected with the meaning of the formative elements that compose them.

3.1   Semantic Relations and Morphological Families

The morphosemantic approach allows the analytical description of the meaning of the words that belong to the same subdomain or to the same "morphological family" [17]. In this subsection we will introduce the possibility to exploit morphemes in order to detect and describe the semantic relations existing between those words that share portions of meaning.

With our method it is easy to find *(almost-)synonym sets* [27] on the base of the words that share morphemes endowed with a particular meaning (e.g., *-acusia*, hearing disorders). Moreover, we can infer the domain of the medical knowledge to which the synonym set belongs (e.g., "otolaryngology") and, in the end, we can differentiate any item of the set by exploiting the meaning of the other morphemes involved in the words.

– synset: *iper-acusia, ipo-acusia, presbi-acusia, dipl-acusia*;
– subdomain: *-acusia* "otolaryngology";
– description: *ipo-* "lack," *iper-* "excess," *presbi-* "old age," *diplo-* "double").

On the base of the morphemes meaning, we can also infer relations between words that are not morho-phonologically related, but which are composed of morphemes that share at least one semantic feature and/or the medical subdomain. Examples of this are reported below.

– related to tumors: *cancero-, carcino-, -oma,* "oncology";
– related to stomach disorders: *stomac-, gastro-,* "gastroenterology";
– related to skin fungus: *fung-, miceto-, mico-,* "dermatology".

It is for all these benefits that we grounded the automatic creation of medical lexical databases on specific formative elements that are able to define the meaning in a univocal way, thanks to the regular combination of modules independently defined. Such elements do not represent mere terminations, but possess their own semantic self-sufficiency [16].

3.2   Natural Language Processing Tools

The NLP tool that we used in this work for both the language formalization and the corpus processing is NooJ[1] [36].

---

[1] www.nooj4nlp.net.

Among the great number of modules, developed by the international NooJ community, the Italian Lingware [40] has been built by the Maurice Gross Laboratory of the University of Salerno, which focuses its research interest on language formalization and text parsing and grounds its works on the Lexicon-grammar (LG) theoretical and practical framework since the beginning of the '80s [13].

The Italian module for NooJ can be any time integrated with other *ad hoc* resources.

The lexical and grammatical resources that the NooJ user can build in order to parse texts and analyze their semantic content are the followings.

- *Electronic Dictionaries.* Characterized by completeness, explanation and coding, electronic dictionaries are lexical databases, which are usable with every kind of computerized document.
- *Local Grammars.* They are algorithms on the form of finite-state automata (FSA) that, thanks to grammatical, morphological and lexical instructions, contribute to the formalization of linguistic phenomena and in the parsing of texts. FSA are non-deterministic graphs characterized by a finite set of nodes and transitions that allow us to locate patterns related to a particular path. They are called finite-state transducers (FST) if the pattern recognition goes together with the pattern annotation; in other words, if the grammar not only matches specific linguistic sequences, but also writes outputs on them.

4   Lexical Resources

In the present work, the corpus analysis has been preceded by the planning of a number of subclasses of the medical domain. With the support of a domain expert the macro class of the medicine has been divided into 22 subcategories, shown in Table 1.

A class "undefined" has been used as residual category, in order to collect the words particularly difficult to classify.

Thanks to the electronic version of the GRADIT [8] it has been possible to collect the morphemes (prefixes, suffixes and confixes) related to the medical domain, to classify them on the base of their subdomain of origin and to enrich them with other semantic information, concerning the meaning they express.

Each of these morphemes has been compared with the morphemes presented into the Open Dictionary of English by the LearnThat Foundation[2]. The respective English translation has been added to the NooJ Dictionary (Table 2).

The electronic dictionary of medical morphemes is classified in the following way:

- Confixes (CPX): neoclassical formative elements with a full semantic value (i.e. *pupillo-*, *mammo-*, *-cefalia*);
- Prefixes (PFX): morphemes that appear in the first part of the word and are able to connote it with a specific meaning (i.e. *-ipo*, *-iper*);

---

[2] https://www.learnthat.org/.

Table 1. Tag set for the morphemes description

Label	Description	Number
Intern	Internal medicine	108
Ortoped	Orthopedics	78
Cardio	Cardiology	54
Neuro	Neurology	42
Ginec	Gynecology	42
Urolog	Urology	38
Gastro	Gastroenterology	36
Endocrin	Endocrinology	36
Chirur	Surgery	26
Otorino	Otolaryngology	24
Oftalmo	Ophtalmology	20
Oncol	Oncology	13
Pneumo	Pneumology	12
Dermat	Dermatology	10
Dermat	Dermatology	10
Trauma	Traumatology	10
Psic	Psychiatry	6
Pediat	Pediatrics	6
Virolog	Virology	6
Farmaco	Pharmacology	4
Allergo	Allergology	2
Geriatr	Geriatrics	2

Table 2. Morphemes of the bilingual dictionary of medical morphemes

Manner of use	Category	Number	Translated
Medicine	Confixes	451	349
Medicine	Suffixes	14	13
Medicine	Prefixes	7	7
Anatomy	Confixes	45	27
General	Suffixes	19	18

– Suffixes (SFX): morphemes that appear in the final part of the word and are able to connote it with a specific meaning (i.e. *-oma*, *-ite*);
– Suffixes for the adjectives formation: derivational morphemes that make it possible to derive and distinguish in the medical domain the adjectives

(i.e. *polmonare*, "pulmonary") from the nouns that have a morpho-phonological relation with them (i.e. *polmone*, "lung").

```
#     PREFIXES
emo,PFX+SensP=sangue+EN=hemo
iper,PFX+SensP=eccesso+EN=hyper
ipo,PFX+SensP=poco+EN=hypo
normi,PFX+SensP=normale+EN=normo
para,PFX+SensP=affinità+EN=para

#     CONFIXES
angio,CFX+SensCP=vasoSanguigno+Med=CARDIO+EN=angio
bronchio,CFX+SensCP=bronchi+Med=PNEUMO+EN=bronchio
cerebro,CFX+SensCP=cervello+Med=NEURO
dacrio,CFX+SensCP=lacrime+Med=OFTALMO+EN=dacryo
osteo,CFX+SensCP=ossa+Med=ORTOPED+EN=osteo
presbi,CFX+SensCP=vecchiaia+Med=GERIATR+EN=presby

#     SUFFIXES
asi,SFX+SensS=interventiPatologie+EN=asis
iasi,SFX+SensS=infestazioniParassitarie+EN=iasis
ite,SFX+SensS=infiammazione+EN=itis
oma,SFX+SensS=tumoriInfiammazioni|+Med=ONCOL+EN=oma
osi,SFX+SensS=lesione+EN=osis
```

Fig. 1. Electronic dictionary of morphemes

As shown in Fig. 1 the medical morphemes have been formalized into an Electronic Dictionary that specifies their category (PFX, SFX, etc.), and provides semantic descriptions about the meaning they confer to the words composed with them. Such semantic information regard the three following aspects:

- Meaning: introduced by the code "+Sens," this semantic label describes the specific meaning of the morpheme (e.g., *-oma* corresponds to the descriptions *tumori*, "tumours" and *-ite* to *infiammazioni*, "inflammations");
- Medical Class: introduced by the code "+Med," this terminological label gives information regarding the medical subdomain to which the morpheme belongs (e.g., *cardio-* let the machine know that every word formed with it pertains to the subdomain of cardiology);
- Translation: introduced by the code "+EN," presents the corresponding translation of the morpheme in English.

The dictionary, compiled into the file "morphemes_IT_EN.nod," contains the three categories presented in Fig. 1 (CFX for the confixes, SFX for the Suffixes and PFX for the Prefixes).

Another category, CFXS, includes all the Confixes that can appear before a suffix, with its correspondent English morpheme deprived of the final part, in order to avoid vocal repetition in case of suffixation. The word *Ateroscelrosi*, "Atherosclerosis," for example, that is composed by three morphemes, *atero*, *sclero* and *osi,* with the respective translation of morphemes, "athero," "sclero" and "osis"; when translated, produces the sequence "atheroscleroosis." Since is not possible to operate directly on English morphemes, to prevent these kind of errors, the system contemplates the new category CFXS for Confixes that are followed by a Suffix. While the sequence of morphemes CFX-CFX-SFX produce "Atheroscleroosis," a sequence CFX-CFXS-SFX translate correctly the medical term.

A supplemental resource used to annotate our corpus is a dictionary composed of more than 700 concrete nouns of body parts ("+Npc," e.g., *braccio,* "arm") and organism parts ("+Npcorg," e.g., *cervello,* "brain") and of more than 400 concrete nouns of drugs and medicines ("+Nfarm," i.e., *morfina,* "morphine") developed by the Maurice Gross Laboratory of the University of Salerno.

Also this dictionary, shown in one of its parts in Fig. 2, is enriched with Parts of Speech ("N," nouns), Inflectional ("+FLX," that specifies the inflectional paradigm followed by the lemmas) and Semantic properties (e.g., "+Conc": concrete; +Npcorg: organism part; "+Med=NEURO": neurology).

```
carioplasma,N+FLX=N15+Conc+Npcorg
cariotipo,N+FLX=N5+Conc+Npcorg
carne,N+FLX=N46+Conc+Ncibo+Npcorg
cartilagine,N+FLX=N46+Conc+Npcorg+Med=ORTOPED
cava,N+FLX=N41+Conc+Nloc+Npcorg
cellulite,N+FLX=N46+Conc+Npcorg+Med=NUTRI
cerebello,N+FLX=N5+Conc+Npcorg+Med=NEURO
cerebro,N+FLX=N5+Conc+Npcorg+Med=NEURO
cerume,N+FLX=N5+Conc+Npcorg+Med=otorino
cervelletto,N+FLX=N5+Conc+Npcorg+Med=NEURO
cervello,N+FLX=N24+Conc+Npcorg+Med=NEURO
chemiocettore,N+FLX=N5+Conc+Npcorg
chemiorecettore,N+FLX=N5+Conc+Npcorg
```

Fig. 2. Electronic dictionary of organism parts

5   Grammatical Rules

It has been shown in the previous section how to formalize the electronic dictionaries required for the annotation of our corpus and for the medical lexical databases creation. However, this represents just the first step of our method, which, in order to automatically recognize and tag medical words occurring in real texts, needs the support of morphological and syntactic local grammars, which take the shape of FST. The grammar net designed for this work includes two kinds of grammars: syntactic grammars, in which every node represents a word and morphological grammars, in which every node represents a morpheme.

5.1 Rules for the Automatic Population of Medical Lexical Databases

The recognition of medical terms is based on seven parallel morphological grammars that automatically assign semantic tags to the simple words found in free texts, according to the meaning of the formative elements that compose the same words. Below are summarised the seven grammars built with *NooJ*, which include the following combination of morphemes:

1. *confix-confix/prefix-confix/prefix-confix-confix*;
2. *confix-suffix/prefix-confix-suffix*;
3. *confix-confix-suffix/prefix-confix-confix-suffix*;
4. *noun-confix*;
5. *prefix-noun-confix*;
6. *confix-noun-confix*;
7. *noun-suffix*;

Together, the morphemes dictionary and the morphological grammar net allow the recognition and the annotation of simple words of the medical domain.

In Fig. 3 is presented a sample of the morphological grammar: the graph is composed by a finite number of states which are always included between an *input node* and an *output node*. Yellow nodes represent *metanodes*, nodes that contain other embedded graphs. The code ⟨+MEDICINA$1S$2S⟩ allows the grammar to assign to the words the information inherited by the morphemes that compose them.

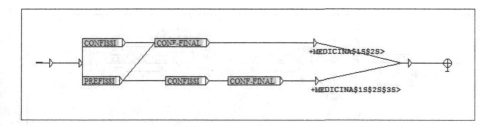

Fig. 3. Extract from the morphological grammar

Figure 4 shows the content of the metanode "CONFISSI", which connects the local grammar with the dictionaries of medical morphemes and human body/organism parts. In order to enable the machine to extract and "understand" also the multiword expressions, we exploited a network of NooJ syntactic grammar. The one designed for this work includes seven main paths based on different combinations of Nouns (N), Adjectives (A) and Prepositions (PREP).

1. N;
2. N+N;
3. A+N;

158   A. Elia et al.

4. N+A;
5. N+N+A;
6. N+A+A;
7. N+PREP+N;

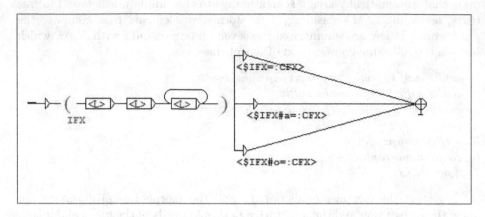

Fig. 4. Example of the confix metanode of the morphological grammar

Every path attributes to the matched sequence the label that belongs to the head of the compound. In the case in which the head is not endowed with a semantic label, the compound receives the residual tag "undefined". The first path matches the simple words, all the other paths match multiword expressions.

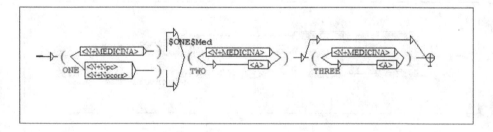

Fig. 5. Extract from the syntactic grammar

Figure 5 shows the syntactic grammar number 6, in which the restriction *ONEMed* is used to assign to the compound the grammatical category corresponding to its head (in this case N).

In technical languages the presence of multiword expressions is extremely relevant. Often these expressions exceed the 90 % of the amount of the words that are characteristic of a specialized jargon [12].

A terminological compound is a particular sequence of simple words separated by blanks, which is characterized by a restriction of distribution, by a shared and established use and, above all, by a want of ambiguity.

Their semantic atomicity is extremely important in the annotation of texts, e.g., the simple word *cisti*, "cyst" alone cannot provide the specific information contained in the compounds *cisti ovarica*, "ovarian cyst" (GINEC, "genecology") or *cisti spinale* "spinal cyst" (NEURO, "neurology").

5.2   Rules for the Machine Translation of Medical Words

Similarly to the task presented in Sect. 5.1, the machine translation of medical words in English is based on a morphological grammar, and a syntactical grammar or a finite-state transductor that transform the Italian term into the English term.

The morphological grammar, named *"MOMENIT.nom"*, recognizes Italian medical terms and tag every morpheme that composes the word with information regarding its meaning. In order to preform this operation, the morphological grammar includes seven patterns which recognize different sequences of morphemes (Fig. 6):

– CFX-CFX
– PFX-CFX
– PFX-CFX-CFX
– PFX-CFXS-SFX
– CFXS-SFX
– CFX-CFXS-SFX
– PFX-CFX-CFXS-SFX

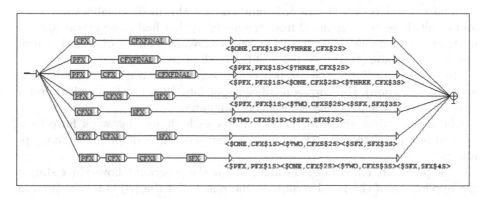

Fig. 6. The morphological grammar for recognition of Italian medical terms of the Machine Translation Module

Subsequently, the syntactic finite-state transducer *"TRANSITEN.nog"* takes as input the morphemes and, then, outputs the respective translations, see Fig. 7. In the end, using the same morpheme sequences defined for the morphological grammar, it tags every Italian Medical Term with the respective English translation.

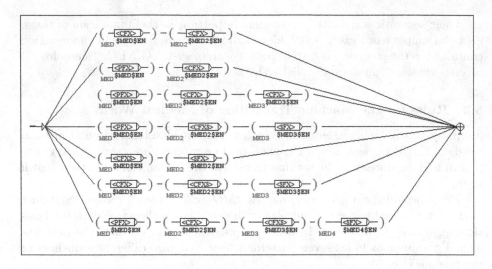

Fig. 7. Syntactic finite-state transducer

6   Discussion and Results

The corpus on which the annotation has been performed consists of 5,000 medical records, from the Italian region Campania, in electronic format. The hospitals' information and the sensitive data of patient they belong to have been hidden, due to privacy reasons.

The medical codes, the record numbers and the medical laboratory tests and results have been excluded from the analysis, that had to be carried out on unstructured texts. So, the annotation has been realized on the diagnoses, which are the largest non-structured fields of the medical records.

In order to facilitate the pre-processing stage (tokenization, normalization and lemmatization), the corpus has been split into 20 subsections with a total of 64, 360 *tokens* and 41, 468 *word forms* annotated.

Then the lexical and grammatical resources built for this work have been applied in tandem to the texts, thanks to the command-line program "noojapply.exe".

The procedure followed by the algorithm of the program follows three stages: the application of the NooJ resources; the removal of the redundancies and, in the end, the proper extraction of the classes. All that provides two kinds of outputs exemplified below:

– an Electronic Dictionary of simple medical words, in which the lemmas extracted from the diagnoses are systematically associated with their terminological ("Med") and semantic ("Sens") descriptions:
  Gastrite acuta. Cardiopatia ipertensiva. Insufficienza aortica lieve-moderata.
  "Acute gastritis. Hypertensive heart disease. Mild-to-moderate aortic regurgitation"

gastrite,N+SensCP=apparatoGastrico+Med=GASTRO+SensS=infiammazione
cardiopatia,N+SensCP=cuore+Med=CARDIO+SensCS=malattia
ipertensiva,A+SensP=eccesso+SensCP=tensione+Med=CARDIO
aortica,A+SensCP=aorta+Med=CARDIO

– a Thesaurus of simple and compound medical words, which are grouped together on the base of their medical classes:

#⟨CARDIO⟩
insufficienza aortica
cardiopatia ipertensiva
vasculopatia aterosclerotica
aritmia ectopica sopraventricolare
aritmia extrasistolica ventricolare

#⟨GASTRO⟩
duodenite bulbare
colonpatia discinetica
gastrite erosiva
coliche addominali resistenti
colecistite litiasica

#⟨PNEUMO⟩
broncopatia cronica
broncopenumopatia cronica enfisematosa
enfisema polmonare
fibrosi polmonare
insufficienza respiratoria

In order to have a measure of the performances of our morphosemantic medical analyser we evaluated its Precision (on a sample of 500 entries of the Thesaurus automatically extracted from a sample of about 5,000 medical diagnoses), that underlined strong variances connected with the different medical classes. A summary of the obtained results is reported in Table 3. Although the Precision percentage on the whole sample (69.50 %) is more than satisfying for a complex semantic task like the one performed in this work, many improvements must be carried out on the dictionaries and grammars of the domains with the lowest levels of Precision.

The medical classes on which the results have been evaluated are the ones located in the sample of the corpus. The size and the nature of the lexical databases that can be created with the proposed method depend on the largeness and on the content of the corpus on which the NooJ resources are applied. Therefore, in order to obtain widespread medical databases, it is preferable to use corpora that cover many areas of the medicine.

Table 3. Evaluation of the automatically generated thesaurus

Classes	Precision %
Traumatology	100.00
Surgery	97.82
Pneumology	95.83
Gastroenterology	89.18
Orthopedic	80.95
Urology	76.19
Intern medicine	69.04
Cardiology	66.96
Endocrinology	23.80
Undefined	50.80
Tot	69.50

At a later stage, the syntactic transducer have been applied to the same corpus in order to generate a list of English medical terms preceded by the respective Italian words.

Table 4. Morphological machine translation

Italian word	English translation	Morpheme 1	Morpheme 2	Domain
Encefalo-patia	Encephalo-pathy	Brain	Disease	Neurology
Cardio-patia	Cardio-pathy	Heart	Disease	Cardiology
Ipo-tensione	Hypo-tension	Under	Tension	Cardiology
Colon-scopia	Colon-scopy	Colon	Medical exam	Gastroenterology

In Table 4 we exemplify the information generated by our lexical and grammatical resources. The procedure extracted 3,138 English medical terms, 2,103 of which were correct, with a Precision score of 67.87 %.

Although the Precision percentage on the whole sample is more than satisfying for complex semantic tasks like the ones performed in this work, many improvements must be carried out on the dictionaries and grammars of the domains with the lowest levels of Precision.

7   Conclusion

In the present work we presented a morphosemantic method for the automatic population of medical lexical databases in the Italian language and for the Ita-Eng machine translation of medical words. Our outputs, in its electronic format, can be used as Knowledge base by every kind of NLP tools or Clinical Decision Support Systems.

We demonstrated, with satisfactory results, that starting from a corpus written in technical-scientific language and from a small sized dictionary of neoclassical formative elements it is possible to "understand" the meaning of a large number of medical simple and compound expressions.

Moreover, we introduced the possibility to compare languages that share a significant number of morphemes, in order to take advantages from such similarities in machine translation tasks.

Because the creation of the medical dictionary and thesaurus comes from the annotations produced by our linguistic resources, a collateral output of this work is a large annotated corpus that can be used for the training of many machine learning tools that deal with the medical domain. Another secondary effect of our work is a multilingual electronic dictionary of semantically annotated medical words, which can be tested and applied on many multilingual medical corpora for many statistical purposes.

We conclude our contribution by specifying that, in order to enlarge and to perfect our medical sub-domain classification, the work of domain experts would be needed. Thus, the performances of our tool could be improved by making medical practitioners enhance our morphological and grammatical resources.

References

1. Amtrup, J.W.: Morphology in machine translation systems: efficient integration of finite state transducers and feature structure descriptions. Mach. Transl. **18**(3), 217–238 (2003)
2. Berruto, G.: Sociolinguistica dell'Italiano Contemporaneo. Carocci, Roma (1987)
3. Cartoni, B.: Lexical morphology in machine translation: a feasibility study. In: Proceedings of the 12th Conference of the European Chapter of the Association for Computational Linguistics, pp. 130–138. Association for Computational Linguistics (2009)
4. D'Achille, P.: L'italiano contemporaneo. Il Mulino, Bologna (2003)
5. Dardano, M.: I linguaggi scientifici. Storia della Lingua Italiana 2, 497–551 (1994)
6. Dardano, M.: La formazione delle parole nell'italiano di oggi, vol. 148. Bulzoni, Roma (1978)
7. Daumke, P., Schulz, S., Markó, K.: Subword approach for acquiring and cross-linking multilingual specialized lexicons. In: 5th International Conference on Language Resources and Evaluation (LREC '06) Workshop on Acquiring and Representing Multilingual, Specialized Lexicons (2006)
8. De Mauro, T.: Grande Dizionario Italiano dell'Uso, vol. 8. UTET, Torino (1999)
9. De Mauro, T.: Nuove Parole Italiane dell'uso, GRADIT, vol. 7. UTET, Torino (2003)
10. Deléger, L., Naner, F., Zweigenbaum, P.: Defining medical words: transposing morphosemantic analysis from French to English. In: Kuhn, K.A., Warren, J.R., Leong, T.Y. (eds.) MEDINFO 2007: Proceedings of the 12th World Congress on Health, pp. 535–539. IOS Press, Amsterdam (2007)
11. Dujols, P., Aubas, P., Baylon, C., Grémy, F.: Morpho-semantic analysis and translation of medical compound terms. Meth. Inf. Med. **30**(1), 30 (1991)

12. Elia, A., Cardona, G.R.: Discorso scientifico e linguaggio settoriale. un esempio di analisi lessico-grammaticale di un testo neuro-biologico. In: Cicalese, A., Landi, A. (eds.) Simboli, linguaggi e contesti. Carocci, Roma (2002)

13. Elia, A., Martinelli, M., D'Agostino, E.: Lessico e Strutture sintattiche: Introduzione alla sintassi del verbo italiano. Liguori, Napoli (1981)

14. Grabar, N., Zweigenbaum, P.: Automatic acquisition of domain-specific morphological resources from thesauri. In: Proceedings of RIAO, pp. 765–784. Citeseer (2000)

15. Hahn, U., Honeck, M., Piotrowski, M., Schulz, S.: Subword segmentation-leveling out morphological variations for medical document retrieval. In: Proceedings of the AMIA Symposium, p. 229. American Medical Informatics Association (2001)

16. Iacobini, C.: Composizione con elementi neoclassici. In: Grossmann, M., Rainer, F. (eds.) La formazione delle parole in italiano, pp. 69–95. Niemeyer, Tübingen (2004)

17. Jacquemin, C.: Syntagmatic and paradigmatic representations of term variation. In: Proceedings of the 37th Annual Meeting of the Association for Computational Linguistics on Computational Linguistics, pp. 341–348. Association for Computational Linguistics (1999)

18. Kirkness, A.: Aero-lexicography: observations on the treatment of combinemes and neoclassical combinations in historical and scholarly European dictionaries. Willy Martin ua (Hrsg.): Euralex, pp. 530–535 (1994)

19. Lee, Y.S.: Morphological analysis for statistical machine translation. In: Proceedings of HLT-NAACL 2004, Short Papers. pp. 57–60. Association for Computational Linguistics (2004)

20. Lovis, C., Baud, R., Rassinoux, A.M., Michel, P.A., Scherrer, J.R.: Medical dictionaries for patient encoding systems: a methodology. Artif. Intell. Med. 14(1), 201–214 (1998)

21. Lovis, C., Michel, P.A., Baud, R., Scherrer, J.R.: Word segmentation processing: a way to exponentially extend medical dictionaries. Medinfo 8(pt 1), 28–32 (1995)

22. Martinet, A.: Syntaxe générale. Armand Colin, Paris (1985)

23. Migliorini, B.: Saggi sulla lingua del Novecento, chap. I prefissoidi (il tipo "aeromobile, radiodiffusione)", pp. 6–90. Sansoni, Firenze (1963)

24. Miller, G.A.: Wordnet: a lexical database for English. Commun. ACM 38(11), 39–41 (1995)

25. Minkov, E., Toutanova, K., Suzuki, H.: Generating complex morphology for machine translation. ACL 7, 128–135 (2007)

26. Möbius, B.: Rare events and closed domains: two delicate concepts in speech synthesis. Int. J. Speech Technol. 6(1), 57–71 (2003)

27. Namer, F.: Acquisizione automatica di semantica lessicale in francese: il sistema di trattamento computazionale della formazione delle parole dérif. In: et Maria Grossmann, A.M.T. (ed.) Atti del XXVII Congresso internazionale di studi Società di Linguistica Italiana: La Formazione delle parole, pp. 369–388 (2005)

28. Namer, F.: Morphologie, lexique et traitement automatique des langues. Hermès-Lavoisier, Cachan (2009)

29. Norton, L., Pacak, M.G.: Morphosemantic analysis of compound word forms denoting surgical procedures. Methods Inf. Med. 22(1), 29–36 (1983)

30. Pacak, M.G., Norton, L., Dunham, G.S.: Morphosemantic analysis of-ITIS forms in medical language. Meth. Inf. Med. 19(2), 99–105 (1980)

31. Pratt, A.W., Pacak, M.: Identification and transformation of terminal morphemes in medical English. Meth. Inf. Med. 8(2), 84–90 (1969)

32. Salvi, G., Vanelli, L.: Grammatica essenziale di riferimento della lingua italiana. Le Monnier, Firenze (1992)
33. Scalise, S.: Morfologia Lessicale. Clesp, Padova (1983)
34. Serianni, L.: Grammatica italiana: italiano comune e lingua letteraria: suoni, forme, costrutti. UTET, Torino (1988)
35. Sgroi, S.C.: Per una ridenizione di "confisso": composti confissati, derivati confissati, parasintetici confissati vs etimi ibridi e incongrui. Quaderni di semantica **24**, 81–153 (2003)
36. Silberztein, M.: NooJ manual (2003). www.nooj4nlp.net
37. Tekavčić, P.: Grammatica storica della lingua italiana: Lessico, vol. 3. Il Mulino, Bologna (1980)
38. Thornton, A.M.: Morfologia. Carocci, Roma (2005)
39. Toutanova, K., Suzuki, H., Ruopp, A.: Applying morphology generation models to machine translation. In: ACL, pp. 514–522 (2008)
40. Vietri, S.: The Italian module for NooJ. In. In Proceedings of the First Italian Conference on Computational Linguistics, CLiC-it 2014. Pisa University Press (2014)
41. Virpioja, S., Väyrynen, J.J., Creutz, M., Sadeniemi, M.: Morphology-aware statistical machine translation based on morphs induced in an unsupervised manner. Mach. Transl. Summit XI **2007**, 491–498 (2007)
42. Wolff, S.: The use of morphosemantic regularities in the medical vocabulary for automatic lexical coding. Meth. Inf. Med. **23**(4), 195–203 (1984)

Grammar Debugging

Michael Maxwell[✉]

University of Maryland, College Park, MD 20742, USA
maxwell@umiacs.umd.edu

Abstract. Perhaps the dominant method for building morphological parsers is to use finite state transducer toolkits. The problem with this approach is that finite state transducers require one to think of grammar writing as a programming task, rather than as providing a declarative linguistic description. We have therefore developed a method for representing the morphology and phonology of natural languages in a way which is closer to traditional linguistic descriptions, together with a method for automatically converting these descriptions into parsers, thus allowing the linguistic descriptions to be tested against real language data.

But there is a drawback to this approach: the fact that the descriptive level is different from the implementation level makes debugging of the grammars difficult, and in particular it provides no aid to visualizing the steps in deriving surface forms from underlying forms. We have therefore developed a debugging tool, which allows the linguist to see each intermediate step in the generation of words, without needing to know anything about the finite state implementation. The tool runs in generation mode; that is, the linguist provides an expected parse, and the debugger shows how that underlying form is converted into a surface form given the grammar. (Debugging in the opposite direction—starting from an expected surface form—might seem more natural, but in fact is much harder if that form cannot be parsed, as presumably it cannot be if the grammar needs debugging.)

The tool allows tracing the application of feature checking constraints (important when there is multiple exponence) and phonological rules. It will soon allow viewing the application of suppletive allomorphy constraints, although we describe some theoretical linguistic issues with how the latter should work. The tool can be run from the command line (useful when repeatedly testing the same wordforms while tweaking the grammar), or from a Graphical User Interface (GUI) which prompts the user for the necessary information. The output can be displayed in a browser.

In addition to its use in debugging, the debugger could have an educational use in explicating the forms in a paradigm chart: each cell of the paradigm could be run through the debugger to produce the cell's derivation, showing how forms which might seem counter-intuitive or irregular are derived. We have not yet implemented this.

1 Introduction

When converting descriptive grammars of some language to a computational implementation as a parser, one often finds problems with the descriptions:

© Springer International Publishing Switzerland 2015
C. Mahlow and M. Piotrowski (Eds.): SFCM 2015, CCIS 537, pp. 166–183, 2015.
DOI: 10.1007/978-3-319-23980-4_11

vagueness, gaps, and contradictions (generally contradictions between different linguists' descriptions, but sometimes within a single linguist's description). This is in part a result of the difficulty of providing an unambiguous and clear description of any complex system; another example of this would the difficulty of providing clear and explicit software specifications (cf. [2]).

Our own work at the University of Maryland on writing descriptive grammars is not immune to this, and it has shown up especially clearly where one linguist (or team of linguists) is writing the description, while another person or team of computational linguists is building a parser. While having both teams under the same roof allows resolution, we are now trying a different approach: making parser building easier for the linguists themselves to do.

For at least a decade, the standard resource for building morphological transducers has been finite state tools such as the Xerox Finite State Tool (XFST and LEXC, [1]) and the Stuttgart Finite State Tools (SFST, [19]). However, linguists with whom we have worked, who are mostly not computer scientists or even computer programmers, have found using such computational tools daunting. We have therefore created a descriptive mechanism—a way of formally modeling grammars—that more closely models views of morphology and phonology that linguists are already familiar with.[1] Our formal grammars are written as XML documents adhering to a schema that defines such constructions as parts of speech, affixes, allomorphs, morphosyntactic features, and phonological rules. Allomorphs can be listed and conditioned by phonological features and inflection classes (modeling an item-and-arrangement morphology), or they can be derived by phonological rules, which can also be sensitive to phonological features and inflection classes (modeling an item-and-process morphology, in one sense of that term). Affixation can also be modeled as affix process rules, including reduplication (modeling item-and-process morphology, in the other sense in which that term has been used). All these sorts of descriptions can be mixed when modeling a single language. For example, some allomorphs of a given affix can be listed, while forms of that same affix are derived by affix process rules.[2]

---

[1] Another approach to writing computational grammars is the 'Grammatical Framework' (http://www.grammaticalframework.org/). To an even greater extent than most finite state toolkits intended for linguists, the Grammatical Framework takes a programming language approach to writing rules. Indeed, the first lesson in the tutorial (http://www.grammaticalframework.org/doc/tutorial/gf-tutorial.html#toc4) starts out by saying "we learn the way of thinking in the GF theory." In contrast, our approach is to assume the linguist already knows linguistics, and prefers to think in linguistic terms, not in "a typed functional language, borrowing many of its constructs from ML and Haskell" (http://www.grammaticalframework.org/doc/gf-refman.html#toc1). For the same reason, we have not attempted to model two-level sorts of analyses; as [1] note, that formalism tends not to appeal to most linguists.

[2] Some linguistic issues arise when combining different models. For example, should phonologically conditions on listed allomorphs be applied before or after phonological rules are applied?

In order to build a parser, such a formal grammar description must be automatically translated into a different form, which can be used by available parser-building tools. We have therefore built a Python program which converts our XML-based descriptions into the programming language of a parsing engine; we are currently using SFST as that engine, but the converter could easily be ported to another such engine. For this conversion to succeed, the constructs of the model must be mappable into the constructs available in the transducer, and this mapping must work for all instances of such constructs.

Many linguistic structures indeed have a fairly straightforward mapping into the formalism of finite state technology. Phonological rules (in rule-based theories of phonology) for example map reasonably well to replace rules in XFST and SFST (although phonological rules expressed in terms of phonological features would not map so easily[3]).

However, not all linguistic structures have such a straightforward mapping. Some structures are simply beyond the reach of finite state systems; recursive syntactic structures are an obvious example. Within morphology, full (unlimited) reduplication is another, although XFST provides a work-around for this. In some cases, however, a linguistic structure may be finite state, but still difficult to express in a natural and general way using existing finite state formalisms.

One linguistic phenomenon which has proven surprisingly hard to map to our chosen finite state formalism (particularly since it is obviously finite state) is suppletive allomorphy. We have succeeded in developing and implementing an algorithm to map a simple description of suppletive allomorphy into SFST code; while each allomorph can be described in a single XML element, this translates in about half a dozen steps in SFST [16].

We have also broken some other linguistic constructs into multiple steps in SFST, for efficiency reasons. Early on, we noticed that compiling complex finite state expressions in SFST was sometimes very slow. It turned out that we could speed up the compilation by breaking it into several sub-steps. For example, in order to compile a phonological rule, we first separately compile the left- and right-hand sides of the environment, storing each of those compiled results as variables, and then compile the rest of the rule using the stored environment variables. This means that phonological rules are compiled in three steps.[4]

The use of two different representations—an XML-based representation which the linguist writes, and an SFST-based representation which the parser

---

[3] To my knowledge, the only morphological parser that directly supports the use of phonological features is SIL's Hermit Crab. An outdated description of this program is at http://www.sil.org/computing/hermitcrab/. Hermit Crab has been re-implemented in SIL's Fieldworks Language Explorer system, FLEx: http://www-01.sil.org/sil/news/2009/flex3.htm. Alternatively, it would be possible to convert feature-based descriptions of phonological environments into phoneme-based descriptions; so far as I know, there is no computational tool which does that. There has been only a little work on implementing Optimality Theory-based descriptions, see [9].

[4] Rules of epenthesis require additional steps, as do rules which apply to a lexically defined subclass of words (e.g., to a particular conjugation class).

uses—creates a problem: debugging the grammar is difficult, because there is no longer a one-to-one relation between what the user wrote and how the user's construct is implemented. The method I have used when debugging such grammars (and more often when debugging the output of the converter program, which I wrote) is to edit the file containing the SFST code produced by the converter, so that I can see intermediate results. While this works, it is clumsy; and more importantly, since our goal is to allow the linguist to write grammars using linguistic constructs without having to know anything about SFST, the linguist cannot be expected to debug the grammar in this way.

The problem is of course similar to the difficulty faced by computer programmers who use a high level programming language, particulary one compiled into assembly code (and eventually machine language code). Most such programmers are not familiar with assembly language, nor do they want to see that code. Programming language debuggers therefore provide ways to step through the code and examine intermediate stages. The solution to our problem is analogous: we provide a debugger, which allows the linguist to step through the application of their constraints and rules, examining the input and output at each intermediate step.

The rest of this paper describes briefly how our formal grammar system works, and then turns to the implementation of the debugger. The debugger currently explains to the user any conflicts in morphosyntactic features (which can arise when there is multiple exponence), and then steps through the phonological rules, showing the output at each stage. The debugger does not yet explain to the user how listed (suppletive) allomorphs are constrained; this capability will be added in future work.

2   A Descriptive System for Morphology

Our descriptive system is an XML-based representation of morphology and phonology, which readily accomodates most morphological and rule-based phonological structures. A converter translates this linguistic representation into the SFST code needed to build a parser. For the working linguist who does not consider him or herself to be a programmer, the XML representation offers several advantages over encoding grammars directly in the programming language of finite state transducers:[5]

Software Independence: The use of XML means that we can create formal grammar specifications which are independent of any particular transducer.

Longevity: As a result of software independence, our formal grammar descriptions will be portable to future generations of software (an important consideration when documenting endangered languages).

Linguistic Basis: By basing our XML schema on linguistically recognized concepts, we ensure that the resulting descriptions are linguistically sound.

---

[5] The motivations behind this work have been more thoroughly documented elsewhere, e.g., [5,14,15,17].

Theory Agnosticism: At the same time, adhering too closely to a particular linguistic theory would both limit the current audience and threaten the longevity of data encoded in the schema, limiting the potential audience of users to those linguists who know (and like) that theory. Our schema therefore attempts to follow as much as possible the notion of "Basic Linguistic Theory" [6,7].[6]

Alternative Analyses: It not always possible to provide a schema that is general enough to accomodate a wide variety of theories; instead, the schema must provide options—different ways to analyze phenomena—which jointly allow for different theoretical approaches, or different analyses within a single approach.

Ease of Use by Linguists: A linguistically-based description language allows linguists to construct grammars in a way that should already be familiar to them, making it easier for them to build and maintain parsers. This is particularly evident where a linguistic structure is not straightforwardly mappable into a finite state transducer's programming language: our system is adapted to the user, rather than the user having to adapt to the programming language.

In order for such a system to be useable by linguists, a number of tools must be provided:

XML Schema: An XML schema is used to provide an explicit format for writing formal grammars. We have written such a schema, and used it to build a number of grammars for typologically distinct languages.

Editor: While it is possible to edit XML documents in an ordinary text editor (or better, a programmer's editor, which helps ensure proper matching and nesting of XML tags), most linguists will balk at this. Rather, an editor which can present an editable view of the XML document looking more like a traditional linguistic description (paradigm tables, templates with slots for agglutinating languages, phonological rules and so forth) is needed. In addition, the editor should enforce the restrictions of our XML schema, so that information cannot wind up in the wrong place.

We have not yet implemented this editing environment, but it will probably be done in a specialized XML editor such as XMLMind[7] or oXygen[8], both of which allow for displaying styled versions of XML code using Cascading Style Sheets (css), and which use a specified XML schema to prevent users from building XML structures which violate the schema.[9]

---

[6] The caveat "as much as possible" refers to the inherent conflict between informal verbal descriptions and formal descriptions which can be processed computationally. One example of this is affix processes (such as reduplication), for which the model presents an explicit formalism based on early work in reduplication by generative linguists [13].

[7] http://www.xmlmind.com/xmleditor/.

[8] http://www.oxygenxml.com/.

[9] SIL's Fieldworks Language Explorer (FLEx) provides similar capabilities for editing grammars conforming to a slightly different schema.

Typesetting: In some cases, one is writing a descriptive grammar of a language for publication and human consumption, and building the parser is a way of testing the description against real data, as well as making the descriptive grammar less ambiguous. It would be helpful if the formal grammar, which is used in our approach to build the parser, could also be typeset as part of the descriptive grammar. Typesetting an XML document as XML (which we can currently do) is not helpful to the reader, for much the same reason that an editable view of the grammar which displays all the XML tags and attributes is not helpful to the linguist writing the grammar. We therefore wish to provide automatic conversion from our XML-based formal grammars into a format useable for typesetting to give a more typical linguistic view. This work remains to be done; it will probably use Extensible Stylesheet Language Transformations (XSLT), or else the existing Python converter could be used to produce LaTeX code, which can then be directly typeset.

Parsing Engine: A parsing engine takes as input a formal grammar written in some format (typically a programming language specific to the parsing engine), plus one or more lexicons (also in the parsing engine's required format), and produces a parser. As discussed, present-day parsing engines are usually finite state transducers, which come with a way to "compile" such a formal grammar and lexicons into the internal finite state representation.[10]

Converter: There must be a way of converting an XML-based formal grammar into the code which will be acceptable to the parsing engine. We have built such a converter. It takes as input the XML file representing the formal grammar, and converts each XML element into an internal representation as an object; it also derives from the name of each part of speech the expected location of lexical files for that part of speech (see below for how those files are created). Some of the elements in the XML grammar are full descriptions of linguistic objects, such as natural classes of phonemes or phonological rules, while others are named references to such definitions elsewhere. After the initial object-based representation is created, the converter then replaces all such references with a pointer to the actual object (this is analogous to the linking step in traditional programming language compilers). The converter then traverses this object-based representation, beginning at the root object, and outputs the formal grammar in the format required by the parsing engine, by calling on each object to produce a representation of itself in the parsing engine's format. (Most objects have more than one representation, depending on how they are being used.) This representation of the formal grammar is then ready for "compilation" by the parsing engine.

Dictionary Importation: A parser needs both a grammar and a machine-readable dictionary. Electronic dictionaries may use any number of XML formats or HTML formats, or they may be PDF or text documents.

---

[10] The scare quotes around the word "compile" are intended to indicate that this compilation is not the same thing as compiling a C program, say, to executable code. Rather, it represents the conversion of some text-based format into a highly compressed and rapidly interpretable internal format as a finite state network.

A mechanism therefore needs to be provided to import the relevant information from such dictionaries and convert it to the format needed by the parsing engine. In addition, dictionaries (or their digitized forms, if they were born as print media) often have inconsistencies, ranging from the trivial (e.g., spelling the name of a part of speech as 'noun' or 'Noun') to the complex (representing the inflection class of each word implicitly by some aspect of the citation form, such as an affix, or by the citation form plus one or more other paradigm forms). Thus far, we have needed to approach each dictionary as a separate importation task, even when they conform to a single model (such as Lexical Markup Framework, LMF). We have no reason to suppose we can eliminate all the dictionary-specific aspects of importation, but we hope to provide at least a generic framework for importation.

Debugger: As discussed above, the user must be able to follow how the implementation treats the grammar rules and lexical elements to generate surface forms from underlying forms.

As the reader can tell, this represents a work in progress. Some of the pieces are more or less complete (the converter from the XML representation to SFST code is mature), other pieces (the editor, for instance) are only envisioned. This paper presents a part of the project which is partially mature, the debugger.

To demonstrate how the XML-based representation differs from the parsing engine's internal representation, and how this difference makes it hard for the linguist to debug a grammar, we now turn to a description of how finite state transducers are built, and then to the representation of suppletive allomorphy in these two representations.

3   Construction of Finite State Transducers

It will help in the following discussion to know how finite state transducers (or FSTs) are built (or "compiled"). The following description pertains to transducers which are built by creating something like the traditional notion of an underlying form of a word, and then applying phonological rules (usually called "replace rules" in the finite state terminology) to produce a surface form. This method should sound familiar to most practicing linguists; it is used in the Xerox xfst program, in FOMA (a re-implementation of xfst and related programs, see [8]), and can be used in the Stuttgart finite state tools (SFST). Another approach, dubbed "two level morphology" [12] is perhaps less familiar to most linguists, and will not be discussed here.

The FST may be viewed as consisting of two "sides" or levels, which I will refer to as the lexical side and the surface side.[11] These two sides are generally, but not always, distinct. The network is organized into a large number of "paths,"

---

[11] Descriptions of FST implementations use the terms "upper" and "lower," but inconsistently: documentation of xfst refers to the lexical side as upper and the surface as lower, while documentation of SFST uses the opposite convention.

where each path represents the pairing of some underlying representation with a possible wordform at some non-underlying level of representation.

The initial form of such an FST is created by concatenating the morphemes of each word according to the morphotactics of the language. At this initial stage, the lexical side and surface side often use the same representation for the stem, or the lexical side may contain the dictionary citation form, while the surface side (which is obviously not the true surface form, as this term is used in rule-based generative descriptions) contains the stem, not including for instance any affix found on the citation form. Affixes are most often represented by their glosses on the lexical side, and by an underlying form on the surface side. The representation is character-based, where each character on the surface side may represent a grapheme, phoneme, or boundary marker. Other characters—auxiliary symbols—may be used to represent such things as morphosyntactic features, part of speech, or inflection classes, generally on the lexical side.[12]

After this initial representation of the network is created, some paths may be eliminated because they violate some constraint—in the cases we are considering here, a path may be eliminated because it violates an allomorph constraint. A path may also be changed, e.g., by replacing one phoneme with another because of the application of a phonological rule.

Finally, any boundary markers and auxiliary symbols are removed from the surface side (and possibly from the lexical side).

At the end of a derivation—after all the constraints have been satisfied and all phonological rules have applied—the result should be a network in which each path represents a word of the language in its underlying and surface forms.

4   Suppletive Allomorphy

Suppletive allomorphy is phonologically conditioned allomorphy (that is, it is not driven by inflection classes) for which phonological processes cannot reasonably be posited. Carstairs [4, p. 21] and Paster [18] give examples, of which one is the Turkish passive suffix. This takes the form –n after a vowel-final stem, and –l elsewhere. While this *can* be expressed using phonological rules, it is not natural to do so, and attempting to do so could easily lead to improper application of the rule elsewhere.

Generative phonologists often avoid the use of allomorphs, assuming instead a single underlying form of each affix, and generating alternative forms of morphemes by the use of phonological rules. Where such rules can be easily defined, and when they handle the allomorphy of a large number of morphemes (for instance stem allomorphy, or suffixal allomorphy due to vowel harmony, as in Turkish), this makes sense. But phonological rules have a drawback: if not written carefully, they can apply to the wrong forms. Working linguists often use allomorphy in situations where they could write a reasonable phonological rule,

---

[12] FST tools often provide for multi-character symbols, which can be useful to represent such non-phonemic entities. The FST engine generally views them as if they were single characters.

but have not gotten around to writing it yet, or because the rule would require refinement in order to prevent incorrect application. In fact even generative linguists debate the boundary between suppletive allomorphy and allomorphy that can be attributed to general phonological rules [3,11]. This situation thus presents an example of our desideratum mentioned in Sect. 2, namely to allow alternative descriptive methods, rather than forcing the linguist to model a phenomenon in a particular way.

Hence, the need for our system to handle suppletive allomorphy has two motivations: some allomorphy cannot reasonably be treated with phonological rules, and even where it can, the linguist may simply prefer to use suppletion.

Allomorphs by definition appear in mutually exclusive phonological environments. While it is always possible to state each allomorph's environment as mutually exclusive, it is often easier to represent them as a sequence from most specific to least specific; the first allomorph in this list whose environment is satisfied in a particular inflected wordform is chosen. The last allomorph in such a list is usually an elsewhere case, chosen if none of the preceding allomorphs in the list have environments which are satisfied [10].

As a simple example, consider the English noun plural suffix.[13] This suffix has three phonologically conditioned allomorphs: a voiced /z/, a voiceless /s/, and /əz/.[14] While these may be derived by phonological rules (which could also handle the verbal third person singular and the possessive clitic, and perhaps the verbal past tense –ed), for illustrative purposes assume the allomorphs are to be represented suppletively:[15]

/əz/: (s|z|ʃ|ʒ|ʧ|ʤ) __
/s/: (p|t|k) __
/z/: elsewhere
      (after b, d, "hard" g, vowels...; but not after s, z, ʃ...p, t, k...)

The order is important. In particular, the elsewhere case must apply last, lest it bleed the application of the other cases. This is represented here as extrinsic ordering. The first and second cases do not need to be ordered in this character-based formulation.[16]

---

[13] We use this affix and its allomorphs for illustrative purposes precisely because of its simplicity. A full regular expression capability is available in the XML formalism, and can be translated into SFST code, allowing much more complex allomorph (and phonological rule) environments.

[14] We will not discuss unusual plurals, such as the –en of *oxen* or the –i/–us alternation of words like *octopus˜octopi*; nor irregular plurals such as *geese, mice*. I also ignore stems ending in /f/, since in many words this voices to become /v/, which then takes the /z/ suffix allomorph: *wife/wives*.

[15] The examples are represented using IPA characters, since the standard orthography does not make the distinctions in a consistent way.

[16] If the allomorph environments were stated intensionally in terms of phonological features, rather than extensionally as lists of phonemes, the first and second allomorphs of this affix would be need to be extrinsically ordered with respect to each other as well.

The representation in our XML-based formalism of the above affix looks
something like this:[17]

```
<affix gloss="-PL">
    <allomorph>
        <form spelling="-əz"/>
        <environment>
            <leftEnvironment>
                <AlternativesContext>
                    <SimpleContextNC>
                        <NCSegment>
                            <refPhoneme idref="S"/>
                            <refPhoneme idref="Z"/>
                            <refPhoneme idref="Sh"/>
                            <refPhoneme idref="Zh"/>
                            <refPhoneme idref="J"/>
                            <refPhoneme idref="Ch"/>
                        </NCSegment>
                    </SimpleContextNC>
                </AlternativesContext>
            </leftEnvironment>
        </environment>
    </allomorph>
    <allomorph>
        <form spelling="-s"/>
        <environment>
            <leftEnvironment>
                <AlternativesContext>
                    <SimpleContextNC>
                        <NCSegment>
                            <refPhoneme idref="P"/>
                            <refPhoneme idref="T"/>
                            <refPhoneme idref="K"/>
                        </NCSegment>
                    </SimpleContextNC>
                </AlternativesContext>
            </leftEnvironment>
        </environment>
    </allomorph>
    <allomorph>
        <form spelling="-z"/>
    </allomorph>
    <fs>
```

---

[17] I have simplified this somewhat, e.g., the prefixes on the XML tags designating the
namespace for our XML schema are not shown.

```
        <f name="Number>
          <symbol value="plural"/>
        </f>
      </fs>
  </affix>
```

The correspondence of the above, apart from the verbosity caused by XML tags, to the linguistic description should be apparent;[18] In particular, this XML representation is directly mappable to the linguistic display, and this mapping will be leveraged when we implement the editor and typesetting goals described in Sect. 2.

It is not, however, immediately obvious how to express such a structure in finite state terms. In general, one of two methods might be used: either the allomorphs could be tested one by one on each wordform, and the first one that matches would be chosen; or each allomorph in the list could be allowed to occur in its phonological environment, and also forbidden to occur in any of the environments of the allomorphs preceding it in the list. Both approaches result in essentially the same finite state network, but the way that network is derived differs.

The approach we have taken is a form of the first method. First, we concatenate all allomorphs of all affixes with the set of stems for the appropriate part of speech; if relevant, we limit the allomorphs to those which are consistent with each stem's inflection class; but we do not attempt at this step to constrain allomorphs to appear in their specific phonological environments. This is simply the first step of building an FST, as described in Sect. 3. But in addition, we tag each allomorph with the name of its affix.[19]

We then proceed through the allomorphs of each affix in order from most specific to least specific (usually the elsewhere case). For each allomorph, we copy into an SFST variable all paths through the finite state network which contain that allomorph, and remove those paths from the main finite state network. At this point, then, the allomorph under consideration is found in only this auxiliary network, not in the main network.

We then apply the phonological environment specified for this allomorph to the auxiliary network, eliminating all paths in which the desired allomorph does not appear in its environment; we then remove all instances of the affix name tag. Likewise, we eliminate from the main network all instances of the affix which are (still) tagged by the affix name, regardless of the allomorph, and which appear

---

[18] One point that may be unclear is the use of the 'idref' attribute to refer to phonemes. The phonemes are defined elsewhere in the XML grammar, with unique IDs, and these IDs are referred to here. The representation of morphosyntactic features would use a similar notation, but for reasons of compatibility with the TEI and ISO encodings of features and feature structures, we instead use the 'name' and 'value' attributes.

[19] The name we use is a multi-character symbol containing the affix gloss. The tag appears on both sides of the allomorph, bracketing it; this allows us to avoid confusion between the allomorph and any homographic sequence of characters.

in the allomorph's environment. Now the auxiliary network contains only paths in which the allomorph appears in its specified environment, while the main network contains no intances of the affix in that environment.

Finally, we combine the two networks. The allomorph appears in its desired environment, and no other allomorphs of that affix appear in that environment. We then cycle through the loop again, with the next allomorph.

The removal of the affix tag from the each allomorphs as it is processed allows us to ignore that allomorph in subsequent passes through the loop. This is crucial, since in general the environment of each successive allomorph represents a superset of the environment of preceding allomorphs. If we did not remove the affix tags, we would therefore incorrectly remove allomorphs which were licensed by previous passes through the loop. The SFST code for one pass through this loop is similar to the following:

```
$TemporaryLexicon$ =
    $TemporaryLexicon$
    || (.*(s|z|ʃ|ʒ|ʧ|ʤ)<PL>\-əz<PL>.*))
    || (<PL>:<> ^-> <> __)
$Lexicon$ =
    $Lexicon$
    || (!(.*(p|t|k)<PL>.*<PL>.*))
$TemporaryLexicon$ =
    $TemporaryLexicon$
    || (.*(p|t|k)<PL>\-s<PL>.*))
    || (<PL>:<> ^-> <> __)
$Lexicon$ =
    $Lexicon$ | $TemporaryLexicon$
```

While the steps in this SFST code correspond to the description of the algorithm given above, the relationship of the code to what the linguist intended is less clear. In particular, the use of the temporary variable$TemporaryLexicon$, the negation of the environment in the second step, and the deletion of the affix tag <PL> are explict representations of information which is implicit in the linguist's notation, and their appearance in the SFST code may therefore seem extraneous, confusing and even impenetrable. It is for this reason that we have built a debugger, which steps through the constraints and rules not at the level of the SFST code, but rather at the level of the linguist's constraints and rules.

5   How the Debugger Works

The purpose of the debugger is to determine why the parser—and hence the grammar—does not give the expected results. One usually tests a morphological parser by having it parse a list of words; the words may be obtained from a corpus, from examples (including example paradigms) in a computer-readable document, or from the user. The parses returned for each word may be validated against a set of expected parses, or (less accurately), one may simply look at the un-parsed words. In either case, the question then arises of why some words parse incorrectly, or not at all. In some cases, this will be obvious; the word which fails to parse is not an ordinary word at all: it is a number; or perhaps a proper name, abbreviation, or acronym which is not in the dictionary that the parser was built from; or the word is misspelled. But some incorrect or failed parses will be for less obvious reasons.

Given the nature of finite state transducers, it is quite difficult to determine why a word does not parse. An FST parses by generating from the dictionary and affixes, and perhaps phonological rules, all possible surface forms. A form that does not parse is therefore not in the FST's network at all, and it is futile to attempt to trace its parse to find the failure point.[20]

The approach we have taken to parser debugging is therefore to work from the parse that the linguist expects for a given word, and to generate the surface form[21] from that. This generated form will be different from the form the linguist expects, else the parse would not have failed. The linguist may immediately realize why the unexpected form results, but if not, the debugger provides a way to visualize why the unexpected form results. In some cases, no surface form will result, because the user has tried to combine incompatible affixes, or for other reasons discussed below.

We have implemented the debugger with two different interfaces; apart from the interface, both debuggers share programming code. One uses a graphical user interface (GUI) to elicit the lexeme, its part of speech, and either the affixes or the morphosyntactic features which should select the affixes; the surface form is generated from this input; the other debugger obtains the input information from parameters on the command line. We use the GUI version of the debugger to illustrate the steps.

The linguist is first prompted to enter the lexeme whose stem is to be inflected, along with its part of speech (in case the lexeme has more than one); this is shown in Fig. 1.

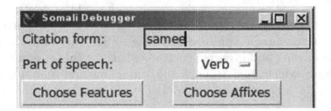

Fig. 1. Lexeme selection

---

[20] One can build a parser-as-guesser, in which the "lexicon" is a regular expression representing all possible lexemes, including those which do not correspond to real lexemes. But this seldom reveals the problem with a failed parse either.

[21] Or forms, should there be optional phonological rules.

The system then allows the user to choose a set of affixes to be attached to this lexeme, or a set of features to be realized by inflectional affixes. The choice of affixes is illustrated in Fig. 2, and the choice of features in Fig. 3.

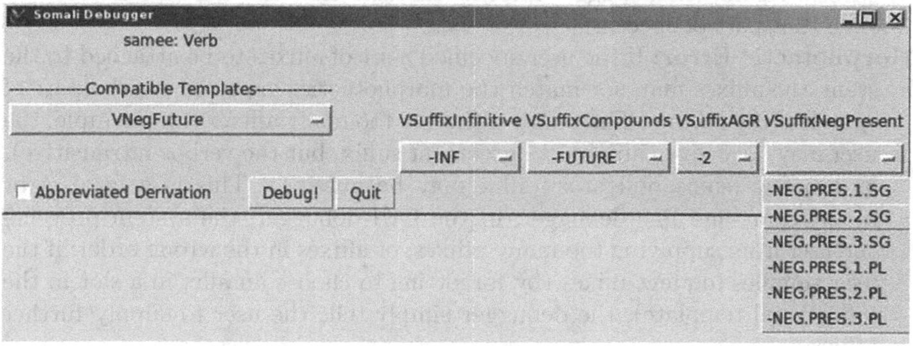

Fig. 2. Affix selection

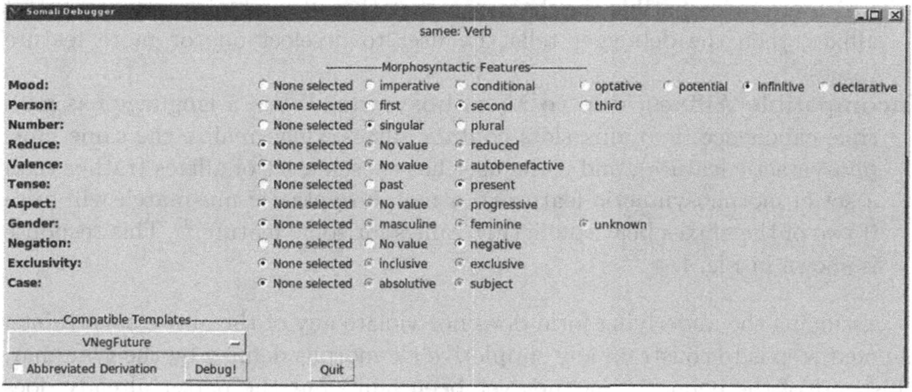

Fig. 3. Feature selection

The parser attempts to construct an underlying form representing the requested lexeme plus affixes or morphosyntactic features, using the morphotactics of the grammar (the morphotactics are specified in inflectional templates). Several things can go wrong here:

Non-existent Lexeme: The user may have chosen a lexeme which is not in the parsers's dictionary for any of several reasons: the user misspelled the lexeme, the lexeme is misspelled in the dictionary (or was incorrectly digitized), the grammatical information is incorrect, or some defect in the digital dictionary or the dictionary import process prevented the lexeme from being imported. The debugger informs the user that the specified word does not exist in the expected form in its lexicon. The non-parse thus becomes a lexicographic problem.

Grammatical Mismatch: The user may have requested a lexeme with one part of speech, but it does not appear in the dictionary with that part of speech. Again, the debugger informs the user that the word does not exist with that part of speech.

Morphotactic Error: If the user specified a set of affixes to be attached to the stem, the affixes may not match the morphotactics expected for the part of speech of the lexeme. There may either be too many affixes (for example, the user may have given an object agreement suffix, but the verb is intransitive), or too few (some obligatory affix may be missing). This is a fatal error in the command line debugger; in the GUI debugger, the system prevents the user from supplying too many affixes, or affixes in the wrong order; if the user supplies too few affixes (by forgetting to choose an affix in a slot in the inflectional template), the debugger simply tells the user to supply further affixes.

Morphosyntactic Feature Error: If the user has selected too few features to pick out a unique set of affixes, then the debugger tells the user to select additional features. If on the other hand the user has selected feature values which are incompatible, in the sense that they do not pick out any set of affixes, then the debugger tells the user to deselect one or more feature values.[22]

Incompatible Affixes, due to Morphosyntax: When a language has multiple exponence (two affix slots contain affixes which realize the same morphosyntactic feature), and if the user has chosen a set of affixes (rather than a set of morphosyntactic features), a morphosyntactic mis-match will arise if two of the affixes bear conflicting values for some feature.[23] This response is shown in Fig. 4.

Assuming the underlying form does not violate any of the above constraints, the next step is to constrain any suppletive allomorphs defined by the grammar. This part of the debugger has not yet been built, but the parser already does this selection in a step-wise fashion. What remains is to display each step in this constraint process, showing how each allomorph is licensed in its allowable environments, or disallowed (removed from further processing) in other environments.

---

[22] This problem happens when two features are not completely orthogonal. For example, in Spanish the feature value of [Mood subjunctive] is incompatible with the feature value [Tense future]: while there is a present subjunctive and a past subjunctive in Spanish, there is no future subjunctive.

[23] The situation is somewhat more complicated than this, since the formal grammar treats features as part of feature structures. There may thus be conflicting values for features which appear in distinct parts of the feature structure. For example, a language which marked transitive verbs for agreement with the person of both subject and object could have distinct values of the number feature for subject and for object, without conflict.

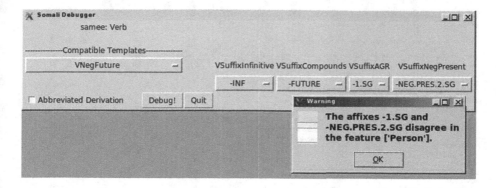

Fig. 4. Incompatible affixes

Finally, after the allomorphs have been chosen, each remaining form is passed through the phonological rules; the output of each rule application is displayed.[24] If a rule applies vacuously, or does not apply at all, a ditto mark is shown, indicating that the rule made no change. This has proven easier to interpret than showing the unchanged form each time.

Figure 5 illustrates the view of a derivation in a browser. In this example, there are two sources of multiple derivations. First, the affix glossed --INF (infinitive) has two variant forms, −n and −i. Second, there are two optional phonological rules, here named LongEEtoE (which applies only to the first form) GlideInsertion (which optionally applies to both forms). Optional application of a phonological rule results in a choice point, hence the derivation is shown as splitting at the application of these rules.

If the environment in which a phonological rule applies is complicated, it is possible that the reason for non-application of a rule will not be obvious. (It is possible, but perhaps less likely, that the reason for over-application of a rule will not be obvious.) A planned enhancement will allow for the rule's environment to be iteratively simplified until the rule does apply, thus helping the user debug the environment of a rule by finding what part of the rule's environment prevents application.

The debugger outputs rule applications in the form of an XML file, which is a simple table. Columns represent ambiguities (such as dialectal variant forms of an allomorph, or the optional application of a phonological rule). The first row represents the input forms (currently, the stage after suppletive allomorph selection); the last row represents the final output form (after deletion of boundary markers); and intermediate rows represent each rule's application.

---

[24] In the case of multiple application of a rule, e.g., vowel harmony rules, the output of the entire rule application is shown.

Mozilla Firefox

file:///home/m...ebugTrace.xml ✕ / file:///home/m...ebugTrace.xml ✕ ＋

◄ ⟳ ⓖ file:///home/mmaxwell/Data/Somali/DebugRe ✔ ⟳ | ⑧ ✔ Google   ⚲ ★ 🗐 ⬇ ⌂

Derivation of stem="samee" with glosses="<-INF><-FUTURE><-2><-NEG.PRES.2.SG>"				
Underlying Forms	samee+n+ doon+t+o		samee+i+ doon+t+o	
StemShiftLANtoLM	"		"	
NGemination	"		"	
LongAAtoAY	"		"	
LongEEtoE	"	samey+n+ doon+t+o	"	
GlideInsertion	"	sameey+n+ doon+t+o	"	sameey+i+ doon+t+o
TbecomesS	"	"	"	"	"
BGemination	"	"	"	"	"
WtoOB	"	"	"	"	"
LNtoLL	"	"	"	"	"
RNtoRR	"	"	"	"	"
MidVowelCollapseGeneral	"	"	"	"	"
MidVowelCollapseRFinal	"	"	"	"	"
StemShiftGtoK	"	"	"	"	"
LTtoSH	"	"	"	"	"
DhdeGemination	"	"	"	"	"
AfterWVoicing	"	"	"	"	"
DGemination	"	"	"	"	"
TdeGemination	"	"	"	"	"
IYtoSH	"	"	"	"	"
DictionaryNtoUnderlyingM	"	"	"	"	"
Gemination	"	"	"	"	"
DeGemination	"	"	"	"	"
DeGemination2	"	"	"	"	"
UnderlyingMtoN	"	"	"	"	"
UnderlyingMtoN2	"	"	"	"	"
NVowelDrop					
Surface Forms	sameendoonto	sameeyndoonto	sameyndoonto	sameeidoonto	sameeyidoonto

Fig. 5. Derivation

6   Conclusion

We have described a debugger for morphological and phonological parsing. This debugger enables linguists to think in terms of concepts they are familiar with, without worrying about how they are encoded in a parsing engine like SFST. At present, the debugger enables the user to debug errors arising from lexical, morphotactic, and morphosyntactic feature choices, as well as errors arising from the unexpected application of phonological rules. Future work will also enable debugging of phonological constraints on allomorph selection.

References

1. Beesley, K.R., Karttunen, L.: Finite State Morphology. University of Chicago Press, Chicago (2003)
2. Berry, D.M., Kamsties, E.: Ambiguity in requirements specification. In: do Prado Leite, J.C.S., Doorn, J.H. (eds.) Perspectives on Software Requirements, vol. 753. Springer, US (2003)
3. Bonet, E., Harbour, D.: Contextual allomorphy. In: Trommer, J. (ed.) The Morphology and Phonology of Exponence, Oxford Studies in Theoretical Linguistics, vol. 41. Oxford University Press (2012)
4. Carstairs, A.D.: Allomorphy in Inflexion. Croom Helm, London (1987)

5. David, A., Maxwell, M.: Joint grammar development by linguists and computer scientists. In: Third International Joint Conference on Natural Language Processing, IJCNLP 2008, Hyderabad, India, 7–12 January, 2008, pp. 27–34. The Association for Computer Linguistics (2008). http://aclweb.org/anthology/I/I08/I08-3007.pdf
6. Dixon, R.M.W.: Basic Linguistic Theory. Methodology, vol. 1. Oxford University Press, Oxford (2009)
7. Dixon, R.M.W.: Basic Linguistic Theory. Grammatical Topics, vol. 2. Oxford University Press, Oxford (2009)
8. Hulden, M.: Foma: a finite-state compiler and library. In: Proceedings of the ACL, pp. 29–32. ACL, Athens (2009). http://www.aclweb.org/anthology/E/E09/E09-2008.pdf
9. Karttunen, L.: The proper treatment of optimality in computational phonology. In: Karttunen, L., Oflazer, K. (eds.) Proceedings of the International Workshop on Finite State Methods in Natural Language Processing, pp. 1–12. Bilkent University, Ankara (1998). http://www.aclweb.org/anthology/W/W98/W98-1301.pdf
10. Kiparsky, P.: 'elsewhere' in phonology. In: Anderson, S.R. (ed.) A Festschrift for Morris Halle, Holt, New York, pp. 93–106 (1973)
11. Kiparsky, P.: Allomorphy or morphophonology? In: Singh, R. (ed.) Trubetzkoy's Orphan: Proceedings of the Montreal Roundtable "Morphonology: Contemporary Responses", Montreal, 30 Sept–2 Oct, 1994, pp. 13–31. Benjamins, Amsterdam (1996)
12. Koskenniemi, K.: Two-level Morphology: A General Computational Model for Word-Form Recognition and Production. Ph.D. thesis, University of Helsinki (1983). http://www.ling.helsinki.fi/koskenni/doc/Two-LevelMorphology.pdf
13. Marantz, A.: Re reduplication. Linguist. Inquiry 13, 435–482 (1982)
14. Maxwell, M.: Standardization as a means to sustainability. In: Workshop on Language Resources: From Storyboard to Sustainability and LR Lifecycle Management, LREC 2010, pp. 30–33 (2010)
15. Maxwell, M.: Electronic grammars and reproducible research. In: Nordoff, S., Poggeman, K.L.G. (eds.) Electronic Grammaticography, pp. 207–235. University of Hawaii Press (2012)
16. Maxwell, M.: Accounting for allomorphy in finite state transducers. In: Finite-State Methods and Natural Language Processing (2015)
17. Maxwell, M., David, A.: Interoperable grammars. In: Webster, J., Ide, N., Fang, A.C. (eds.) First International Conference on Global Interoperability for Language Resources (ICGL 2008), Hong Kong, pp. 155–162 (2008). http://hdl.handle.net/1903/11611
18. Paster, M.E.: Explaining phonological conditions on affixation: Evidence from suppletive allomorphy and affix ordering 1. Word Structure 2(1), 18–37 (2009)
19. Schmid, H.: A programming language for finite state transducers. In: Yli-Jyrä, A., Karttunen, L., Karhumäki, J. (eds.) FSMNLP 2005. LNCS (LNAI), vol. 4002, pp. 308–309. Springer, Heidelberg (2006)

Author Index

Printed in the United States
By Bookmasters